# THE FUTURE OF IRAQ

# THE FUTURE OF IRAQ

## DICTATORSHIP, DEMOCRACY, OR DIVISION?

Liam Anderson
and Gareth Stansfield

First published 2004 by
PALGRAVE MACMILLAN™
175 Fifth Avenue, New York, N.Y. 10010 and
Houndmills, Basingstoke, Hampshire, England RG21 6XS.
Companies and representatives throughout the world.

PALGRAVE MACMILLAN is the global academic imprint of the
Palgrave Macmillan division of St. Martin's Press, LLC and of Palgrave
Macmillan Ltd. Macmillan® is a registered trademark in the United
States, United Kingdom and other countries. Palgrave is a registered
trademark in the European Union and other countries.

ISBN 1–4039–6354–1

**Library of Congress Cataloging-in-Publication Data**
Anderson, Liam D.
The future of Iraq : dictatorship, democracy, or division? / by Liam
Anderson and Gareth Stansfield.
   p.  cm.
  Includes bibliographical references and index.
  ISBN 1–4039–6354–1 hardcover
   1. Iraq—Politics and government—1958-  2. Iraq War, 2003.
3. Democracy—Iraq.  4. Iraq—Ethnic relations.  I. Stansfield,
Gareth R. V.  II. Title.

DS79.65.A687   2004
956.7044'3—dc22

2003058846

A catalogue record for this book is available from the British Library.

Design by Letra Libre, Inc.

First edition: February 2004
10  9  8  7  6  5  4  3  2  1

Printed in the United States of America.

*To our parents*

# CONTENTS

*Acknowledgments*                                                          ix
*Maps*                                                                     xi

Introduction                                                               1

Chapter 1   Iraq 1920–1958: The Hashemite Monarchy                        13

Chapter 2   Iraq 1958–1968: Revolution, Republic, and Renaissance         31

Chapter 3   Iraq 1968–1988: The Ba'ath Regime                             49

Chapter 4   1988–2003: The Destruction of Iraq                            83

Chapter 5   The Shi'a                                                     117

Chapter 6   The Sunnis                                                    139

Chapter 7   The Kurds                                                     155

Chapter 8   The Democracy Dilemma                                        185

Epilogue                                                                 225

*Notes*                                                                  237
*Index*                                                                  255

# ACKNOWLEDGMENTS

THE INITIAL IMPETUS TO WRITE A BOOK FOCUSING on the instabilities inherent within Iraq came in the latter half of 2001, particularly after the appalling events of September 11. By this time, we had been discussing Iraq and watching its development for several years, starting from a Kurdish orientation for one of us, and a political science outlook for the other. Our idea of Iraq being characterized by the existence of strong sectarian and ethnic identities was not new, but was certainly "untrendy" as academics particularly remained focused on the unifying strength of an "Iraqi" identity. As such, our proposal commenced life as controversial to say the least, and almost certainly remains so today in 2004. However, it is now perhaps tinged with a heightened degree of realism as Iraq continues forlornly to struggle to find some form of stability as a plethora of forces governed by, at times, exclusive agendas emerge from within the state to either make Iraq in their own image, as is the case of the Shi'a and Sunni, or to make something new, as, perhaps, the Kurds may try.

In undertaking the research and writing of this book, we have received the support of many individuals. Indeed, the controversial nature of our argument and the highly charged atmosphere surrounding anything to do with Iraq from 2001 onwards meant that we needed wise counsel and "sounding boards" at very regular intervals. This is not to say that our supporters necessarily agree with the arguments we've developed, but more to recognize the need of such arguments to be aired in public and contribute to the ongoing debate regarding the future of Iraq that promises to dominate world affairs for some time to come. In particular, we would like to thank our editor at Palgrave Macmillan, David Pervin, who kept us focused on the job at hand, showing an unswerving faith in our convictions and cutting through the fogs of conceptual ambiguity which occasionally threatened to limit our vision with brutal logic. Similarly, Professors Ewan Anderson and Tim Niblock remained constant fonts of advice, always willing to perform the role of devil's advocate for our ideas. In the UK, we benefited from being associated with one of the leading centers of study on Iraq at the Institute of Arab and Islamic Studies at the University of Exeter where the input of several staff and students (and especially Lise Storm Grundon, John Measor, and Hassan Abdulrazak) provided a most fertile environment for honing our ideas. Similarly, the members of the Middle East Programme at the Royal Institute of International Affairs (Chatham House), and especially Ali Ansari, Toby Dodge, Mai Yamani, and Rosemary Hollis, provided an unparalleled critical venue for us to discuss and develop the ideas behind this book. Nearly last, but by no means least, we would like to thank those who helped in background research and turning our rough pages into a finished book. Thanks to Heather Wiehe, Rosemary Baillon and Lise Storm Grundon, and Azos Rashid for always being available with up-to-the-minute breaking news and shrewd analysis, and Alan Bradshaw at Palgrave for putting it all together.

Finally, we reserve our greatest thanks for our parents, Sian and Ewan Anderson, and Lynn and Roy Stansfield. They have been our greatest supporters and it is to them we dedicate this book.

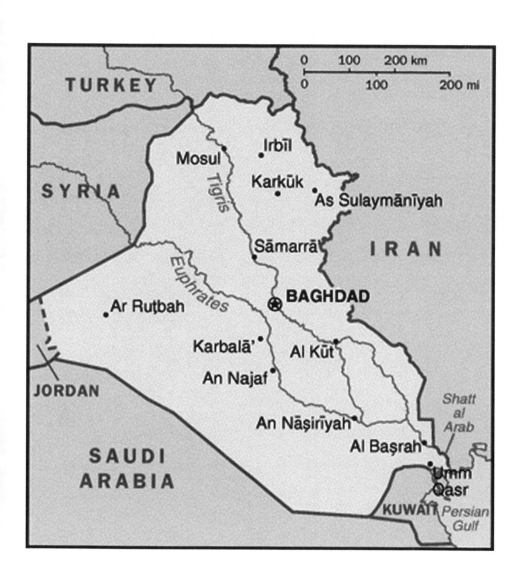

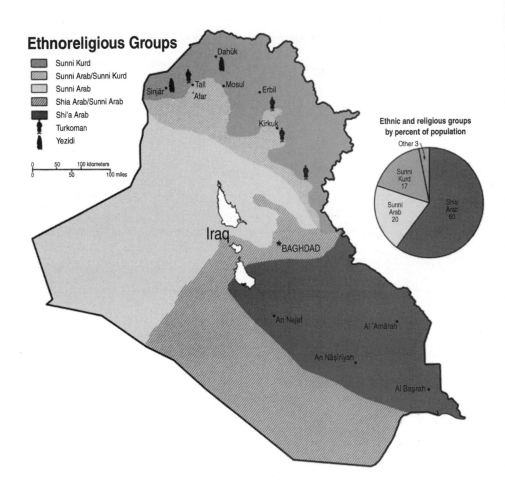

## Ethnoreligious Groups

- Sunni Kurd
- Sunni Arab/Sunni Kurd
- Sunni Arab
- Shia Arab/Sunni Arab
- Shi'a Arab
- Turkoman
- Yezidi

0    50    100 kilometers
0    50    100 miles

Dahūk

Sinjār    •Tall    •Mosul    •Erbil
          'Afar

Kirkuk

Iraq

★ BAGHDAD

•An Najaf    Al 'Amārah•

An Nāşirīyah•

Al Başrah •

**Ethnic and religious groups
by percent of population**

Other 3

Sunni
Kurd
17

Sunni
Arab
20

Shia
Arab
60

# INTRODUCTION

"OPERATION IRAQI FREEDOM," a U.S. and British military invasion of Iraq to remove from power the regime of Saddam Hussein, began on Wednesday, March 19, 2003. Barely three weeks later, coalition forces arrived at the gates of Baghdad to find that Saddam's forces had simply melted away. The military phase of the conflict was over; what remained was the far more daunting challenge of occupying and reconstructing an Iraq that had been devastated by decades of sanctions and war.

Five months earlier, in mid-November 2002, support among the American people for "the use of force to overthrow the regime of Saddam Hussein" hovered around the 68 percent mark—down from a previous high point of 70 to 75 percent, but a respectable majority nonetheless. At the same time, a troubling survey conducted by *National Geographic* magazine revealed that only one in seven Americans aged 18 to 24 were able to locate Iraq on a map of the world. Intrigued, the British *Daily Mirror* newspaper dispatched a reporter to the streets of New York to investigate. The Mirror's ad hoc poll of 100 New Yorkers yielded similar results; of the 100 polled, 80 "didn't have a clue where Iraq was."[1] These included a New York cop who selected Austria as the new Iraq, and others who placed Iraq in France, Albania, northern Italy, and South Africa. One respondent, described as a "burly construction worker," probably captured the sentiments of many with the words, "don't know, don't care, there'll be nothing left of it soon anyway."

No doubt similar results could have been obtained from any major Western city. However, that a significant majority of Americans supported overthrowing the regime of a person whose country they could not locate on a map is indicative of a deeper reality. Most Americans may have known little about Iraq the country, but they would almost certainly recognize the name of its former leader, Saddam Hussein. Demonizing the "Butcher of Baghdad" was scarcely a daunting challenge; there was ample ammunition to draw on; his authorization of the repeated use of chemical weapons against the Iranians during the Iran–Iraq war of the 1980s; the gassing of his own countrymen—the Kurds of northern Iraq—at Halabja in 1988; the widespread use of torture and rape as instruments of political control; and so the list could go on. Lurid, though not necessarily reliable, accounts of life under Saddam's regime penned by recent defectors merely added fuel to the fire. Personalizing a conflict through the demonizing of the target country's leader has one great advantage: it makes conflict much easier to sell to a potentially skeptical public. The goal of military action becomes to rid the world of an evil dictator and to liberate his oppressed people. The target of such an attack is not the country itself, or its citizenry, but a single individual and his attendant regime. But the personalization of conflict has at least two important drawbacks. First, the demon himself must be caught before victory can be considered complete. Osama Bin Laden is still "wanted, dead or alive," but until a dead body is produced, two thirds of the American people will not accept the war on terror as won. Second, and much more important, by focusing the public's attention on a single individual, the implication is that his successful removal (and, or, destruction) is the major task at hand. The conflict with Iraq was always sold in these terms by the Bush Administration. Administration officials, most notably those in the Department of Defense, assumed that once freed from the oppressive yoke of dictatorship, the Iraqi people would embrace democracy and the associated pantheon of Western values and retake their rightful place within the community of civilized nations. Iraq is a democracy in waiting, lacking only the opportunity to express itself, or so the assumption goes. The truth of course, is somewhat more complex. The difficult part of the war against Iraq was never going to be military, few would have backed Iraq's ramshackle army against history's most powerful fighting force, but rather, political. The key question was not how to remove Saddam's regime from power but what to put in its place.

## THE PLAN

At the time of the U.S. presidential election in 2000, the issue of Iraq barely registered on the political radar screen. Yet it was already clear to many that something would have to be done, and soon. The Clinton Administration's muddled policy of containment, based largely on the maintenance of a multilateral sanctions regime, was unraveling at an alarming rate. The original pretext for the sanctions—the destruction of the Iraqi regime's capacity to produce weapons of mass destruction (WMD)—had long since been replaced by a policy of regime change. The official position of the Clinton Administration was that sanctions would only be lifted once Saddam was no longer in office, regardless of the level of cooperation between regime officials and weapons inspectors. At this point, any incentive the regime might have had to yield to the demands of inspections evaporated. The predictable consequence was Iraqi noncooperation, the removal of the UN inspection team (UNSCOM), and the initiation of the toothless bombing campaign (Operation Desert Fox) in December 1998. Meanwhile, reports of Iraqi civilian deaths in the millions as a direct consequence of the sanctions generated huge resentment in the Arab world, creating a rapidly escalating public relations nightmare for the Clinton Administration. Bereft of ideas, the Clinton Administration handed over the reins of power to an Administration with a far clearer vision of the appropriate way to deal with Saddam's regime in Baghdad. While scarcely mentioned during the election campaign, the issue of Iraq was evidently firmly on the agenda by the time the new Bush Administration assumed office in January 2001. In September 2000, for example, the Project for the New American Century (PNAC)—a neoconservative think tank with strong links to the incoming administration—had advocated a "more permanent role" for the U.S. in the Gulf region, arguing that "while the unresolved conflict with Iraq provides the immediate justification, the need for a substantial American force presence in the Gulf transcends the issue of the regime of Saddam Hussein."[2] Perhaps more surprisingly, the group identified one of the key missions of the military as being to "secure and expand zones of democratic peace." However, the issue of Iraq remained on the back burner—at least until September 11, 2001. The president's State of the Union address the following January placed Iraq firmly in the crosshairs. Making a heroic link between the war on terror and what had been termed "rogue states" under the Clinton Administration, Bush located Iraq firmly at the center of a newly identified "Axis of Evil." While fellow members included North Korea and Iran, the real target was plainly evident. The qualifications required for Axis membership remained somewhat obscure—apparently some combination of a propensity for WMD and state support for terrorism. Only Iran seemed to convincingly fulfill both requirements—yet increasingly obviously, the Bush Administration's goal was regime change in Iraq.

Desperate attempts to integrate Iraq into a broader war on terror yielded scant evidence of any connection between Saddam and terrorism, still less between the regime in Baghdad and Al Qaeda. Osama Bin Laden has made no secret of his contempt for the secular regime in Iraq, even offering his services to the Saudis to help drive Iraqi armed forces out of Kuwait in 1991. Absent a smoking gun, much of the world, including many American observers, remained skeptical about how regime change in Iraq would affect the war on terror in anything but a negative way. A U.S. invasion of an Arab, Muslim state at the heart of the Middle East ran the serious risk of exacerbating rather than diminishing regional hostility toward the U.S.

Taken at face value, the explanations offered by Bush Administration officials remained unconvincing. However, increasingly, astute political observers began to identify the strategic vision underlying the Administration's commitment to regime change in Iraq. The National Security Strategy (NSS), released in September 2002, provided many with the missing pieces of the jigsaw. In an op-ed piece in the *New York Times*, columnist Mark Danner recognized the "chasm between the justifications proffered and the more elaborate geopolitical enterprise motivating many in the Bush Administration."[3] According to Danner, the nature of this enterprise is simple; the entire reconstruction of the Middle East along democratic, capitalist lines. The creation of "the first Arab democracy" in Iraq will encourage moderates in Iran in their struggle against hardline leaders, leading eventually to a more open, and even democratic society east of Baghdad. Simultaneously, control over vast Iraqi oil reserves will eliminate, for the immediate future at least, the West's dependence on Saudi Arabian oil supplies, permitting U.S. troops to withdraw from "holy ground" and removing one of the major bones of contention in the Arab world. Most importantly, the spread of democracy and prosperity in the region will serve to "drain the swamp" by removing the root causes of terrorism—namely, poverty and political repression. According to this vision, American policies toward the Middle East are not the primary cause of terrorism; rather, they serve as a lightning rod that focuses resentment generated by underlying societal forces. Address these underlying forces, and terrorism can be neutralized at its source. Therefore, the invasion of Iraq *is* connected to the war on terror, but at a far grander level than has so far been articulated openly by the Bush Administration.

Danner was not alone in this interpretation of the true significance of the NSS. Esteemed historian John Lewis Gaddis arrived at almost identical conclusions, describing the NSS as a "plan for transforming the entire Muslim Middle East: for bringing it, once and for all, into the modern world."[4] According to Gaddis, this "truly grand strategy . . . can set in motion a process that could undermine and ultimately remove reactionary regimes elsewhere in the Middle East, thereby eliminating the principal breeding ground for terrorism."[5]

The key assumption underpinning the strategy is that, as the NSS states, there is now "a single sustainable model for national success: freedom, democracy, and free enterprise . . . These values of freedom are right and true for every person, in every society."[6] In essence, the Administration's strategy is a battle for the "hearts and minds" of the region's people. To say the least, this is an ambitious project. As Gaddis observes, "There's been nothing like this in boldness, sweep, and vision since Americans took it upon themselves, more than half a century ago, to democratize Germany and Japan."[7] It is also a highly risky enterprise. This will be one of history's more difficult sales pitches. The Bush Administration will somehow need to convince a deeply skeptical Arab world that the grand strategy is not a cynical exercise in neo-imperialist domination, but actually has the best interests of the region's people at heart. Some idea of the scale of this task can be appreciated by examining the results of a recent Gallup poll conducted across nine predominantly Muslim countries.[8] The 11 percent favorability rating obtained by President Bush probably surprised no one. Far more shocking was that over 60 percent of those polled did not believe that Arabs were responsible for the attacks of 9/11. This included 89 percent of Kuwaitis polled. As observers of the "Arab street" have often noted, the most widespread opinion among Arabs is that the attacks of 9/11 were carried out by Israeli agents in cahoots with the Central Intelligence Agency (CIA), in order to provide a pretext for a subsequent war against the Islamic world. That such opinion flies in the face of the empirical evidence merely reinforces the point that utter cynicism about U.S. policies in the region is deeply embedded. On the positive side, the U.S.'s reputation in the Arab world can only improve. Commenting on the poll, President Bush said, "there is no question that we must do a better job of telling the compassionate side of the American story."[9] Indeed.

If the U.S. is unable to bridge this chasm of perception effectively, efforts to reconstruct Iraq along liberal democratic lines cannot possibly succeed. The foisting of a largely alien system of government on a conquered people will be bitterly resented not just in Iraq, but throughout the Middle East. There is a difference between assuming that the Iraqi people want "freedom, democracy, and free enterprise," and assuming that they will tolerate this being imposed on them by an external power at the point of a gun. As the Bush Administration embarks on its grand moral crusade to reconstruct the Middle East, it does so in the middle of a region with a long history of animosity toward the U.S. Moreover, in selecting Iraq as the test case, the U.S. has chosen perhaps the most difficult case of all.

## THE RAW MATERIAL

The history of Iraq as a modern political entity dates back to the immediate post–World War I period when Great Britain pieced together the provinces of

Basra and Baghdad from the ruins of the Middle East.[10] The addition of the northern territory of Mosul in 1925 established the geographical outlines of the Iraqi state that persist to this day. Iraq gained formal independence from British rule in 1932, and was then governed by a (British imposed) monarchy until its violent overthrow in a military coup in 1958. A decade of political chaos (1958–1968) gave way to rule by Saddam Hussein's Ba'ath Party and, from 1979 onward, to a totalitarian dictatorship under the direct (and violent) control of the "Great Leader" himself. Throughout this period, Iraq has maintained its territorial integrity as a state. What it has never succeeded in becoming is a nation. In part this failure can be attributed to the deep and often violent ethnic, tribal, economic, and sectarian divisions that persist to the present day; in part it is a function of the failure of a succession of rulers to establish a coherent and inclusive framework for the emergence of a distinct Iraqi national identity.

In the complex tapestry of Iraqi society, traditional geographical divisions are reinforced by sectarian and ethnic divides. The former Ottoman province of Basra was (and still is) populated predominantly by Shi'a Muslims; Baghdad and Mosul, by Sunnis. Overall, the Shi'a constitute approximately 60 percent of Iraq's population, Sunnis 35 percent, with the remaining 5 percent a mixture of Christians and a host of smaller religious groups. The sectarian divide is potentially explosive for political and religious reasons. Since the days of the Ottoman Empire, military and political power has been concentrated almost exclusively in the hands of the Sunni Arab minority. Sunni control over the levers of power and the distribution of the spoils of office has had predictable consequences—a simmering resentment on the part of the Shi'a that periodically erupts into open and violent rebellion.

In addition to the sectarian divide, Iraq is also fractured along ethnic lines. The central and southern parts of Iraq are ethnically Arab, while the northeastern portion of the country is populated by Kurds and smaller populations of Turkomen and Assyrians. Numerically, Arabs comprise 80 percent of the population and Kurds between 15 and 20 percent. The formal incorporation of Mosul province into the Iraqi state in 1925 was intended, in part at least, to help reduce the numerical dominance of the Shi'a.[11] In practice, this decision was to have fateful repercussions. The Kurds of northern Iraq have never accepted central rule. During the brief, turbulent history of the modern Iraqi state, one of the few constants has been Kurdish resistance to central Arab authority. More often than not this resistance has manifested itself in violent uprisings against rule from Baghdad. These rebellions have been suppressed with a brutality that has only intensified over time. This pattern was repeated in the aftermath of the second Gulf War in 1991—a full-scale Kurdish revolt against the defeated and detested regime of Saddam that succeeded in occupying all the major cities of northern Iraq was dismantled with the utmost severity by troops loyal to the regime. Subsequently, under the protection of a U.S.- and British-enforced no-fly zone, and flush with the receipts of a thriving trade in illegal oil exports across the border with Turkey, and with 13 percent of Iraq's legal oil revenues, the Kurds continue to enjoy their "golden era" of autonomous development outside the control of the Iraqi state apparatus. This they are unlikely to sacrifice without a fight.

Given the depth of these societal divisions, it is scarcely surprising that no ruler of Iraq has been able to forge a clear and inclusive vision of national identity for the Iraqi people. When and where a sense of Iraqi identity has emerged, it has normally been a negative rather than positive force—driven by hostility to internal "enemies of the state," or external demons such as imperialism or Zionism. Historically, far more energy has been devoted toward the generation of a pan-Arabist identity than toward a uniquely Iraqi identity.[12] Moreover, by definition, pan-Arabism is inaccessible to the Kurdish minority. Those who have tried to construct an inclusive vision of nationhood have failed, and many have not even tried, preferring instead to exploit societal divisions to preserve power and retain the perquisites of office. Faced with the difficult, perhaps impossible task of constructing a positive vision of Iraqi identity, all regimes have relied heavily and frequently on the use of patronage and violence to preserve the geographical integrity of the state. Saddam Hussein may well have transformed the use of violence into an art form, but in reality, he is merely the latest in a line of Iraqi rulers who have realized the necessity of holding this fractious state together by force. In this respect, Saddam is not a unique figure in Iraqi history, but rather the logical product of the difficulty of successfully governing the state by peaceful means.

## THE LEGACY OF SADDAM HUSSEIN

On October 16, 2002, Iraqi voters went to the polls to decide whether to extend Saddam's presidency for another seven years. Unsurprisingly perhaps, the Iraqi people returned a 100 percent vote of confidence in their leader. As British journalist Mark Steel wryly noted, "Saddam must have been especially pleased after the disappointment of only getting 99.96 percent last time."[13] Yet however farcical this exercise in Iraqi democracy Saddam-style appeared to Western journalists, the real story here was largely ignored. After a crushing military defeat in the second Gulf War, a subsequent rebellion that at one

point saw 15 of Iraq's 18 provinces in open revolt, numerous coup and assassination attempts, and over a decade of stringent economic sanctions, Saddam's
regime could still exercise sufficient control over the Iraqi people to turn out
the vast majority of the population and to get them to vote the "right" way at
the polling booth. Regardless of why people voted the way they did, this was
still an impressive exercise in mobilizing the masses. As of October 2002, Saddam's regime was still very much in control of things in Iraq.

Apparently, Saddam is no longer in control of things in Iraq, but it took
the military might of history's most powerful fighting forces to remove him.
Alongside figures such as Stalin and Castro, he will still go down as one of the
twentieth century's great survivors. Measured by almost any criteria (economic, social, political, or military), the rule of Saddam Hussein was a disaster
for the people of Iraq. Measured in terms of durability, Saddam has been the
most successful ruler of modern Iraq. Saddam's aptitude for survival was truly
astonishing. Understanding how Saddam survived in power for 35 years is essential to understanding the magnitude of the task confronting those seeking
to reconstruct Iraq.

Clearly, fear was an important factor. Saddam's reputation for ruthlessness
and brutality, while probably exaggerated, was no doubt deserved. But it cannot be the only factor. No regime, however brutal, could survive as long as
Saddam's based purely on fear. A more nuanced assessment would recognize
that Saddam was highly skilled at playing the political game in Iraq. As Saddam understood early on, the keys to political survival in fractious Iraq were,
and probably still are, fear and organization. Under Saddam's sole leadership
after 1979, the Ba'ath party largely shed its ideological baggage, evolving instead into a vehicle for the extension and sustenance of his own leadership.
Modeled closely on the Communist Party of the Soviet Union, the cellular
structure of the Ba'ath enabled the party to infiltrate and control all aspects of
Iraqi life. Major efforts during the 1970s to reduce illiteracy through the expansion of access to education have been hailed as one of the important
achievements of the Ba'ath. But they also enabled the party to inculcate into
successive waves of children the tenets of Ba'athist dogma and the importance
of defending the Ba'athist "revolution" against internal and external enemies.

In tandem, Saddam moved to either co-opt, neutralize, or simply eliminate
rival power structures within the state. The Iraqi Communist Party (ICP)—the
only large-scale political organization other than the Ba'ath Party in Iraq's
stunted political history—was first co-opted, then eliminated. The military, the
traditional arbiter of political power prior to the Ba'ath, was neutralized from
within. Most top-ranking military officials were staunch Ba'ath party men, or

tied to Saddam by bonds of familial or tribal loyalty. Periodic purges served to remind the military in the clearest possible terms who was really in charge in Iraq. To further safeguard against the threat of a military coup, Saddam created a number of "unconventional" military forces outside the traditional military chain of command, ranging from urban militia forces such as the *Fedayeen Saddam* (Men of Sacrifice), to the rather more daunting Republican and Special Republican Guards. By channeling resources to these forces at the expense of the regular army, Saddam bought their ultimate loyalty, and ensured his own survival against internal uprisings. Keeping a watchful eye over Saddam's architecture of control was a complex network of security services, ranging from the Department of General Intelligence (the infamous *Mukhabarat*) to the less well-known Special Security Service (*Jihaz al-Amn al-Khas*). These various agencies monitored internal and external threats on behalf of the regime, and, critically, monitored each other.

Beyond Saddam's aptitude as an organizer, the hallmark of his regime's durability was his capacity to exploit existing societal divisions to serve his own purposes. Thus during the war with Iran, Saddam appealed to Arab identity to solidify the ranks against the Persian threat from the East. In the aftermath of the second Gulf War, faced with a major Shi'a uprising in the south, the appeal was along sectarian lines. What probably saved the regime in its gravest hour was Sunni fear of a successful Shi'a rebellion—fear that was intentionally stoked by a desperate regime. Saddam also proved adept at exploiting ethnic (Arab/Kurd) divisions, and even the factional divides among the Kurds themselves. During the 1990s, the regime made a conscious effort to appeal selectively along tribal lines. Particularly in the south, Saddam strenuously wooed certain tribal leaders, rewarding some at the expense of others. In this way, Shi'a tribal leaders were drafted to help the regime maintain its grip on the rebellious south. Ironically, in co-opting selected Shi'a leaders, the regime reversed a decades-old tradition by which the Shi'a were largely excluded from access to the spoils of office. Saddam's incarnation as the *sheikh mashayikh* (chief of chiefs) cut across the sectarian divide with an appeal based on tribal rather than sectarian identity.[14] In so far as this was a more "inclusive" mode of governance, it came at a considerable cost. The underlying social and political order in Iraq became yet more fragmented and dysfunctional. It is in this environment that the architects of a postwar reconstruction of Iraq will be required to operate.

Complex issues arise regarding the nature of the democratic arrangements to be implemented in defeated Iraq. By definition, democracy will invert the existing power structure in Iraq. This is purely a function of numbers. Sunni Arabs—rulers of Iraq throughout its modern history—constitute less than 20 percent of the population, while Shi'a Arabs make up 60 percent. In any meaningful democratic order, the Shi'a will dominate, and the Sunnis will have to take it on trust that the Shi'a will not use their position of dominance to exact retribution (violent or otherwise) for decades of subjugation at the hands of the Sunni. Likewise the Kurds (15 to 20 percent of the population) will be expected to accept at face value the pledges of the overwhelming Arab majority to respect Kurdish autonomy, culture, and language—despite the overwhelming historical evidence to the contrary. Of course, constitutional scholars in the West will be busy designing elaborate systems of checks and balances to ensure minority representation; the executive branch will probably be some form of collegial presidency with all three groups represented; the parliament will no doubt be elected by proportional representation to ensure that representation faithfully reflects the society's major groupings; each major group will be granted veto power over important decisions; and so the list could go on. Iraq's first democratic constitution will almost certainly resemble the fragmented institutional monstrosity imposed on the Bosnians as part of the Dayton Peace Accords in 1995. It has not worked there, and it will not work in Iraq because two critical ingredients are missing. First, at the most fundamental level, democracy requires the existence of an implicit consensus on the legitimacy of the underlying order. Put simply, all of Iraq's social groups must recognize the state of Iraq as a legitimate territorial entity. It is questionable whether the Kurds have ever fully accepted the legitimacy of an Iraqi state that includes them within its boundaries. Second, any form of democracy requires trust. Assigning vetoes to minority groups, devising complex forms of checks and balances—these can all help to minimize the occasions on which the majority can tyrannize the minority, but ultimately, some decisions have to be made according to majority rule, or else the state simply cannot function. In these areas, the minority has to be able to trust that the majority will not abuse its power. The history of modern Iraq indicates that trust among society's major groupings has mostly been in pitifully short supply. In the absence of any developed sense of national identity, a basic consensus over the legitimacy of the Iraqi state, and a reservoir of mutual trust and understanding to draw upon, it is difficult indeed to locate the foundation on which a liberal democratic Iraqi state can be constructed.

## ALTERNATIVES

An alternative option involves genuinely allowing the Iraqis themselves to determine their own future. At present, the oft-stated U.S. intention to "let the

Iraqi people decide their own leaders" sounds entirely reasonable. Yet what it really means is that Iraqis get the opportunity to elect their chosen representatives within the confines of a political and economic framework dictated to them from outside. If self-determination is really the intention, then the starting point is to address a fundamental question. Do the Iraqi people want the state of Iraq to continue in its present configuration? Without a basic shared emotional commitment to preserving a unitary state, democracy cannot take root. If, as seems likely, the Kurds opt to pursue their historical dream of an independent Kurdish state, then this outcome must be accepted and respected by the international community. After all, this would be no more than the long-overdue fulfillment of a promise made to the Kurds as far back as 1920. Some states in the region—notably Turkey and Iran—would consider the establishment of an independent Kurdistan to be destabilizing to the region. A powerful counterargument can be advanced that it is precisely the absence of a Kurdish state that makes the Kurds a perpetually destabilizing force in the Middle East. Removing the Kurds from the state of Iraq would increase the numerical dominance of Shi'a over Sunni in the remaining territory. It is possible that Arab identity will transcend sectarian differences, and the bulk of Iraq will remain intact. However, it is also possible that traditional sectarian divisions will prevail, and that a further division of Iraq into Sunni and Shi'a zones will be the outcome. Hence, if the Iraqi people are genuinely given the right to shape their own future, it is possible that what emerges out of contemporary Iraq could be three distinct entities. Each would be relatively homogenous, so each would also be much more viable as an independent state than is the current state of Iraq.[15] Of course, many argue that the removal of Saddam's regime from power will ultimately result in the disintegration of Iraq in any case. The key difference then is how this occurs—through a managed and orderly process, or through bloodshed and civil war. The option of "managed partition" has yet to be seriously contemplated, and it is certainly not without its problems and complexities.[16] Clearly, it is not the "ideal" solution to the problem of what comes after Saddam. But it does not have to be; rather it only needs to be demonstrably more viable than the current alternative. This is the case we make in the chapters that follow.

## CHAPTER ONE

# IRAQ 1920–1958:
# THE HASHEMITE MONARCHY

## INTRODUCTION

THE RELENTLESS DEMONIZATION OF SADDAM HUSSEIN over the last decade or so imparted a deeply personal flavor to the conflict with Iraq. War with Iraq was a moral crusade to rid the world of an evil tyrant and to liberate the Iraqi people from the yoke of a murderous dictator; but the fact that successive U.S. administrations apparently had an inexhaustible reservoir of synonyms for the word "evil" to apply to the Iraqi leader does not alter the fact that his removal may well create more problems than it resolves.

Placed in historical context, the regime of Saddam Hussein appears less as an aberration, and more as a logical culmination of the pathologies embedded in the state of Iraq since its creation in 1921. Iraq was assembled according to great power (mainly British) strategic calculations rather than with a view to creating a coherent, functional, self-sustaining state. Governing this deeply fractious product of British geopolitical engineering has traditionally entailed the skillful manipulation of tribal, ethnic, and sectarian divisions (the classic "divide and rule" technique of colonial domination), supplemented periodically by the application of generous doses of violence. The removal of Saddam's regime does not alter this, it will simply require the violence to be administered by someone else: the U.S. perhaps.

## THE BIRTH OF IRAQ

By the end of World War I, the once proud Ottoman Empire[1] lay in ruins and the victorious Allied combatants—primarily France and Great Britain—were in control of large swathes of former Ottoman territory in the Middle East. The colonial carving up of Ottoman lands had already begun long before the war's end. In January 1916, a British member of Parliament and Middle East expert, Sir Mark Sykes, and a French Government representative, François Georges Picot, met in London to divide up the future spoils of war. The resulting Sykes–Picot Agreement provided for French control over Greater Lebanon and Syria, while Britain was to retain control over the former Ottoman provinces of Basra and Baghdad. The Agreement was kept secret for two years, primarily for fear of alienating Arab opinion, which was, at that time, vital in the military struggle being waged against the Ottomans.[2] The covert establishment of mutually acceptable spheres of influence in the Middle East was accorded a fig leaf of legitimacy when the Supreme Council of the League of Nations convened in San Remo in 1920.

Article 22 of the League's founding charter (the Covenant) outlined a mandate system to deal with "those colonies and territories which as a consequence of the late war have ceased to be under the sovereignty of the States which formerly governed them and which are inhabited by people not yet able to stand by themselves under the strenuous conditions of the modern world." The "tutelage" of such entities was to be the mandate of "advanced nations" who would "prepare" them for self-government. Idealistic (or patronizing) in intent, the mandate system was, in practice, little more than a means of ensuring continued colonial dominance over conquered territory. Anglo-French dominance of the League ensured that the spoils of war were appropriately allocated. The French were awarded the mandate for Lebanon and Syria, while Britain was assigned tutelage over the territory that became officially known as Iraq in March 1921.

To oversee its recent acquisition, Britain required a suitably pliant leader and a system of governance that would ensure British dominance without incurring unnecessary economic costs. British authorities thus turned to the Hashemite Amir Faisal. A veteran of the Arab Revolt against the Ottomans during the war, Faisal had at least three major selling points: his prominent participation in the Arab Revolt endowed him with natural authority in the Arab world; he enjoyed generally good relations with the British; and, from 1920 onward, he was available, following his unceremonious eviction from the abortive Syrian Kingdom by the French.[3]

Iraq's first great exercise in fake democracy did not occur under the leadership of Saddam Hussein. In July 1921, the British staged a rigged referendum to impart legitimacy to Faisal's rule. The resulting vote indicated that a highly implausible 96 percent of the population favored Faisal's accession to the newly created throne. Hence, in August 1921 a man who had never even visited Iraq previously, was duly installed as the new nation's first leader. During a somewhat surreal investiture ceremony on August 27, 1921, the new Iraqi flag was proudly raised, but the military band, in the absence of an Iraqi national anthem, played "God Save the King"—an apt indication as to who really controlled the levers of power in the nascent Iraqi state.[4]

## Appending the Kurds

The precise territorial configuration of the new state had yet to be determined. There was no dispute that the provinces of Baghdad and Basra were components in the fledgling Iraqi state. However, the northernmost of the three former Ottoman provinces—Mosul—raised a number of important strategic concerns.[5] Most notably, initial assessments by the British suggested that large reserves of oil were located in Mosul. Access to oil reserves was almost certainly the primary motivating factor behind the British decision to incorporate Mosul into the new state of Iraq—yet this decision was to have tragic repercussions for the unity and coherence of Iraq for decades to come.

The problem was simple. Unlike the vast majority of the populations of Baghdad and Basra, who were ethnically Arab (though divided along sectarian Sunni/Shi'a lines), the province of Mosul included a significant population of ethnic Kurds. In the aftermath of World War I, it was generally assumed that the Kurds, as a significant ethnic presence in the Middle East, would be awarded their own state. A treaty to this effect—the Treaty of Sèvres, concluded in August 1920 between the victorious allies and the defeated Ottoman Empire—had indeed envisaged a separate Kurdish state. The state was to combine the Kurds of what is now Turkey with those of northern Iraq, and the resulting entity, an independent Kurdistan, would be allowed to apply for admission to the League of Nations within a year of the signing of the Treaty.

Tragically for the Kurds, their dream of an independent existence was thwarted almost immediately by geopolitical realities. A successful nationalist movement in Turkey led by Mustafa Kamal Atatürk swept away the remnants of Ottoman rule in Turkey and reestablished Turkish control over Kurdish areas in the southeastern part of Turkey. Atatürk then laid claim to Mosul as Turkish territory, and backed up his claim by an invasion of the province. Faced with the prospect of losing control over oil-rich Mosul, the British successfully repelled the Turkish advance, driving the Turks back across what was subsequently to become the Iraqi–Turkish border. In 1925 a League of Nations commission officially recognized the legality of this border. Thus, Mosul was recognized (along with Baghdad and Basra) as part of the modern state of Iraq.

This decision divided the bulk of the Kurdish nation between Turkey, Syria, Iran, and Iraq—thus shattering hopes of an independent Kurdish homeland. The Kurdish nation was not to have its own state, mainly because an independent Kurdistan was simply not in the strategic interests of the great powers.

## Governing the New State

Negotiations over an Anglo–Iraq Treaty to govern relations between Britain and Iraq during the mandate began in late 1921 and were eventually approved by the Iraqi Parliament (Constituent Assembly) in 1924. Simultaneously, a new constitution and electoral law were devised and adopted. On paper at least, the political system possessed all the trappings of democracy. The electoral law established a two-stage system of elections to the parliament. All male taxpayers aged over 21 were eligible to vote for secondary electors in one of the three large electoral districts into which Iraq was divided. Secondary electors then elected parliamentary deputies. The king was granted the power to appoint cabinet members, to confirm all laws, to dismiss parliament, and to call for general elections.

Most important from the British perspective, the king could completely bypass parliament and issue executive orders to fulfill treaty obligations. British rule was exercised largely behind the scenes through a system of political "advisors" appointed to the major departments of government to ensure that British interests were adequately represented within the system. Critically, the British provided the military muscle to guarantee security within the nascent state. This was exercised through an indigenous army of Assyrians numbering over 5,000 and the firepower of the Royal Air Force (RAF).[6] Economic control was ensured by requiring Iraq to pay half the costs of the British mandate, and, subsequently, through British dominance over the emerging Iraqi oil industry.

The democratic facade did little to mask British colonial dominance and placed King Faisal in a deeply unenviable position. Deprived of real power, the king's major function was to serve as a symbol of unity for Iraq. But crafting a coherent national identity from a deeply divided and fractious society proved beyond even the politically experienced and, by all accounts, very able

Faisal. The two forces that Faisal could potentially have harnessed to unify his people—a profound and widespread anti-British sentiment and a burgeoning sense of Arab nationalism—were both inimical to his status as a *de facto* British puppet. Faisal was caught between the aspirations of the Iraqi people to be free of British influence and the cold, hard reality of British power. Ultimately, his failure to provide the foundations for the emergence of a strong, stable, and united Iraq must be placed in the appropriate context. Faisal failed to accomplish an impossible task.

This was a failure that was explicitly recognized by the King himself in his later years. Shortly before his death in 1933, Faisal provided a perceptive and prescient analysis of the problems confronting his fragmented inheritance—

> In Iraq . . . there is still no Iraqi people, but unimaginable masses of human beings, devoid of any patriotic ideal . . . connected by no common tie, giving ear to evil, prone to anarchy, and perpetually ready to rise against any government whatsoever. Out of these masses we want to fashion a people which we would train, educate, and refine . . . The circumstances being what they are, the immenseness of the efforts needed for this cannot be imagined.[7]

The year before Faisal's death, Iraq gained formal independence from Britain and was accepted as a member of the League of Nations. However, Iraq still owed certain obligations to the British as a consequence of a revised version of the Anglo–Iraq Treaty agreed to in 1930. Under its terms, British advisors already present in Iraq (by 1931 these totaled about 260) were to remain, Britain was permitted to lease two air bases in Iraq, and the two countries agreed to consult closely on Iraq's foreign policy and to provide mutual assistance in time of war.[8]

While the Treaty effectively guaranteed Iraq's independence, it did little to assuage anti-British sentiment in Iraq, not least because it entailed the perpetuation of considerable British influence for the foreseeable future (the Treaty had a duration of 25 years).

## Decline of Monarchical Rule

Following Faisal's death in 1933, his son Ghazi acceded to the throne. Lacking the talents of his father, Ghazi nonetheless enjoyed popularity, mainly because his thinly disguised contempt for the British played well among pan-Arabist politicians and average Iraqis alike.[9] Much to the chagrin of the British, Ghazi disseminated pan-Arabist ideas and spread anti-British sentiment throughout the Middle East. To facilitate this process, Ghazi went as far as to establish his own radio station at the royal palace of Al Zuhour from which daily propaganda broadcasts were beamed out to the region.[10] King Ghazi's unwillingness to play the role of pliant monarch enhanced his prestige among ordinary Arabs, but disturbed the delicate political balance that had prevailed in Iraq under his father's rule.

In the absence of the late Faisal's steadying influence, the political fabric of Iraq began to unravel with alarming rapidity. Between 1936 and 1941, there were seven political coups involving extra-constitutional transfers of power. The first of these—a military coup apparently instigated by Ghazi, but executed by General Bakr Sidqi and the Iraqi Army—marked a critical turning point in Iraq's history. The removal, at gunpoint, of Prime Minister Yasin al-Hashimi and his entire cabinet from office indicated with some clarity that the military was now a key power broker in Iraqi politics. The 1936 coup also signaled the beginning of the end of constitutional order in Iraq. Whatever the failings of King Faisal, elections had been held and changes in Prime Minister and Cabinet had been accomplished according to constitutional principles. After 1936, extra-constitutional, often violent transfers of power became the rule rather than the exception. Symptomatic of Iraq's descent into political disorder, General Sidqi's assassination in 1937 (by a disgruntled group of army officers) was followed in quick succession by the death of Ghazi in suspicious circumstances (1939), another military coup by Iraqi army officers (1941), a military invasion of Iraq by the British Army (May 1941), and a vicious pogrom conducted against Jews in Baghdad (June 1941) in which some 150 Jews were slaughtered by a rampaging mob in full view of occupying British forces.

Of these events, the most significant was probably Ghazi's death. The official British version of events was that Ghazi had died instantly (and in a drunker stupor) when his car crashed at high speed head-on into a telephone pole. Many remain unconvinced by the official version of events, and have concluded that Ghazi was, in all likelihood, assassinated by the British.[11]

Truth often matters less than perception, and most Iraqis simply assumed that Ghazi had been the victim of regicide. According to one observer, the true significance of Ghazi's death was that it

> proved that the British would never accept anything except "their" king or regent. The people of Iraq wanted the opposite, a king who would be more than a figurehead symbol of unity and would unite their country through expressing their desires. They wanted a king who would close their divisions, heal their social wounds and become a magnet for all the Arabs of the Middle East.[12]

Although the monarchy survived to rule Iraq for another 18 years—first in the form of a regency (of Ghazi's cousin Abdul Ilah, from 1939 to 1953), then through the brief reign of Ghazi's only son, Faisal II, from 1953 to 1958—after the suspected complicity of the British in the death of Ghazi, the days of Hashemite rule in Iraq were numbered. Abdul Ilah was deeply unpopular in Iraq. Just how unpopular became evident in 1958 when the regent met his grisly end. A group of army officers (the so-called "Free Officers") overthrew the monarchy in a coup that wiped out almost the entire royal family. Whereas Faisal II's lifeless body was conveyed to a secret location for burial, Abdul Ilah's body was thrown to the mob. After being dragged through the streets, it was dismembered, and the remains hung on public display for two days outside the Ministry of Defense in Baghdad.

This gruesome termination of Hashemite rule in Iraq was probably inevitable. The Hashemite dynasty was an invention of British rule, and was always perceived as such by the majority of Iraqis. For 38 years, successive Hashemite rulers were unable to resolve the central contradiction embedded in the idea of monarchical rule in Iraq. The essential function of the monarchy was to serve as a symbol of unity for the Iraqi people—to rally Iraq's disparate and factious elements around a common project of nation-building. Ultimately, however, the sorts of political message that could successfully span both sectarian and ethic divides were limited; possibilities included an appeal for a more equitable distribution of power and privilege, or some form of pan-Arabist, anti-British theme. But the Hashemite monarchy could never credibly harness these appeals and channel them toward a common purpose. As a creation of the British, the monarchy presided over a system that relied for its stability on rewarding the few at the expense of the many. King Ghazi's efforts to arouse Arab sentiment against the British had, at least according to popular perception, been dealt with in short order by the British. It is ironic then that after 38 years of Hashemite rule, during which the monarchy struggled hard to create a coherent sense of national identity, the most potent source of Iraqi national identity was one forged around the idea of opposition to the continued monarchical rule.

## LEGACIES OF MONARCHICAL RULE

### Sunni Dominance

Despite constituting only about 20 percent of Iraq's population, Sunni Arabs have controlled the levers of economic and political power throughout the history of modern Iraq. Under the Ottomans, the three provinces of Mosul,

Baghdad, and Basra were administered by Sunni Arabs, a tradition that the British intentionally did little to disturb. Sunni dominance was manifest not just in the form of the Hashemite dynasty, but throughout the political elite. For example, between 1921 and 1936, of the 57 men who held cabinet positions, only 5 were either Shi'a or Kurds. Over the entirety of monarchical rule (1921–1958), the five power ministries were controlled almost exclusively by Sunnis.[13] Dominance was even more pronounced at the local level. In 1933, for example, Sunnis governed in 13 of Iraq's 14 provinces, and comprised 43 out of 47 heads of district.[14] According to one estimate, of the most important political leaders in Iraq over the 1920–1958 period, close to 60 percent were Arab Sunni, about 25 percent were Arab Shi'a, and 15 percent were Kurdish.[15] Over the same period, Sunnis comprised approximately 20 percent of Iraq's population, the Shi'a, 55 to 60 percent, and the Kurds 20 percent. Thus, not only did Sunnis dominate, they dominated out of all proportion to their numerical presence in the population.

A similar pattern prevailed within the armed forces. While the Shi'a were well represented in the lower ranks (particularly after the introduction of conscription in the 1930s), the officer corps was almost exclusively a Sunni domain. Sunni dominance of the military was to become increasingly important over the course of the period as the armed forces began to assume a more active role in the political life of Iraq.

The exclusion of Shi'a and Kurds from power was by no means absolute. The expansion of Iraq's armed forces over the period of the monarchy provided some means of advancement. Numerically, the army increased from less than 12,000 in 1933 to 15,000 by 1935, and had reached 20,000 by the time of the military coup in 1958. Key to the army's growth was the introduction of conscription in 1934 (and the popularity of the army's role in the 1933 Assyrian massacre); thereafter, the numerically superior Shi'a came to comprise the bulk of the army. For Kurds, too, the armed forces were accessible, and offered the potential for political advancement. Of the ten Kurds who came to play a significant political role across the 1920 to 1958 period, all owed their positions of prominence to careers in the armed forces.[16]

The British adopted a conscious policy of strengthening the power of certain tribal leaders through a variety of measures, including acknowledging their possession of tribal lands; cash payments; arms supplies; and the implementation of a special tribal disputes code that enabled leaders to administer local justice within their recognized spheres of jurisdiction. This policy benefited Sunni, Shi'a, and Kurdish leaders alike (though the number of individuals who benefited was obviously very small). The British also ensured that prominent tribal leaders were well represented in parliament. Approximately one-fifth of seats in the Iraqi parliament were reserved for tribal leaders. By 1954, this had risen to 38 percent.[17] These manipulations were not driven by an egalitarian impulse to spread power, wealth, and influence across the sectarian divide. Rather, they were cynical but highly effective divide-and-conquer tactics. By favoring certain Shi'a tribal leaders at the expense of others, the British, and subsequently the Sunni-dominated regime, preempted the emergence of a unified Shi'a opposition to the status quo. Perhaps even more significantly, they drove a wedge between the two key foci of organized Shi'a power—the tribal leadership and the religious leaders of the south.[18]

Many Shi'a also made progress in the economic realm. With access to the military and political elite largely denied them, upward mobility for the Shi'a was achieved mainly through land accumulation or entrepreneurial activities. Thus, in 1958 Shi'a Arabs comprised close to 50 percent of Iraq's largest land owners, and 7 of Iraq's 15 millionaires.[19] Nonetheless, the clear pattern throughout the period was of extensive Sunni political dominance out of all proportion to their numerical presence within Iraq. This dominance persisted, largely unchecked, throughout the twentieth century.

## Governing Iraq

One of the most significant consequences of British hegemony and Sunni political dominance was the failure of representative democracy to take root. In simple terms, embracing truly representative democracy would have required the Sunni Arabs to relinquish their stranglehold over political power in favor of the numerically superior Shi'a. The British, of course, were complicit in this arrangement, preferring to govern through those elements of the Sunni Arab elite deemed to be dependably pro-British. A more inclusive system would almost certainly have meant a more anti-British polity, and this the British were naturally unprepared to tolerate.

Hence what was in theory a relatively democratic constitution—involving elections and some attempt to separate legislative from executive power—was in practice a stillborn political creation. The key positions of executive power—Prime Minister and the power positions in the Cabinet—were dominated throughout by the same small number of (mainly) elite Sunni Arabs. Typical in this respect was the prolific political career of Nuri al-Said—a reliably pro-British Sunni Arab who held a total of 47 cabinet posts (14 times as Prime Minister) during the monarchical period. As a political operator of considerable dexterity, Nuri was ideally equipped to succeed in a political environment where ideology meant little, and the politics of personality meant everything.

Political competition, such as it was, was driven not by the power of ideas, but by the clash of rival factions that cohered around prominent individual politicians. For those involved, the key concern was to preserve the status quo, thus ensuring continued access to the privileges and benefits of office for themselves, their families, and their supporters. As stated by political scientist Charles Tripp, "intense rivalry for patronage and fierce competition between client networks for influence characterized this regime of power."[20]

The three centers of power under the Hashemite regime—the British, the monarchy, and a relatively small cabal of Sunni Arab politicians—all had a vested interest in preserving the status quo, and none had an incentive to liberalize the political process. For the most part, elections were carefully stage-managed, with the outcomes determined in advance.[21] In this context, opposition groups had few incentives to abide by the rules of a game they could not hope to win. Of the numerous political parties that emerged over the period, only three had an enduring influence on the political process. Of these, two were licensed: The *Istiqlal* (Independence) Party, which championed pan-Arabist causes and was strongly anti-British, and the National Democratic Party (NDP), which favored political liberalization and a more equitable distribution of wealth. While both parties participated in several elections from the 1930s onward, their willingness to work within a system that was so obviously stacked against them declined significantly over time. Had the system permitted, these two parties could have formed the nucleus of a moderate and progressive party system. As it was, they ended up becoming deeply alienated from the regime.

The third major organized political force was the Iraqi Communist Party (ICP). It was not licensed to participate in elections and so did not even try to work within the established system. While initially a party of the literate urban middle classes, the ICP evolved into Iraq's first genuine grassroots political force. More ominously for the regime, the ICP's political message—an anti-imperialist appeal for a more egalitarian distribution of wealth and privilege—resonated beyond the Sunni heartland to embrace Shi'a, Kurds, and other disaffected minorities. Continually harassed and persecuted by the regime, the ICP relied on the ideological commitment of its leadership to organize a tightly knit, disciplined operation that spearheaded a political assault on the legitimacy of the political system. By the later 1940s, the ICP had become the best-organized political force in Iraq and was at the forefront of efforts to mobilize popular resistance to the established political order. The organizational skills of the ICP and its capacity to mobilize dissent was evident in the numerous strikes and demonstrations that convulsed Iraq during the latter years of the Hashemite monarchy.

The success of the ICP highlights the fundamental weaknesses inherent in the country's flawed democratic experience. Opposition was tolerated to the extent that it did not meaningfully threaten the existing status quo. This pattern was established early on by the British, and was sustained by an oligarchy of mainly Sunni Arab elites for whom the status quo entailed continued enjoyment of the material benefits of political office. Opposition groups for whom the status quo (for whatever reason) was unacceptable were excluded from meaningful participation in the "legitimate" political process. As a consequence, their goal became the overthrow of the regime from without, rather than peaceful change from within. Through its failure to accommodate opposing voices, the regime unwittingly nurtured the seeds of its own destruction. Moreover, it gave birth to a new dynamic in Iraqi political life. Henceforth, control over the political machinery of the state shifted to those with the capacity to mobilize "the street" (the ICP), those who controlled the instruments of coercion (the armed forces), or those with the ability to manipulate both (the Ba'ath Party under Saddam Hussein).

## The Use of Violence

It is tempting to view the brutality of Saddam Hussein's regime as an anomaly in the modern history of Iraq. Without underestimating the *extent* to which Saddam relied on coercion to maintain his grip on power, it is undeniable that the use of force to remove a regime, to sustain a regime, or to ensure the territorial integrity of the state is scarcely without precedent in the annals of Iraqi history. Those who focused on the "evilness" of Saddam invariably point to the use of chemical weapons against the Iraqi Kurds during the so-called *Anfal* campaign in 1988. That a leader could use such weapons *against his own people* was apparently the epicenter of the moral argument calling for his removal by force.

Perhaps the extensive British use of chemical weapons against rebellious Kurdish tribes during the 1920s provided the model for the *Anfal* campaign. Certainly it was Winston Churchill rather than Saddam Hussein who spoke of the "excellent moral effect" of using gas against the Iraqis in 1920, and the British rather than Iraqi air force that pioneered the use of phosphorus bombs and a rudimentary form of napalm to subdue Iraqi Kurdistan.[22] The casual and persistent use of violence to maintain order has been the norm rather than the exception. As stated by one historian, "Beginning with the British ideas of order, the use of violence to suppress dissent, much of which took violent form itself, has been reproduced and elaborated by central governments in Baghdad since the foundation of the state."[23]

Very early on, the nature of "British ideas of order" became evident. As early as 1920, before the pieces of Iraq had even been officially conjoined, a major rebellion broke out against British rule. The rebellion, which mainly involved Shi'a tribes from the mid- and lower-Euphrates region (but was also supported by Sunni tribes and the Shi'a religious establishment) was suppressed with efficient brutality by the British. By October 1920, barely four months after it had begun, the rebellion was over, at a cost of 500 British and Indian lives, and the lives of over 6,000 rebels. Throughout the first half of the 1920s, the British relied heavily on air power to administer discipline to the perpetually rebellious Kurdish tribes in the north. As Wing Commander Gale of the RAF noted, "If the Kurds hadn't learned by our example to behave themselves in a civilized way then we had to spank their bottoms. This was done by bombs and guns."[24]

Repressing the "uncivilized" Kurds through the liberal use of violence was to become something of a national sport in Iraq over the next 80 years, but the Kurds have not been the only victims. During the 1930s there was almost perpetual unrest in the Shi'a south fueled by a variety of motives, but underpinned throughout by their continued exclusion from the upper echelons of political power.[25] Denied the opportunity to express discontent through democratic means, the Shi'a often opted for open revolt.

The most serious Shi'a rebellions occurred in 1935 and 1936. In each case, the response of the now independent Iraqi government was to use armed force to crush the rebellions ruthlessly. The task of administering forceful discipline to the Shi'a tribes fell to General Bakr Sidqi—a man not renowned for his squeamishness in the face of adversity. The same man achieved infamy (and considerable popularity) through his orchestration of the massacre of hundreds of Iraqi Assyrians in 1933. The Assyrian massacre was a government instigated attempt to target a minority "scapegoat" group, deemed to constitute an enemy of the state. During the course of the violence, Kurds, Arabs, and Yazidis found common cause in the persecution of the Assyrians. In the words of one commentator, "In short it was open season on Assyrians in Iraq in the summer of 1933."[26]

The military's role in the affair was unsavory. On August 11, 1933, a motorized machine-gun unit under the command of General Sidqi entered the Assyrian-populated village of Sumayl, and proceeded to exterminate systematically the inhabitants—men, women, and children. Far from being a cause of national shame, the Assyrian massacre became a symbol of national pride and unity. Triumphal arches were erected in the army's honor in the city of Mosul; the army enjoyed a tickertape parade through the streets of Baghdad on its return to the capital; and recruitment to the army increased dramatically as a consequence of the army's "heroic" elimination of the Assyrian threat.[27] According to one commentator, "The Assyrian pogrom was the first genuine expression of national independence in a former Arab province of the Ottoman Empire."[28]

Yet the infliction of violence on minority groups was merely the most visible manifestation of a deeply troubled political system. As opposition to the regime intensified during the latter years of the 1940s, coercion increasingly became the standard response to political dissent. In 1946, a strike instigated by the ICP among oil workers in Kirkuk resulted in police opening fire on a crowd of workers, killing 8 and injuring up to 50. The so-called "Kirkuk Massacre" was followed in 1948 by the *wathbah* (uprising), a student-led demonstration against the continued British influence that resulted in police killing five students.[29] Eleven days later, a more serious clash between police and demonstrators—the most serious in Iraq's short history—led to the deaths of 77 demonstrators and the wounding of several hundred. Widespread rioting in 1952 (the so-called *intifada*), which ultimately spread to most of Iraq's urban centers, was dealt with equally harshly. While less gratuitously violent than the Assyrian pogrom, the regime's response to these political challenges, and the nature of the challenges themselves (which were all expressed through violence) emphasized how far removed the system was from being a functioning, stable democratic order. Deprived of access through legitimate means, opposition groups staged violent demonstrations designed to undermine the regime; a predictably violent response from the regime merely added further fuel to the fire. That the end point of this cycle of violence was the overthrow of the regime in a bloodbath in 1958 served to reinforce an important lesson— namely, that violence was a much more effective way to achieve meaningful political change than peaceful, democratic means. One of the enduring legacies of the monarchical regime, then, was the institutionalization of violence as a political instrument, a process that began with British "ideas of order" and reached its logical culmination under the regime of Saddam Hussein.

## National Unity

Whether there was any more deeply rooted sense of Iraqi national identity in 1958 than there had been in 1921 is questionable. The most powerful unifying force throughout the period was opposition to British influence, and, subsequently, opposition to the regime imposed by the British on Iraq. By channeling their animosity against a common enemy, sharply divergent groups were able to unify around a common cause. But this unity was inherently negative. Groups could agree on what they did not want Iraq to be, but lacked a shared, *positive* vision of Iraqi national identity.

Crafting an inclusive sense of national identity was always going to be a challenge given the ethnic and sectarian makeup of Iraq. Of the various fault lines that fracture Iraqi society, the ethnic Arab/Kurd divide has always proven the least tractable. The Kurds were never willing participants in the creation of the new Iraqi state and have consistently, often violently, resisted the imposition of rule from Baghdad. The identity of the power at the center mattered little; the Kurds rebelled against British rule in 1919 and proved a permanent source of irritation for the RAF throughout the 1920s. Simmering resentment was periodically punctuated by serious rebellions, such as those of 1930 and 1945. Both rebellions were crushed with large-scale military force, but the fundamental problem was never resolved. The Kurds have a distinct historical, cultural, and linguistic identity that resolutely refuses to be assimilated into something broader. Hence the search for an inclusive national identity for Iraq was destined to fail, for the simple reason that a sizable minority (Kurds constitute 15 to 20 percent of the total population) has little interest in participating in the search.

The sectarian, Sunni/Shi'a Arab divide is altogether more complex and will be dealt with in greater detail in subsequent chapters. For the moment, it is worth noting that tensions between Sunni and Shi'a were seldom driven by purely sectarian differences. Certainly, the secular Sunni regime viewed the political role played by prominent religious leaders in the south with some concern;[30] but the major problem was the congruence of sectarian divisions with divisions of wealth and political power. Sunni control over political and economic power effectively relegated the majority of Shi'a to a position of permanent subordination. A shared Arab ethnicity (potentially at least) could have been exploited to transcend these divisions. However, the particular version of Arab nationalist ideology adopted and promoted by the Sunni regime was an additional barrier, as it stressed the historical glories of the Arab empire and viewed Shi'ism as a heretical, Persian-inspired threat to the unity of the Arab world.[31] This Sunni-defined Arab nationalism thus engendered mutual suspicion rather then internal unity. In foreign policy terms, the prevalent Sunni Arab vision was one of unifying the Arab world into one single coherent entity. This vision was unlikely to appeal to the Shi'a. While constituting a significant majority within Iraq, the Shi'a would be outnumbered approximately nine to one in a unified Arab state that embraced all the Arab countries of the Middle East. Thus the Shi'a were relegated to the status of second-class Arabs—or worse, perceived by Sunnis as a potential fifth column for the extension of Persian (Iranian) influence into Iraq.

This vision of pan-Arab unity was actually part of a far broader debate based on the future direction of Iraq's foreign policy. Subsumed within this was a more profound disagreement about the future identity of the Iraqi state. Iraqi nationalists argued that Iraq was an independent nation-state with a distinct Arab identity, while pan-Arabists considered it to be Iraq's destiny to become an administrative unit within a larger, unified Arab nation. This debate was still awaiting definitive resolution in 1958. While the pan-Arabist view prevailed, as it did throughout much of the period, the internal unification of the Iraqi nation was always less of a concern than the ultimate goal of broader Arab unity.

By 1958, Iraq had been an independent state for over a quarter of a century but had failed to become a coherent nation. There remained no enduring ideological "glue" that bound together Iraq's disparate factions into something larger. In large part this reflected the difficulty (perhaps impossibility) of forging a national identity that could simultaneously transcend sectarian and ethnic divides. In part it reflected the reality that the debate over the nature of Iraqi identity was never an inclusive one.

The exclusivity of the political system generated resentment and division rather than consensus and unity. The institution that probably came closest to imparting a sense of national unity was the army; yet the army's contribution was always something of a double-edged sword. On the one side, the army was one of the few institutions established under the monarchy that served as a source of integration rather than division. On the other hand, as was the case in all important national institutions, the distribution of power within the armed forces failed to reflect the broader social makeup of Iraq. With a few significant exceptions (General Bakr Sidqi was ethnically Kurdish, as was the executor of the 1958 coup, Brigadier Abdel Karim Qassim), the officer corps was dominated by Sunni Arabs. Indeed, the introduction of conscription was strongly opposed in large parts of the Shi'a south and the Kurdish north largely because of the (generally accurate) perception that while Sunni Arabs would make the important decisions, it would fall on the Kurds and the Shi'a to provide the cannon fodder.

Initially, the political significance of the army was largely symbolic. Whereas the other political institutions of the regime were always viewed as legacies of imperial domination, the army was the first institutional expression of independent Iraqi statehood. As such, it commanded the respect of Iraq's population in a way that the monarchy and parliament never could. As the Assyrian massacre made clear, however, the army's role as a source of popular unity was not necessarily benign.

Controlling both the instruments of coercion and the broader loyalties of the Iraqi people, the armed forces had, by 1958, become the ultimate arbiters of political power in Iraq. When it came to the crunch, as it did in 1958, tens of thousands of Iraqis took to the streets in support of the military coup. Popular resistance to the overthrow of the regime was invisible. This new reality made prospects for the emergence of a peaceful, democratic political order in Iraq appear grim indeed.

Ominously, one of the most powerful sources of Arab unity that emerged over the 1920 to 1958 period was a common hatred of the state of Israel. After Israel's creation in 1948, the most reliable way to unify Iraq's Arab population was to focus attention on hostility toward Israel. Iraq's significant military contribution to the Arab–Israeli war in 1948 was immensely popular among Arabs in Iraq, and the ultimate humiliation of the Arab forces irreparably undermined the prestige of the regime at home. But the message was clear, and not lost on subsequent leaders of Iraq. Iraq's Arab population could be reliably unified around an aggressive anti-Zionist posture.

## CONCLUSION: FUTURE PATTERNS ESTABLISHED

The pathologies of contemporary Iraq—the internal repression, the widespread and systematic use of violence, and the threat the country presents to its neighbors and the international community as a whole—are deeply rooted in the troubled history of Iraq. The real damage was inflicted on the fabric of Iraq long before Saddam Hussein arrived on the scene. Two critical decisions—both attributable to the British—stand out in this respect. First, the decision to attach the province of Mosul to the Arab-populated provinces of Baghdad and Basra to create the state of Iraq confronted subsequent leaders of Iraq with an inescapable dilemma: how to integrate a sizeable minority of perpetually rebellious Kurds into a larger Arab entity. All of Iraq's leaders have struggled with this problem, and in the last analysis, all have addressed it through the use of violence. Second, the conscious decision on the part of the British to favor the Sunni Arab minority at the expense of the more numerous Shi'a effectively precluded the emergence of meaningfully representative government.

The Sunni Arabs were the chosen agents of indirect British rule. Their status as a numerical minority ensured that the constitutional trappings of democracy could never amount to much more than an organized sham. Safeguarding Sunni rule required the implementation of classic divide-and-conquer tactics. Certain powerful Shi'a tribal leaders were systematically favored at the expense of others, thus dividing the Shi'a elite against itself. Once again, when all else failed, the stranglehold of the Sunni oligarchy on power was maintained through coercion. This basic pattern persisted throughout the 1920–1958 period.

## CHAPTER TWO

# IRAQ 1958–1968:
# REVOLUTION, REPUBLIC, AND RENAISSANCE

## INTRODUCTION

THE MILITARY COUP OF 1958 COULD HAVE MARKED a critical turning point in the history of Iraq. This "revolution" swept away the last institutional vestiges of colonial domination, finally severing the deeply unpopular umbilical cord linking Iraq to Britain. It brought to power an individual—Brigadier Abdel Karim Qassim—who appeared the very personification of Iraq's ethnic and sectarian diversity. Qassim's father was a Sunni Arab and his mother a Shi'a Kurd; hence Qassim could, with some legitimacy, claim to be Iraq's first truly representative leader.

Sadly, the first decade of the newly established Iraqi republic was scarred by violence, internal conflicts, and gross political instability. A succession of coups and counter-coups yielded a series of leaders who were simply unable to control the forces unleashed by the popular revolution; from the midst of the chaos emerged triumphant the one force—the Ba'ath Party—that proved capable of administering discipline to Iraq's anarchic political order.[1] It was a ruthless form of discipline, but it was highly effective nonetheless; so effective indeed, that after 1968, when the Ba'ath assumed sole control over the Iraqi state, no other organized political force came close to successfully challenging its hegemony.

This dominance was expressed initially in the form of tightly structured one-party rule; after 1979, when Saddam Hussein offically assumed leadership of the party, the Ba'ath increasingly functioned as a well-oiled vehicle for the personal ambitions of Saddam. The Ba'ath succeeded in sustaining hegemony where others had failed. Understanding the durability of the Ba'ath and its leader yields critical insights into the underlying dynamics of Iraqi political history.

## THE 1958 COUP: BIRTH OF THE IRAQI REPUBLIC

The military coup that overthrew the Hashemite monarchy in 1958 was, by all accounts, popular and violent.[2] The coup was spearheaded by two disaffected army officers—Brigadier Qassim and General Abdul Salam Arif, backed by a group of predominantly Sunni Arab officers (known collectively as the "Free Officers") and an assorted collection of opposition political parties (the Iraqi Communist Party [ICP], the National Democratic Party [NDP], the Independence Party, and the Ba'ath). Collectively, these disparate forces were united by little more than staunch opposition to the existing regime. There was shared agreement on the need to eliminate all traces of the prevailing political order, but profound disagreement about what to put in its place.

For some—notably the Free Officers and the Ba'ath—the revolution provided the opportunity to pursue long cherished pan-Arabist aspirations. The other groups favored an Iraq-first approach—one that focused on rectifying internal economic and social problems and emphasized Iraq's development as an independent nation-state. Unity among these groups, which had been forged in the heat of hostility toward a common enemy, dissipated with startling rapidity after 1958. Politics became a naked and increasingly ugly struggle to control the future trajectory of Iraq.

The violence associated with the coup itself was an ominous indicator of things to come. On July 14, 1958, while the Free Officers focused their forces on liquidating the royal family (decisively and permanently terminating Hashemite rule) and seizing key points in the capital, the political parties set about mobilizing the Baghdad streets to protect the unfolding revolution. At the forefront was the ICP, whose capacity to mobilize large numbers of supporters in short order was, at the time, unrivalled.

After seizing control of the radio station, General Arif broadcast a short statement declaring an end to the monarchy, the beginning of the Iraqi Republic, and urging the people to take to the streets. Over the following days, tens of thousands of people poured onto the streets of Baghdad—some simply to observe first-hand the drama of the unfolding events, but many to exact violent retribution on the figures and symbols of the hated former regime. The armed forces looked on as popular will was expressed in the form of wide-spread looting, beatings, and revenge killings.

Two new realities of Iraqi political life were established as a consequence of the coup. First, from being one of several competing political forces, the military emerged as *the* ultimate source of political power in Iraq. A relatively small group of disgruntled army officers had succeeded in erasing an entire political system. Second, the aftermath of the coup illustrated the vital role of mass mobilization as an instrument of political control. The Free Officers encouraged the Iraqi people to take to the streets in order to present the appearance that the coup was a popular and thus legitimate revolution—the better thereby to preclude outside intervention or a possible counter-coup by loyalist army officers. Henceforth, the relative power of political parties was determined not by size of party membership or by coherence of ideological message, but by capacity for mass mobilization.

## THE NEW REPUBLIC

From the outset, events elsewhere in the Middle East dominated the political discourse in the new republic. The decade after 1948 had been a turbulent time for the region. The Cold War competition between the U.S. and the Soviet Union had steadily moved into top gear; the creation of the state of Israel and the consequent displacement of hundreds of thousands of Palestinian Arabs generated outrage throughout the Arab world; in 1952, a coup in Egypt had overthrown (relatively peacefully) the monarchy of King Farouk bringing Gamal Abdul Nasser to power; and in 1956 President Nasser demonstrated his mettle with a display of defiance against the British, French, and Israeli armed forces during the Suez Crisis. Nasser's performance elevated him to the status of undisputed hero within the Arab world. In February 1958, Egypt and Syria were officially united via the creation of a United Arab Republic (UAR). Though geographically bizarre (the two countries shared no common border), the UAR seemed to many to constitute the first step toward the pan-Arabist goal of creating a larger, unified territorial entity that would embrace the entire Arab world.

Following the coup, the pan-Arabists, led by coup-instigator General Arif, pushed for Iraq's immediate entry into the UAR. Ranged against these pan-Arabists were the ICP, the NDP, and, ultimately, Qassim's group; the favored focus of this latter group was on the social and economic development of Iraq as an independent state. Iraq could not simultaneously join the UAR and remain independent, and thus the stage was set for a protracted and painful struggle between these competing visions of Iraq's future. This struggle dominated the brief regime of Qassim and eventually sabotaged what might otherwise have been a brave new start for the Iraqi nation.

Qassim's reign promised much but ended up delivering very little. Considerable efforts were dedicated to the formulation of a government apparatus that would faithfully reflect Iraq's divergent groupings. A three-man Council of Sovereignty (essentially a collegial presidency) was created in which each of Iraq's three major groups—Kurds, Sunni Arabs, and Shi'a Arabs—were allocated seats. The regime's first cabinet was equally inclusive, with posts for all major political parties, and only one seat (the lowly social affairs portfolio) assigned to the Free Officers.[3] However, most of the power was reserved for Qassim (as prime minister, minister of defense, and commander-in-chief), and Arif (as deputy prime minister, minister of the interior, and deputy commander-in-chief). Even so, on paper at least, this was the most broadly representative system of government enjoyed by Iraq in its brief history.

To further suggest that Iraq was heading for a new dawn of political liberalization, Qassim allowed for the relicensing of formerly prohibited political parties and announced that free and fair elections would be held within a year. Sadly, it was never to be. Politics was to be dominated by a bitter and as yet unresolved dispute over the identity of the Iraqi state. At first this dispute played out as a struggle for power between the two main instigators of the coup, Qassim and Arif; subsequently, it came close to tipping the country into full-scale civil war.

Arif, as leader of the pan-Arab faction, pushed immediately for union with the UAR. This push undoubtedly reflected a genuine commitment to the cause of Arab unity, but was also intended as a direct challenge to Qassim for control of the state. Qassim dealt swiftly with this personal challenge. Arif was first exiled to Bonn, West Germany, under the guise of an ambassadorial appointment. When Arif returned to Baghdad amid rumors of an impending plot to overthrow Qassim, the latter had him arrested, tried, and sentenced to death (later commuted to life in prison). But disposing of an immediate rival did nothing to resolve the underlying issue.

Powerful pan-Arab forces were arrayed against Qassim. Qassim had succeeded in alienating powerful segments of the officer corps both through his lukewarm attitude toward union with the UAR and through his failure to appoint more of the Free Officers to positions of power within the regime. He also alienated the leadership of the Ba'ath, who were deeply disillusioned by Qassim's failure to embrace fully the pan-Arab cause. To counter the threat, Qassim came to rely heavily on the organizational prowess of the ICP. This was a dangerous development. Iraqi politics increasingly acquired a "rent-a-mob" complexion as the ICP, on demand, orchestrated pro-Qassim rallies, through which the "Sole Leader" would stroll, soaking up the adulation of the crowd.[4] But Qassim was playing with fire. The "theatre of the street" was often little more than organized anarchy.[5]

By 1960, the ICP was 25,000 strong—though hardcore, experienced membership was significantly lower than this. As the ICP extended its influence and its membership, it inspired fear among many (such as large land owners) that it would translate this influence into policies of radical wealth redistribution. Partly as a result of its reliance on ICP muscle, the regime that had promised to dedicate itself to the cause of national unity was now presiding over an increasingly polarized society.

At times, Iraq appeared headed for a complete and irrevocable breakdown in law and order. The Mosul Revolt of March 1959 was a case in point. The trigger for the revolt was a massive, Communist-sponsored rally in the northern city of Mosul. Over 250,000 Communist sympathizers poured into the city, unwittingly disrupting plans for a coup attempt that were then being hatched by the commander of the Mosul garrison and two other colleagues from the Free Officers movement. These pan-Arab officers, supported by a significant contingent of sympathizers and local Kurdish tribal groups (and with material support from the UAR), decided to act. They rounded up prominent Communist leaders and launched the rebellion. The action precipitated violent confrontations between pan-Arabists and Communists, which soon escalated into a low-level war. Qassim dispatched the Iraqi air force to bomb the rebels' headquarters in Mosul, fatally wounding one of the leaders of the attempted coup. The rebellion collapsed shortly thereafter.

Later the same year, the ICP organized another large-scale rally to coincide with the first anniversary of the revolution in the northern city of Kirkuk. Once again, the Communist display of strength precipitated violent confrontations, this time between ethnically Kurdish Communist sympathizers and the indigenous Turcoman (ethnically Turkish) community. The body count was lower than in Mosul (all told, about 30 deaths and over 100 injuries), but a disturbing pattern was emerging. Qassim was faced with a difficult strategic decision; on one hand, he relied on the capacity of the ICP to mobilize popular demonstrations of support for the regime. On the other, Communist excesses were solidifying opposition to his regime. Qassim acted to reassert his authority by striking out against the Communists. In the aftermath of the Kirkuk incident, several Communists deemed responsible for instigating the violence were rounded up, tried by military court, and executed.

The Communist press was effectively silenced, and Communists in positions of power within the regime were gradually weeded out. For the remainder of Qassim's rule, the ICP was subdued, but still largely supportive of the regime.[6]

In addition to the chaos created by the excesses of the ICP, the stability of Qassim's regime was also threatened by the pan-Arabist forces. By 1960, three attempts to overthrow the regime had already been conducted—an attempted coup in December 1958, the Mosul Revolt of March 1959, and a Ba'ath-instigated assassination attempt in October 1959. The latter was poorly planned and abysmally executed, but was notable in that it marked the first time that Saddam Hussein (a participant in the attempt) made an impact on the national stage.

The "heroics" surrounding his escape from capture are the stuff of all subsequent authorized biographies of Saddam. The official version of events, as recorded in the autobiographical *The Long Days*, tells of how a wounded Saddam extracted a bullet from his own leg with a razor blade, swam across the Euphrates River (heading for Syria), then completed the last stage of a seven-day journey on horseback across the Syrian desert. Apparently, he was accorded a hero's welcome on his arrival in Syria by fellow Ba'ath Party members.

## THE BA'ATH PARTY TAKES CONTROL

The Ba'ath Party was a minor power in Iraqi politics at the time the monarchy was overthrown in 1958. In 1956, for example, the Iraq branch of the Ba'ath boasted perhaps 300 members. By the first year of the republic under Qassim, membership had increased considerably, to 1,200 hardcore members, supplemented by 2,000 "organized" supporters, and a potential "mob" of 10,000.[7] Relative to the organized power of the ICP, however, this was an insignificant force. The ICP at the time could probably call upon over a million supporters. The ICP's control of the street was amply demonstrated in May 1959 when the Party mobilized a rally of over half a million people in Baghdad. This was to be the high point of the ICP's popularity; over the following years, the Ba'ath picked up new members at about the same rate as the ICP was shedding them.

Three key factors help explain the rise of the Ba'ath at the expense of the ICP. First, as noted above, Qassim's reluctance to embrace the idea of immediate union with the UAR helped mobilize support for the Arab nationalist cause. Second, the ICP's rampages in Mosul and Kirkuk caused many to gravitate toward any organized political force that opposed Communist influence. Third, while the Ba'ath Party's abortive attempt to assassinate Qassim in 1959 ended in farce, the immediate aftermath greatly increased the stature of the Party in the eyes of many.

The regime rounded up 57 Arab nationalist "enemies of the state" (mostly Party members) and herded them into the People's Court for the obligatory show trial. The intention was to provide a public forum for the humiliation and intimidation of these opponents of the regime. To this end, the trials were broadcast live throughout the Arab world. But the tactic backfired as one by one, the accused refused to recant, and instead used the occasion to mount defiant attacks on the regime, accusing it of betraying the Arab cause. It was, as Aburish notes, "the Ba'ath Party's finest hour."[8] Seventeen were ultimately sentenced to death, including Saddam Hussein.

The string of failed attempts at regime change by the pan-Arabists was a setback to the cause, but only a temporary one. The Ba'ath Party regrouped during the early 1960s, focusing its energy on strengthening party organization and improving its capacity to mobilize a presence on the street to challenge the ICP. One major failing of the ICP was its inability to infiltrate the armed forces. The Ba'ath Party was much more effective in this respect.

In 1962, Party secretary Ali Salih al-Sadi established the Military Bureau of the Ba'ath Party, with the express purpose of recruiting members of the officer corps to the cause. The effectiveness of these moves was graphically illustrated in 1963 when a coalition of Ba'ath civilian activists and Ba'athist army officers succeeded in overthrowing the Qassim regime. While units under the control of Ba'athist officers surrounded the Ministry of Defense, well-armed Party supporters took to the streets to neutralize the potential threat of ICP mobilization. After two days of fierce fighting around the Ministry, the rebels broke through the lines of defense, captured Qassim, and executed him. In the aftermath of the successful coup, this civilian contingent formed the backbone of a new paramilitary militia force—the National Guard—which supplanted Qassim's Popular Resistance Force. Qassim's regime had been born in a hail of bullets and ended in similar fashion. Visual confirmation of Qassim's demise was provided when rebels aired pictures of the "Sole Leader's" lifeless corpse on Iraqi national television.

## THE BA'ATH IN POWER

To govern the new regime, the coup instigators established a National Council of the Revolutionary Command (NCRC), to be headed by the recently liberated General Arif. The Ba'ath Party claimed 16 of the 18 seats on the Council, and 12 of the 21 cabinet positions—including that of Prime Minister, which went to General Ahmad Hassan al-Bakr.[9] This was a government totally dominated by the Ba'ath—with power allocated roughly equally between civilian and military wings of the Party.[10] But it was to last only nine months. This provided just enough time for the Party to wreak havoc on the streets of Baghdad, initiating a wave of terror that swept the capital. At the crest of the wave was the National Guard. With its ranks swelled to perhaps 15,000, this force was charged with defending the revolution and rooting out enemies of the state. This task was pursued with the maximum of gratuitous violence.

The targets were predominantly leftists—trade unionists, ICP members, and members of the various ICP-sponsored militia groups. The result was a bloodbath involving the arbitrary execution of up to 3,500 supporters of the former regime. This was also a period during which torture became commonplace—most notably at Baghdad's Qasr al-Nihaya, the infamous "Palace of the End," which would later become one of the most active torture sites under Saddam's rule.

With attention focused on smashing the ICP and its bases of support, there was little time for the Ba'ath Party to achieve anything constructive with its nine months of power. Talks began in April 1963 between the regime and Egypt over possible union, but yielded nothing. Then in June, a new assault was launched against the Kurds—somewhat bizarrely, given that the Kurds had fought to the end against Qassim's regime, and had actually supported the coup that overthrew him.

This latest attempt to squash Kurdish resistance involved razing Kurdish villages using tanks and aircraft, killing hundreds of innocents in the process. This fierce new offensive against the Kurds was designed to illustrate the regime's strength of purpose to an officer corps that had been frustrated by their inability to defeat the Kurds under the previous regime. The context for the assault conformed to the by-now familiar pattern. The Kurds offered a plan for wide-ranging autonomy within the north, and, fearing that granting the Kurdish request would undermine the territorial integrity of the state, the regime opted to settle the matter through violent means. Regardless of the identity of the regime at the center, the cycle of violence inflicted on the Kurds continued unabated.

In 1963, the Ba'ath Party lacked the capacity to govern a country. The regime was hopelessly divided internally, split between a radical socialist wing and a more conservative, pan-Arabist faction. The latter was also divided between those favoring immediate union with Egypt (the pro-Nasserites), and those looking to advance the case of Arab unity through an Iraq–Syria Ba'athist axis.[11] Splits between the military and civilian wings of the Party were also evident, growing rapidly as the National Guard stepped up its campaign of terror. To the military contingent, the National Guard was rapidly becoming a dangerous, destabilizing threat to the integrity of the new regime.

In the midst of chaos, President Arif mobilized those army units on whose loyalty he could rely, seized key strategic points in Baghdad, then launched an assault on the headquarters of the National Guard. Within hours, Arif had successfully achieved Iraq's latest military coup, once more reestablishing the military as the ultimate source of political power in the country.

While largely avoiding the gratuitous excesses of the brief Ba'ath regime, the Arif regime made clear from the outset that democracy was not a serious option. Arif himself maintained his position as president, and officially assumed command of the armed forces. Thus empowered, Arif ruled Iraq as a military dictatorship until his demise in a helicopter crash in April 1966.

As a veteran of the 1958 coup, Arif had a clearer idea than most of how to maintain power in the turbulent world of Iraqi politics. To appease leftists, Arif issued a decree in July 1964 nationalizing banks and leading industrial firms. To placate pan-Arabist sentiment, the 1964 Constitution explicitly outlined Arab union as the ultimate goal of the Iraqi state. Rather than eliminating opponents by unleashing the militia to exact retribution (Arif in fact dissolved the deeply feared National Guard), Arif relentlessly, but no less effectively, weeded out enemies (mainly the Ba'ath Party) behind the scenes. Arif relied on an expanded secret police to either assassinate prominent Ba'ath members or lock them safely away behind bars. To safeguard against the prospect of coups from within the armed forces, he removed known Ba'ath sympathizers from their posts (including Bakr, who was imprisoned), and, in a move that was to have fateful repercussions, established a small army of hand-picked troops, operating outside the established military chain of command (the Republican Guard), to protect him against his own army. This became an enduring contribution to the institutional landscape of Iraqi politics—a buffer force of fiercely loyal, elite troops with a vested interest in defending the regime. To guarantee loyalty, Arif relied on ties of tribal kinship. The force was headed by Colonel Sa'id Slaibi, who like Arif was a member of the al-Jumaila tribe; territory occupied by the tribe became the major source of recruits. The infamous Republican Guard was thus not a creation of Saddam Hussein—though it was subsequently to fulfill an identical function under his regime.

Through a careful combination of such manipulations, Arif was able to impose some order on Iraq. The exception, predictably, was in the north. Despite initial promises to end the Kurdish war peacefully, negotiations between the government and Kurdish leader Mulla Mustafa Barzani broke down with the usual rapidity, and full-scale fighting resumed in the summer of 1964. As in times past, government forces could control the major population centers with relative ease, but were never able to drive the Kurds from their strongholds in the mountains. Stalemate was the predictable result.

The superficial calm that Arif had imposed on proceedings quickly evaporated after his death in April 1966. The National Defense Council, which had replaced the NCRC as the principal organ of governance, elected Abdel Rahman Arif, brother of the deceased general, as President. He proved far less adept than his brother at manipulating Iraq's political forces. A 12-point peace plan was offered to the Kurds to end the war in the north. The plan was perhaps the most generous ever offered to the Kurds, but was withdrawn almost immediately due to intense pressure from the army officers surrounding Arif. The armed standoff persisted in the north.

In an entirely laudable attempt to move the regime away from military dictatorship, Arif threatened to reconstitute Parliament and to hold elections. Prominent Ba'ath Party activists were released from prison—a move that was to have fatal consequences. The death knell of the regime came in the aftermath of the Arab–Israeli War of 1967. The "Six Day War," in which Israelis dismantled the combined forces of Egypt, Syria, and Jordan with consummate ease, was a major blow to the prestige of the Arab world, and in particular, to the military governments that had presided over many countries in the region since the 1950s.

The Israeli victory was so rapid that Iraqi forces had no real opportunity to get involved in the fighting. Nonetheless, the Arif regime paid the price for this combined Arab failure. In the months following the war, turmoil reigned on the streets of Baghdad. In the thick of things was the revitalized Ba'ath Party. The end for Arif, when it came, was an uncharacteristically gentlemanly affair.

Allied with key officers from military intelligence, the Republican Guard, and the Guard's tank regiment, the Ba'ath Party's military wing seized the TV station in Baghdad, the Ministry of Defense, and the headquarters of the Republican Guard. General Hardan al-Tikriti, a Ba'athist army officer, delivered a polite request in person to Arif that he resign and fly to join his wife in London. Arif complied with the request after first sharing a cup of tea with the general.[12]

The Ba'ath Party was once more at the helm of Iraqi politics—and this time, it would prove rather more difficult to displace.

# LEGACIES OF THE IRAQI REPUBLIC

## Sunni Dominance

Brigadier Qassim's assumption of power in 1958 had suggested that, for the first time in the history of Iraq, the Sunni stranglehold over the institutions of state might be loosened. As the product of a Sunni Arab father and a Shi'a Kurdish mother, Qassim possessed the perfect demographic profile to govern the fractious state of Iraq. The creation of the three-man Council of Sovereignty, in which Kurds, Sunni Arabs, and Shi'a Arabs were equally represented, was (apparently) a major step forward in the search for a truly representative political system. Moreover, Qassim's most important political ally—the ICP—was a party that spanned the sectarian and ethnic divide. Indeed, the ICP was a Shi'a stronghold, appealing particularly to the lower-class Shi'a in the slums of Baghdad, as well as to the Shi'a masses in the south. Kurds, too, could identify readily with a political party that emphasized wealth redistribution and was ambivalent, even hostile, toward grandiose pan-Arabist schemes. Under Qassim, for the first time since the creation of the Iraqi state the political system was not dominated by Sunni elites. The problem was that *real* power did not reside in the Council of Sovereignty, the ICP, or even the person of Qassim. During the first ten years of the Iraqi Republic, the power to determine the fate of regimes lay with the military, and the military was a bastion of Sunni power. The armed forces were the key powerbroker in all regime transitions over this ten-year period. Power had simply shifted from civilian Sunni elites under the monarchy to military Sunni elites under the Republic. The seizure of power by General Arif, a committed pan-Arabist and staunch "Sunni nationalist," confirmed that Iraq was still ruled from the Sunni heartland.[13] In fact, it was under the various regimes of the first ten years of the Iraqi Republic that the dominance of Sunnis over positions of political power reached its zenith. Over the 1958–1968 period, of the 38 most important political leaders, 30 were Sunni Arabs, 6 were Shi'a Arabs, and only 2 were Kurds.[14] At lower levels of government the dominance of Sunni Arabs was less pronounced, but the system as a whole was further from being broadly representative of Iraq's diversity than it had ever been.

## Governing Iraq

Iraq's first experience of genuinely independent governance began promisingly. A popular leader of mixed ethnic background, with a clear focus on national unity rather than vague schemes for broader Arab union, made clear his commitment to heal historical wounds from the outset. He instituted a broadly representative government, relicensed political parties, and promised early elections. Moreover, in 1958, the political landscape was populated by a number of ideologically moderate political parties (such as the NDP) with middle-class appeal and a commitment to working within a democratic framework. By 1963, however, most of these parties had simply disappeared, to be replaced by two powerful organizations (the ICP and the Ba'ath Party) of an entirely different pedigree. The political competition between them was never likely to be played out at the ballot box. This was a clash of clandestine organizations in which victory would be determined by capacity to mobilize "the street."[15] Both were ideologically immoderate, and neither was interested in democratic pluralism. Qassim's regime did not create these two forces, but it provided the stage on which this new, fundamentally intolerant style of politics was acted out.

Behind the scenes, the upper echelons of the armed forces were divided and riddled with conspiracy. Qassim's personal charisma ensured him considerable support, but in the end it was not sufficient to survive the violent military coup that terminated his regime. In other respects also, Qassim's regime contributed significantly to the degeneration of Iraqi political life. The establishment of the People's Court in August 1958 was a case in point. Created initially to try leaders of the monarchical regime for certain categories of crime (threatening the security of the nation and corrupting the regime), the Court soon evolved into something less savory. Qassim's total control over the Court ensured that important enemies could be dispatched with the minimum of due process. Carefully staged show trials, designed primarily for public consumption, destroyed the Court's credibility as an instrument of justice. Instead, it became an instrument of dictatorship.[16]

Another dubious contribution of the Qassim regime was the institution of a state-sponsored popular militia. The paramilitary "Popular Resistance Force" was established soon after Qassim assumed power. Its primary functions were to ensure loyalty to the regime on the street, using intimidation where necessary, and to weed out and eliminate clandestine opposition activity. Qassim's two institutional innovations—a Court for staging productions masquerading as justice, and a paramilitary militia—were subsequently to become important elements of the Ba'ath Party's political repertoire.

Under Qassim's watch, Iraq's politics acquired a bitter, violent, and dangerous tone. In 1958, prospects for the evolution of a stable democratic order in Iraq had looked reasonable; by 1963, they had evaporated entirely. Instead, what the regime provided was the perfect training ground for the political force (the Ba'ath Party) that was soon to dominate the totality of life in Iraq. The ICP and the Ba'ath Party, whose struggle for preeminence defined much of the political character of the decade, were never likely to champion the cause of liberal democracy. In the end the Ba'ath Party prevailed, in part because its Arab nationalist message made it more appealing to the officer corps (still the key to political power), and in part because the Party dealt with opposition much more ruthlessly.

The astute and pragmatic General Arif, who ruled Iraq for three years (1963–1966) restored some semblance of order to Iraq's chaotic and violent political life, but the respite was only temporary. His weaker and less able brother who succeeded him was simply incapable of exercising the same degree of control over events. The second Arif's sincere attempts to liberalize a political system that was by then dominated by fundamentally illiberal political forces (such as the Ba'ath) was doomed from the outset. The time for democracy in Iraq had long since passed.

## The Use of Violence

By the latter years of the monarchy, state-controlled violence had become an institutionalized means of dealing with dissent. It was sadly appropriate, then, that monarchical rule was terminated in so violent a fashion in 1958. The events surrounding the 1958 coup provided an ominous indicator of the extent to which violence had permeated the fabric of Iraq. The treatment of the royal family (liquidated almost in its entirety by the Free Officers) was moderate in comparison with the fate meted out to regent Abdul Ilah and the detested symbol of British rule, Nuri al-Sa'id. Abdul Ilah was thrown to the mob and dismembered; then the various body parts were strung up for days outside the Ministry of Defense. Abdul Ilah's treatment at the hands of the mob was matched in barbarity only by the treatment of Nuri al-Sa'id. Nuri escaped the initial retribution, but was apprehended the following day trying to escape dressed as a woman. He was killed and buried quietly that night. The following day his body was dug up by the mob, dragged through the streets, then repeatedly run over by cars until the corpse resembled "Iraqi sausage meat."[17] The body was then cut into small pieces and the remnants held aloft by the triumphant crowd.[18]

A new form of popular political expression was born during the days after the 1958 coup. Control of the street became a critical tool of governance, and the "mob" became a key political actor. This was a form of popular participation

that was inevitably steeped in violence. The massive ICP "rallies" that characterized the first years of Qassim's regime more often than not degenerated into
widespread random acts of violence. In the immediate aftermath of the 1959
Mosul Revolt, for example, Communist forces went on the rampage in Mosul,
slaughtering hundreds of pan-Arabists as well as a number of the city's wealthy
families. They established a mock court, staged show trials, and executed 17
people. Similar events in Kirkuk the same year indicated that the ICP was anything but a peaceful force for change in Iraqi politics. In fact, the ICP helped to
foster precisely the sort of turbulent and violent political environment in which
the Ba'ath Party could flourish. The Ba'ath, however, was always more deliberate and targeted in its use of violence. This was evident during the Party's brief
stint in government in 1963. The wave of terror that swept Baghdad during the
Ba'ath's nine months in power was, in fact, a relatively well-organized campaign
of extermination targeting prominent ICP activists and aimed at decapitating
the leadership of Communist-dominated civic organizations.[19] The fate of the
first secretary of the ICP—Husain Ahmed al-Rahdi—was typical of the brutality
employed. After his capture, al-Rahdi was tortured for 15 days at the Palace of
the End, before being crushed to death.[20] The ICP estimated the death toll of
members at over 5,000—no mean achievement for a 9-month period, and an enduring testament to the Ba'ath's capacity to inflict violence efficiently. But unlike
the violence associated with large-scale ICP rallies, this was violence with a purpose—namely, to terrorize and ultimately eliminate a powerful and dangerous
political opponent. It was this capacity to *focus* violence that separated the Ba'ath
from the ICP, enabling a far less numerically significant political force to dominate Iraq's first genuinely mass political movement. The emergence of the
Ba'ath as a major political power in Iraq was a telling symptom of the prevailing
political climate in Iraq. Iraq, as CIA director Allen Dulles declared in 1959,
"was the most dangerous spot on earth."[21]

It was certainly a dangerous spot for the Kurds. Indeed, the first decade of
the Iraqi Republic witnessed the evolution of the Kurdish struggle against
central authority into a serious military confrontation, initiating an on-off civil
war that was to last until 1991. It is notable that over a ten-year period, four
different central regimes attempted to resolve the "Kurdish problem," initially
through negotiation, but ultimately through violence. Qassim's attempts to
seek a peaceful resolution to the issue were half-hearted, and were over by
September 1961. A political standoff between Kurdish leader Mustafa Barzani
and the regime was resolved when Qassim ordered the bombing of Barzani's
home village of Barzan. Full-scale war erupted and continued until the end of
Qassim's regime. The cost to the Kurds was 500 bombed villages, hundreds of

deaths, and up to 80,000 displaced people.[22] The inability of Qassim's regime to deliver a decisive military victory over the Kurds was one of the major contributory factors to his eventual overthrow.

The most concerted effort to crush Kurdish resistance through the use of force was undertaken by the Ba'ath, who somehow found time away from eliminating Communists by the thousands to launch a major military offensive against Kurdish forces in April 1963. The offensive involved the massive and largely indiscriminate bombardment of Kurdish villages from the air and by heavy artillery; villages that came under central government control were bulldozed, and strategic areas of northern Iraq were "Arabized." Kurdish resistance stiffened rather than crumbled in response to this onslaught. The elusive military solution was pursued by both Arif brothers, but by 1966, the Kurds were receiving significant military assistance from Iran, and were essentially unbeatable fighting on their own terrain. Violence could not yield a solution to the Kurdish problem, but neither (apparently) could negotiation.

## National Unity

Qassim's rise to power offered hopes that Iraq could be unified under a democratic regime at last. Ranged in his support were significant sections of the armed forces, a personal popularity among the Iraqi people, and the ICP—the most powerful political organization of the period, and the only political party with an ideological appeal that could span the ethnic and sectarian divide.[23]

Some of this initial promise was indeed fulfilled in the economic and social realm. Under Qassim's leadership, a conscious effort was made to rectify some of the economic inequities of the monarchical regime. Spending on education almost doubled,[24] social welfare spending increased dramatically, and conditions were improved for workers.[25] An ambitious (though never fully realized) Agrarian Reform Law of 1958 envisaged the large-scale redistribution of land in favor of the peasants and at the expense of major landowners. Meanwhile, the position of women in society improved considerably via revisions to the personal status code, which granted equal inheritance rights regardless of gender, imposed limitations on polygamy rights, and raised the minimum marriage age to 18.[26] These moderately progressive reforms were aimed at diluting the concentration of wealth and privilege that had accumulated in the hands of the few under the monarchy. Inevitably, this generated opposition to the regime. Ominously, it aroused the hostility of the religious establishment in the Shi'a south. This hostility revolved around two issues. First, the communist-tinged reforms of the Qassim regime (particularly changes to the status of women) were perceived as threatening to the traditional social order; second, the ICP began to make significant inroads in terms of membership not only in the Shi'a slums of Baghdad, but also in the holy cities of Najaf and Karbala. The successful recruitment of members by the atheistic ICP in the heartland of Shi'a Islam was perceived as a serious challenge to the status of the religious establishment in the south. The origins of organized resistance to the growing influence of communism can be traced to the late-1950s and the formation of the *Jama'at al-'ulama* (literally, the Society of the Learned)—a body dedicated to strengthening religious awareness within the Shi'a community and to counteracting atheism (i.e., communism). The *Jama'at* spawned not only influential publications such as the periodical *al-Adwa* (the Beams of Light), but also the underground (and often violent) *al-Da'wa* movement. The religious establishment in the south had played no significant role in Iraq's political life since the rebellion against the British in 1920. This changed after 1958 as first the "godless Communism" of the Qassim regime, and then the strident pan-Arabism and "Sunni jingoism" of the Ba'ath and Arif regimes, aroused increasingly organized, vocal, and violent opposition among the Shi'a religious leadership.[27] The reawakening of politicized religion and its potential to exacerbate the sectarian divide was one of the most dangerous legacies of the first decade of the Iraqi Republic. It sparked off a competition that persists to this day between successive secular regimes and the Shi'a religious establishment to win the hearts and minds of the Shi'a "masses."

Ultimately, though, the most significant obstacle to the emergence of a coherent sense of national unity and identity was the problem of the Kurds in the north. From 1961 onward, the successful and peaceful integration of the Kurds into the state of Iraq became progressively less and less likely. A major part of the problem was the internationalization of the Kurdish struggle against the central government. In 1961, the Kurdish struggle against Qassim's regime was supported monetarily and militarily by the U.S. and Israel; after 1963, Iran became the major source of military equipment and financial assistance. A clear pattern was emerging, by which the Kurds were willing to ally with external forces to pursue their goal of autonomy, while external powers were more than willing to use the Kurds as a surrogate army to weaken and destabilize regimes at the center. The significance of this external involvement in the internal affairs of Iraq was that it precluded a military solution to the Kurdish problem. Fighting out of mountainous terrain and supported materially by external powers, the Kurds could not be defeated outright by the Iraqi armed forces. They therefore had few incentives to compromise on their demands for autonomy. This level of autonomy was unacceptable to both the

Iraqi military and the succession of pan-Arabist regimes that ruled Iraq after the fall of Qassim. The result was a stalemate that periodically erupted into full-scale military hostilities.

The renaissance of politicized Shi'ism and the escalation of ethnic (Kurdish–Arab) conflict were the most overt manifestations of the difficulties involved in stitching together Iraq's diverse parts into a coherent whole. Beneath the surface, it was clear that Iraq was not a nation at peace with itself. A telling indicator of this came in the wake of the failed Mosul Rebellion of 1959. The Communist-led rampage against pan-Arabist forces in Mosul precipitated a total breakdown of law and order in the city. In turn, this opened up a Pandora's box of festering hatreds and resentments as the city degenerated into an orgy of violence:

> For four days and nights Kurds and Yazidis stood against Arabs: Assyrian and Aramian Christians against Arab Muslims; the Arab tribe of Albu Mutaiwit against the Arab tribe of Shamar; the Kurdish tribe of Gargariyyah against Arab Albu Mutaiwit; the peasants of Mosul country against their landlords; the soldiers of the Fifth Brigade against their officers; the periphery of Mosul against its center; the plebians of the Arab quarter of Makkawi and Wadi Hajjar against the Arab aristocrats of the Arab quarter of al Dawwasah; and within the quarter of Bab al Baid, the family of al Rajabou against its traditional rivals the Aghawat.[28]

The events in Mosul were essentially a civil war in microcosm, and "the clearest demonstration ever recorded of the divisions racking Iraq."[29] Despite nearly 40 years of shared history, the various ethnic, religious, and tribal groupings that comprise Iraq's complex social fabric were seemingly no closer than ever to achieving a shared sense of national identity.

## CONCLUSION

The 1958–1968 decade was one of extreme turbulence and violence for the state of Iraq. Relatively speaking, the monarchical regime stretched backward in time like a sea of stability and tranquility. The monarchy had failed to create an inclusive identity for the state—one that could be shared by all Iraq's disparate populations. Yet after a decade of the Republic, the formation of this collective identity was as far away from realization as ever. In many ways, the Republic marked a regression rather than progress, as rival factions struggled violently to gain supremacy over the machinery of the state, the better to impose their vision of Iraqi identity on the rest of the population. None of these visions was appealing to the Kurds. As a consequence, the Kurds continued their bitter armed struggle against central forces throughout most of the decade. Like a succession of rulers before them, Republican leaders were simply unable to find a formula for integrating the Kurds into the Iraqi state that was mutually acceptable.

Along with the unresolved Kurdish question, the first decade of the Republic also bequeathed to successive generations the politics of intolerance and a blueprint for dictatorship. Moderate political parties essentially disappeared from the scene, to be replaced by an altogether different breed of political organization. The techniques of governance employed by the Ba'ath after 1968, and Saddam Hussein in person after 1979, were not innovative. Many of the same techniques and institutions were in place before 1968. Thus, the use of show trials for public consumption, the cult of personality, the use of state-sponsored civilian militia groups, and the Republican Guard were all inherited from previous regimes. The instruments of effective dictatorship were already present for all to see: all it required was someone with enough political cunning to piece them together into a coherent whole.

## CHAPTER THREE

# IRAQ 1968–1988:
# THE BA'ATH REGIME

## INTRODUCTION

THE FIRST DECADE OF THE IRAQI REPUBLIC had witnessed four military coups, two of which were bathed in bullets and blood. Politics in Iraq had evolved into a Darwinian struggle to survive, and by 1968 the Ba'ath Party had emerged as the political force best equipped to prosper in such an environment. The daunting challenge was to create a survivable regime within a context in which the average life expectancy of regimes was a little over two years. Beyond this, there was the problem of how to impose some form of unity and shared identity on Iraqi's perennially fractious ethnic and sectarian groupings—a problem that was especially acute in the case of the Kurds. This was connected to a third challenge—how to prevent external forces, most notably the Iranians and the United States, from exploiting Iraq's deep divisions to destabilize or even terminate the regime. Confronting these challenges shaped the logic of the first decade of Ba'ath Party rule. The primary goal was to produce a "coup-proof" regime, and the result was totalitarian rule. Given the violent mess that was Iraqi politics in the late 1960s, it is difficult to see how regime survival could have been achieved in any other way. Ba'ath Party rule was the logical response to the prevailing political context, not a historical aberration. The tactics and techniques of Ba'ath governance were the culmination and consolidation of prior practice. The major distinction was the degree of coercion the Party was prepared to use in order to survive. As threats to regime survival—both internal and external—increased, so the level of violence necessary to sustain power increased correspondingly. As one-party rule gave way to rule by one man after 1979, the "regime" evolved into little more than an extension of Saddam Hussein's persona, but strategies for survival remained largely consistent.

The July 1968 coup that brought the Ba'ath back to power was accomplished with the assistance of four key figures in the Arif regime: Colonel Ibrahim Abd al-Rahman Da'ud (Commander of the Republican Guard), Colonel Abd al-Razzaq Nayif (Chief of Military Intelligence), Colonel Hammed Shihab (Commander of the Baghdad Garrison), and Colonel Sa'dun Ghaydan (Commander of the Republican Guard's armored brigade). Once again, the military demonstrated itself to be the key arbiter of power in Iraqi political life.

## TAMING THE MILITARY

The collaboration of Nayif and Da'ud in the "July Revolution" did not come cheaply for the Ba'ath Party. By prior arrangement the price was the Premiership for Nayif and the Ministry of Defense for Da'ud. Clearly for these two, the July coup was merely the prelude to a sustained period of military dictatorship. Certainly, military officers totally dominated the power positions within the new regime. Aside from Nayif and Da'ud, General Bakr assumed the Presidency, and all seven members of the new administration's ultimate executive body—the Revolutionary Command Council (RCC)—were military officers. However, of the seven, only three (including General Bakr) were also members of the Ba'ath. Seemingly, the stage was set for a military-Ba'athist power struggle similar to that of 1963. But the context was different. The Ba'ath Party had learned a key lesson from their 1963 experience—never share power. Immediately prior to the coup, Saddam had made his post-coup intentions abundantly clear. Referring to Nayif and Da'ud, he stated, "we should collaborate with them but see that they are liquidated immediately during or after the revolution. And I volunteer to carry out this task."[1] True to his word, Saddam moved quickly on behalf of the Party. In July 1968, after Da'ud had allowed himself (rather stupidly) to be lured out of Iraq to inspect Iraqi troops based in Jordan, Nayif was invited to lunch with Bakr at the Presidential Palace. At the end of the meal, Saddam entered, accompanied by a military escort, and led Nayif at gunpoint to Baghdad airport. Nayif was then informed of his (very) recent appointment to the ambassadorship of Morocco, placed on a plane, and flown out of the country, never to return.

For his part, Da'ud was instructed to remain in Jordan, and two years later, was officially retired from his post. He too, was never to return to Iraq. In essence, Saddam had effected Iraq's second coup in the space of two weeks. But while Saddam was the executor, the key figure in these events was General Bakr. Bakr is often considered little more than a warm body—someone who lent a legitimate public image to the Ba'ath regime while Saddam exercised the power behind the throne. Certainly there is truth in this, but initially at least, Bakr's presence proved essential.

As a seasoned army officer and veteran of the 1958 coup, Bakr had a strong following within the armed forces. Critically, when the crunch came, and Bakr had to decide where his true loyalties lay—with the military, or with the Ba'ath Party—he opted for the latter. It is only through Bakr that the Ba'ath Party was able to achieve the seemingly impossible task of bringing the Iraqi military back under civilian (Ba'athist) control. Moreover, it is simply impossible to make sense of the speed of Saddam's rise to the top without reference to the nature of his relationship with Bakr.

As fellow Tikritis and distant blood relatives (Bakr was Saddam's uncle's cousin), both were convinced that in the treacherous world of Iraqi politics, ties of kinship were the only guarantee of loyalty. Accordingly, following the removal of Nayif and Da'ud from their posts (and from Iraq), in the subsequent reshuffle Saddam was appointed Deputy Chairman of the RCC—the second most powerful position in the apparatus of state. Bakr himself added the titles of Prime Minister and Commander-in-Chief to his existing positions, Hardan al-Tikriti was appointed the new Minister of Defense, and Salih Mahdi Ammash (a Ba'ath Party stalwart) remained Minister of the Interior.

Behind the scenes, Saddam began to accumulate power. He voluntarily (and astutely) assumed control over the Party's revamped and expanded security apparatus—the innocuous-sounding Office of General Relations—thus initiating what was to prove a long-term love affair between Saddam and the security services. Control over the flow of internal intelligence enabled Saddam more than once to detect and foil coup attempts against the regime. It also allowed him to manufacture "plots" that had no basis in fact, but provided a convenient means of dispatching dangerous rivals.

A case in point was the first major plot exposed by the regime. While there appears to have been at least some evidence of an Israeli-sponsored spy network centered around Basra in the south of Iraq,[2] and the assassination of a Mossad agent at the Hotel Shattura in Baghdad yielded a notebook containing names of network members, to these Saddam apparently added the names of those people he wanted removed for one reason or another. Arrests and a swift trial followed. On January 27, 1969, to great popular acclaim, 14 of the accused (including 9 Jews) were strung up in Liberation Square.

In the wake of the hangings, moves were also made against the ICP—the Ba'ath's major political rival. In February 1969, prominent ICP official Aziz al Hajji was arrested, and, after a brief sojourn in the Palace of the End, was ready to confess to a Communist conspiracy. Twenty ICP leaders were rounded up, put on trial, and sentenced to death.

Saddam's worth to the regime was amply demonstrated in early 1970, when his security services infiltrated a conspiracy among the military. This time there was no question of fabrication, and Iran's involvement in the plot was clear. With precise knowledge of the nature, date, and time of the coup attempt, Saddam was able to lure the plotters into a trap. The inevitable show trial pronounced a death sentence on 37 military officers, who were then executed with their own weapons—apparently supplied by Iranian secret services. Subsequently, the Iranian Ambassador was deported from Iraq, and Iranian consulates in Baghdad, Karbala, and Basra were closed.

## TAMING THE KURDS

In addition to the urgent task of making the Ba'ath regime coup-proof—especially from the threat of the military—the early days of the regime were dominated by inherited problems. Foremost among these was the ongoing Kurdish problem. On and off, the Kurds had been fighting the central government since 1958, and their stubborn resistance had contributed significantly to the demise of two regimes (those of General Qassim and the second Arif). Saddam dealt personally with the issue, first traveling to the Soviet Union to try and convince the Soviets to curtail their military assistance to Kurdish forces, and then, after being warned by Premier Kosygin against restarting the military campaign in the north, returning to Baghdad with more peaceful intentions. In an uncharacteristically pacific statement, Saddam asserted, "If the Kurdish problem is handled exclusively militarily . . . then we will all lose."[3]

The outcome was the so-called March Manifesto of 1970, which for the first time referred to the "autonomy" of the Kurds, accepted the use of Kurdish languages in Kurdish-dominated areas, guaranteed a share of wealth from the huge Kirkuk oil field, and even promised to implement democracy (complete with elections) in Kurdistan. Quite how democracy in Kurdistan was to coexist with totalitarianism throughout the rest of Iraq was not entirely clear. Nonetheless, the Manifesto was the best offer that the Kurds had ever received.

The March 1970 agreement, like all previous agreements, was never implemented. The terms of the Manifesto were to be phased in over a five-year period, and would, at some point, have had to include a census to determine the boundaries of an autonomous Kurdistan where Kurds were in the majority. This opened up the unacceptable prospect that Iraq's major oil field at Kirkuk (where Kurds were in a majority) might fall under Kurdish control. To change reality on the ground, Saddam embarked on a conscious process of "Arabizing" the city—offering financial inducements to Arabs to move to Kirkuk to change its ethnic makeup. Kurdish leader Barzani urged Kurds to do the same. The early 1970s also witnessed at least two assassination attempts against Barzani. The hand of Saddam was strongly suspected.

As part of the March deal, Barzani had agreed to break off relations with Iran. Presumably predicting a resumption in military hostilities, Barzani was by 1972 back on the Iranian payroll, and also receiving aid and assistance from the United States and Israel. The Kurdish problem had thus acquired a dangerously international dimension.

## TAMING THE SHI'A

The Shi'a—always a significantly more diverse group than the Kurds—required a more nuanced approach. What emerged was the classic Saddam strategy of *tarhib wa-targhib*—literally "terror and enticement"—or stick and carrot. The real threat to the regime stemmed from the potential combination of radical Shi'a religious leaders with the dispossessed masses of ordinary Shi'a. The Ba'ath Party, by the time it assumed power, was almost entirely a Sunni Arab operation; once again, the majority Shi'a were being systematically excluded from access to power and influence. As with the Kurds, the problem for the Ba'ath presented by the Shi'a religious establishment was, to an extent, inherited from previous regimes. During the brief period under the Qassim regime in which licensed political parties were allowed, the *al-Da'wa* Party (The Call) had been established. Under the leadership of Muhammad Baqir al-Sadr—a young religious activist and scholar of some repute—*al-Da'wa* expanded rapidly and organized for armed struggle. The goal of the party was simple: the overthrow of the regime and the imposition of an Islamic state, clearly something of a threat to the avowedly secular Ba'ath.

After initial violent clashes in the fall and summer of 1969 between the regime and the Shi'a religious establishment, the regime enacted anti-*Da'wa* legislation, then used this as a cover to persecute party members. In 1974, five members of *al-Da'wa* were executed. This number would increase considerably over the course of the 1970s. Throughout the decade, the regime relied on confrontation, executions, and deportations to keep the Shi'a threat under control. However, while beating the religious establishment with a large stick, the regime simultaneously dangled carrots in front of the excluded Shi'a masses.

The key to soothing tensions between the Sunni center and the Shi'a majority was to spread wealth and power more equitably. Beginning in 1970, and continuing throughout most of the decade, the Ba'ath embarked on a genuinely revolutionary program of restructuring the entire fabric of economic and social life. In the process, Iraq was to become the most advanced and modern society in the Arab world. The process kicked off with radical land reform in 1970 that established a network of state-run collective farms. Extensive land holdings were broken up and redistributed to the peasants working in these. This achieved the dual effect of earning popular support for the regime while simultaneously reducing the power of large landholders. What emerged was a mixed agricultural sector that permitted small and medium-sized farms to remain in private hands, but "socialized" the largest tracts of land. Ultimately, though, the ambitious plans of the Ba'ath required resources, and this meant establishing direct control over Iraq's massive oil reserves.

## THE NATIONALIZATION OF OIL

At the beginning of the 1970s, oil production in Iraq was largely dominated by the Iraq Petroleum Company (IPC), an operating company owned by a conglomerate of British, French, Dutch, and American interests, and the Basra Oil Company (BOC), a smaller foreign-owned concern. Many of the foreign interests involved in the IPC had concessions in other Arab countries; as a consequence, production from Iraqi wells was often kept deliberately low to ensure a high price for oil. In short, while Iraq benefited financially from oil, it did not control the supply or pricing of its major natural resource.

Nonetheless, any attempt to wrest control over Iraq's oil from foreign hands would be perilous in the extreme.[4] Saddam personally handled the nationalization of the Iraqi oil industry. To ensure a continued market for Iraqi oil, and to secure technological assistance in the development of oil new fields, Saddam traveled to Moscow in 1972. A reciprocal visit by Soviet Premier Kosygin in April yielded a 15-year Treaty of Friendship and Cooperation between the two countries. The Treaty provided access for the Soviets to Iraqi ports and airports, ensured continued Soviet arms sales to Iraq, and most importantly, guaranteed a Soviet market for Iraqi oil. Soon after, on June 1, 1972, Law 69 officially nationalized the IPC. The BOC was nationalized the following year.

The nationalization was a personal triumph for Saddam. The move was exceedingly popular in Iraq (June 1 was officially named "Victory Day"), finally giving Iraq control over its own natural resources and eliminating the last vestiges of colonial dominance. In the process, Iraq had also chosen sides in the Cold War. The benefits were considerable—plentiful supplies of Soviet weaponry, technical assistance with Iraq's oil industry, and a guaranteed market for oil exports. On the down side, to placate the Soviets, Saddam pledged to share power with (rather than persecute) the ICP. This implausible pledge resulted in the formation of a National Progressive Front—a political alliance between Iraq's "revolutionary forces" that included the Ba'ath, the ICP, and a motley collection of carefully selected and pliable Kurdish groups. Two members of the ICP were also appointed to the cabinet, and the harassment of Communists was curtailed—for the time being. This appearance of power-sharing with the ICP was an exercise in deception, but was apparently sufficient to appease the Soviets temporarily. A more dangerous consequence for Iraq stemmed from the logic of the Cold War. In opting for Soviet client status, Iraq had also automatically acquired a new enemy (the United States). Nonetheless, Saddam's masterstroke soon paid handsome dividends. When yet another Arab–Israeli conflict erupted in 1973, the price of oil spiraled. Iraq was ideally placed to cash in on its greatest national asset.

## THE KAZZAR COUP ATTEMPT

Thwarting coup attempts had become something of an annual event for the Ba'ath regime, and 1973 did not disappoint. The 1973 effort, masterminded by Nadhim Kazzar (one of Saddam's right-hand men in the security services, and one of the few prominent Shi'a in the regime) ended in farce, but illustrated the perpetual precariousness of the new regime. Kazzar's cunning plan involved kidnapping the Ministers of Defense and Interior, presumably to ward off a response from the military and police, then organizing an assassination squad to meet President Bakr's plane as it returned from a state visit to Poland.

Unfortunately for Kazzar, the plane was delayed for four hours, and the hit squad fled, believing the plot had been intercepted. Left with two prominent members of the regime held captive in his cellar and his plot in tatters, Kazzar made a dash for the Iranian border with his hostages in tow. Shaken by the actions of so close an associate, Saddam organized the chase, intercepting Kazzar before he could cross the border.

The ensuing trial pronounced death sentences on Kazzar, 8 other security officers, and 13 military officers. The following day, just to make sure that justice had been served, another 36 men were tried, 14 of whom were subsequently executed. Once more the regime had demonstrated its resilience in the face of adversity, and that there would be a high price to pay for opposing the regime.

## TROUBLE UP NORTH

The Ba'ath regime—guided by Saddam's uncanny survival instincts—was proving increasingly coup-resistant, but was, apparently, as unable to bring closure to the Kurdish problem as all previous regimes. By 1974, the March Manifesto agreement was unraveling at an alarming rate. Fortified by extensive international backing, Barzani did not hesitate to provoke the Ba'ath regime, stating, "The Kurdish territory is rich in petrol . . . and it is our territory. It is ours, and therefore we commit no act of aggression by taking it."[5] In a *Washington Post* interview in the summer of 1973, Barzani had deliberately dangled a tempting carrot in front of the United States, promising that "if America will protect us from the wolves . . . we could control the Kirkuk field and give it to an American company to operate." To say the least, the tenor of Barzani's statements did not go down well in Baghdad. Full-scale hostilities looked inevitable and duly erupted in March 1974.

The war with the Kurds came close to toppling the Ba'ath from power. The Kurds were supported by the United States, Syria, Israel, and Iran. Equipped with heavy artillery and surface-to-air missiles, Barzani's experienced guerilla fighters proved more than a match for Iraqi troops. The cost of the war (up to $4 billion) was wreaking havoc with the Iraqi economy, while casualty figures for the 1974–1975 period topped 60,000.

After January 1975, the situation deteriorated still further as Iran deployed two regiments into Iraqi Kurdistan to provide a more direct form of aid to the rebels. Confronted with the prospect of total economic and military collapse, Saddam had little option but to bow down to the superior power of his Iranian neighbor.

In March 1975, Saddam and the Shah of Iran concluded the Algiers Agreement. The Agreement, subsequently codified in the June 1975 Treaty on International Borders and Good Neighborly Relations, represented a humiliating moment for Saddam. A long-standing territorial dispute over the Shatt Al-Arab was settled entirely in Iran's favor, and Iraq was required to renounce any claims to the Arab-populated Iranian province of Khuzistan.[6]

Iraq got little in return, except an Iranian pledge to terminate aid to the Kurds. Within two days of the signing of the agreement, all international aid to the Kurds (from Iran, Israel, and the U.S.) was curtailed; the Kurds were left to their fate. Within the space of two weeks, the Kurdish rebellion was crushed.

## MODERNIZING IRAQ

By the end of 1975, the Ba'ath regime had consolidated its position on all fronts, and had already become the Iraqi Republic's longest-lasting regime. Internally, all potential rivals (the armed forces, the ICP, the Kurds), had either been eliminated, neutralized, or co-opted. Externally, the agreement with Iran, humiliating though it was, had warded off the threat of major war. Flush with burgeoning oil revenues, Saddam turned his attention to the modernization of Iraq. Guided by the suitably flexible socialist principles[7] of Ba'athist ideology, the metamorphosis of Iraq from Third World to developed country in the space of a decade was driven by two major considerations. First, was the need to spread wealth more equitably. In the most basic sense, the legitimacy and popularity of the Ba'ath regime depended on its capacity to deliver a better quality of life to ordinary Iraqis than had previous regimes. Second, the regime needed to diversify Iraq's economy to avoid overdependence on a single commodity (oil). The industrialization of Iraq's economy would make it less vulnerable to violent fluctuations in oil prices, and reduce Iraq's import dependence on the developed world for industrial products.

Regardless of the oppressive (or "evil") nature of the regime in other respects, in the economic and social sphere its achievements were truly impressive. A huge program was initiated to construct hospitals and schools. Free access to high-quality health care and education became a right rather than the privilege it had been previously. The expansion of the social network was accompanied by ambitious infrastructure projects. A drive to electrify rural Iraq resulted in 4,000 villages receiving electricity for the first time. In order to give the people something to do with their newly acquired power source, free refrigerators and televisions were distributed to the masses—starting, not by coincidence, with the Shi'a in the south. Buying off the Shi'a masses was central to Saddam's legitimization strategy.

Saddam also initiated an epic plan of truly Stalinesque proportions to desalinate irrigation waters from the Tigris and Euphrates and reclaim three million hectares of arable land. The plan was aimed at "re-creating the world's granary." The diversification of oil export routes was another priority. To this end, Saddam oversaw the construction of an extensive interconnected pipeline system that would enable oil from anywhere in Iraq to be exported via three different routes (Basra, Turkey, and Syria) as the situation demanded. Industrial production was heavily state-directed and focused on diversification so that the fate of the Iraqi economy would not be entirely beholden to fluctuations in oil prices. Iraq's extensive sulfur and phosphate reserves were extracted and refined for the first time, while a huge petrochemical complex was built from scratch in the city of Basra.

## FROM ONE-PARTY TO ONE-MAN RULE

By the mid- to late 1970s, the Ba'ath Party—with Saddam as its driving force—was at the height of its powers. Thanks largely to the efforts of Saddam, the regime had demonstrated its capacity to survive repeated coup attempts; the political role of the military—long a source of instability in the chaotic Iraqi political arena—had been ruthlessly but effectively curtailed; a long-running dispute with neighboring Iran had, at least temporarily, been prevented from escalating into something more serious; and, as a consequence, the possibility of an Iranian–Kurdish axis ripping the country apart had been neutralized. Moreover, the establishment of state control over most of the important sectors of the economy—critically, over Iraq's huge reserves of liquid gold—and the vast expansion of public services had important consequences for the governance of the country. For the first time in Iraq's history, a stable regime had pursued a conscious policy of dispersing rather than concentrating wealth. On one hand, this policy dramatically increased the quality of life for ordinary Iraqis; on the other, the exponential growth of the state apparatus placed awesome powers of patronage in the hands of those who controlled the state, effectively making the populace ever-more dependent on the center.

In almost all sectors of life—social, educational, economic, political, and military—the state controlled career advancement. State officials determined who was to be punished, and who rewarded. The Iraqi people were confronted with a clear choice: cooperate with the state and benefit from its largesse, or dissent and face some unpleasantly violent consequences. By the end of the 1970s, the state apparatus controlled Iraq, the Ba'ath Party controlled the state apparatus, and Saddam controlled the Ba'ath Party. All that remained was for this hierarchy of power to be officially confirmed. This came about in July 1979 when the aging and ailing Bakr was persuaded to step down by his younger deputy. Bakr's televised resignation speech was timed with some precision by Saddam to coincide with the anniversary of the July Revolution (July 17).

In his speech, Bakr explained that ill health no longer allowed him to carry the burdens of office, obliging him to turn over the reigns of power to

"Comrade Saddam Hussein," the "faithful struggler" and "brilliant leader" of the revolution.[8] Faithful struggler and brilliant leader were only two of the many titles that accrued to Saddam as a consequence of his promotion. In addition, he now became President, Prime Minister, Commander-in-Chief, Secretary-General of the Ba'ath Party's Regional Command, and Chairman of the RCC.

Saddam moved quickly to solidify his newly acquired titles. The targets were potential rivals within the Ba'ath. First on the hit list was Muhie Abdul Hussein Mashadi, whose instinct for survival had apparently deserted him. During an RCC meeting to determine a successor to Bakr, Mashadi displayed a truly staggering lack of judgment by opposing Bakr's imminent retirement and demanding a vote on the succession. Mashadi was accordingly removed from his position on the RCC and tortured until willing to confess to anything.

On July 22, Saddam convened a special Party meeting to permit Mashadi to expose the details of an elaborate Syrian plot to overthrow the regime. Saddam had the meeting videotaped for posterity. Following a well-rehearsed confession from Mashadi, a list of coconspirators' names was read out. As their names were announced, distraught Party members were led from the room by security officials—66 of them in all. The meeting then continued. The remaining delegates had apparently got the message.

Of the 66, 22 were sentenced to death by a hastily convened RCC special court. Two weeks later, Party officials were once more convened to administer collective justice to the condemned. One by one, Party leaders stepped up to put bullets into the brains of the unfortunate 22. In this "glorified tribal bonding session," almost the entire remainder of the Party leadership was now fully implicated in these "democratic executions."[9]

The purge of the RCC was accompanied by a more general purge of Ba'ath Party ranks with the goal of removing any actual or potential opposition to Saddam's leadership. Simultaneously, he added to the regime's growing stable of security organizations with the creation the *Amn al-Khass* (the Special Protection Apparatus) which essentially functioned as a private security agency for Saddam.

Saddam's moment of ultimate triumph, the climax of a relentlessly ambitious career that had taken him from the poverty of Tikrit to the pinnacle of power in Iraq, was to prove short-lived. Within the space of a year, Iraq would be plunged into a hugely destructive eight-year conflict with its powerful neighbor to the east, which would once again test Saddam's capacity for survival to its limits.

## THE THREAT FROM IRAN

The twentieth century's, and perhaps history's, last great war of the masses pitched a secular Sunni Arab regime against a fanatically religious Shi'a Persian regime. Not surprisingly, the resulting war was a hideously bloody, drawn-out confrontation that neither side could afford to lose. The roots of the Iran–Iraq war can be traced back to centuries of ethnic (Arab–Persian) and sectarian (Sunni–Shi'a) animosity. Overlaid on this were a number of territorial disputes, the most significant of which concerned the Shatt al-Arab. The 1975 Algiers Agreement (which favored Iran) had been forged in the context of utter Iranian dominance and Iraqi desperation. But it was the Islamic revolution in Iran and the ascent of Ayatollah Khomeini in 1979 that provided the trigger for conflict. Now a secular, socialist, Sunni-dominated regime in Baghdad faced a radical Shi'a regime in Tehran that pledged to export Islamic revolution throughout the Middle East. Iraq was first in the firing line. Khomeini wasted little time in calling upon Iraq's Shi'a majority to overthrow the detested infidel Ba'athist regime. Mutual hostility soon escalated to border skirmishes and exchanges of artillery fire. Intensive shelling of Iraqi cities in early September 1980 led Saddam to announce Iraq's unilateral withdrawal from the Algiers Agreement on September 17. Subsequently, the Iranians shifted the targets of their artillery attacks to the Iraqi side of the Shatt, targeting residential areas and critical economic installations. On September 22, Iraq invaded Iran. Motives for the invasion were complex. As one expert summarized, "Motivated by fear, opportunism and overconfidence, a mixture of defensive and offensive calculations, Iraq's decision to resort to force was a compound of a preventive war, ambition and punishment for a regional rival."[10]

Regardless of the motivations, Saddam clearly underestimated Iran's will and capacity to resist. Saddam had planned for a lightning advance across the border, the swift capture of territory, including the ethnically Arab province of Khuzistan; then either the Arab population of Khuzistan would join with their Arab brothers and spark a general uprising against the regime in Tehran, or, at a minimum, Iraq would be in a position of strength from which to negotiate a more favorable version of the 1975 Agreement. There was no plan C.

It was clear that Saddam did not anticipate the war lasting more than a matter of days, or weeks at most. Initially, this seemed a reasonable assessment, as Iraqi armored brigades made swift advances into Iranian territory. By early October, Iraqi forces had captured the city of Khoramshahr and were laying siege to Abadan, Iran's second-largest city. At this point, the lack of a plan C became something of a problem. Far from uniting with their Arab brethren, Iran's Arab population mobilized behind the Tehran regime and offered stiff resistance to the invading Iraqis. Iraqi efforts to bring an early diplomatic end to proceedings were rebuffed outright by Khomeini.[11] Nothing less than the removal of Saddam's regime would satisfy Tehran. Iraqi forces were caught occupying increasing swathes of Iranian territory, but with no obvious strategic goal. The result was a temporary stalemate. Then in mid-1982, the Iranians began their counterattack, recapturing Khoramshahr in a human wave assault, and taking 15,000 Iraqi soldiers prisoner in the process.

This marked the first of several major turning points in the conduct of the war. Saddam withdrew his forces from Iranian territory and took up defensive positions along the border. In July 1982, Iranian forces pressed their advantage, mounting an assault that took them into Iraqi territory and placed Basra under threat. Successive Iranian attempts in 1983 to capture Basra were beaten back by the Iraqis with the assistance of chemical weapons, and the war degenerated into another stalemate. Between 1984 and 1986, the only major territorial gain was made by Iran with the capture of the oil-rich Majnoon Islands in the southern marshlands of Iraq. Otherwise, the conflict saw both sides focusing their attention on targeting the others' economic infrastructure—with Iraq launching missile attacks on Iranian oil tankers and terminals, and Iran responding in kind. A major breakthrough by Iranian forces in February 1986 resulted in the capture of 310 square miles of Iraq's Fao Peninsula—a huge strategic victory that placed the city of Basra in direct jeopardy. The U.S., which to this point had busied itself by supplying arms to both countries, now began to intervene overtly on the Iraqi side. At the request of the Kuwaitis, U.S. naval vessels began to escort oil tankers through the Gulf region to protect them from Iranian attack. In October 1987, the U.S. navy sank three Iranian patrol boats in response to an alleged attack on a U.S. helicopter. By this point, there were over 60 Western (U.S., British, and French) warships in the region ready to confront Iran. The tide of battle was turning once again, and Iraq pushed its advantage. During the first half of 1988, Iraq began a sustained surface-to-surface missile assault on Iran's major cities. In April, with significant assistance from U.S. intelligence, Iraqi forces recaptured the Fao Peninsula, and in May, the Majnoon Islands. Confronted by a significant multinational armada in the Gulf, the threat of outright hostilities with the U.S., and a disintegrating army, Khomeini drank from what he termed the "poisoned chalice" and accepted a cease-fire.

## Consequences of the War

In territorial terms, the eight-year war was a colossal waste of effort. More importantly, it was a tragic waste of human life. On the Iraqi side, the death toll was estimated at 200,000, with a further 500,000 wounded.[12] Saddam's deliberate "guns and butter" policy, which had aimed at protecting the Iraqi population from the ravages of war while simultaneously funding the military effort, had required Iraq to borrow over $100 billion, including over $40 billion for military hardware. Despite this, the war halved Iraq's per capita income. In addition, damage to Iraq's infrastructure was estimated at $200 billion.[13] Iraq emerged from the war with the most powerful armed forces in the region—a regular army of some one million men, buttressed by nearly as many members of the Popular Army, and equipped with 4,500 tanks, 400 combat aircraft, and over 3,000 armored fighting vehicles.[14] However, sustaining this force consumed seven-eighths of the revenue gained from Iraq's oil exports—an impossible burden for an economy already crippled by debt.

## LEGACIES OF BA'ATHIST RULE, 1968–88

### Sunni Dominance

By the time the Ba'ath Party assumed power in 1968, its ranks were virtually devoid of Shi'a and Kurdish members. By 1970, Shi'a representation in the higher echelons of the Party had dwindled to 14 percent.[15] For a party that preached the equality of all Arabs (Sunni and Shi'a) within one sovereign Arab nation, the continued exclusion of the Shi'a majority from access to political power was problematic. In some ways the political position of the Shi'a improved over the course of the first 20 years of Ba'athist rule; in other ways, political power became even more concentrated in Sunni hands under the Ba'ath than under previous regimes.

Beginning in the early 1970s, the Party adopted a conscious policy of affirmative action to incorporate more Shi'a into the governing structures. Hence, whereas Shi'a representation on the RCC—the chief decision-making body within the state structure—was precisely zero in 1968, by 1977 it had reached 28 percent. Likewise, Shi'a representation within the Party's highest executive organ—the Regional Command—had reached 26 percent by the same year.[16]

The reinstitution of Parliament (the National Council) by law in 1980 provided another means by which the political exclusion of the Shi'a could be alleviated. Elections to the 250-member body were organized along regional lines to guarantee that Shi'a and Kurds would be elected from regions in which they were dominant numerically. Accordingly, of the delegates elected in Iraq's first parliamentary election since 1958, 43 percent were Shi'a and 12 percent Kurds.[17] According to one expert, this deliberate policy of increasing Shi'a political representation "was designed to signal to Shi'a youngsters that if they towed the line laid down by party and president and acquiesced in de facto Sunni–Arab supremacy, they could realistically expect upward social mobility."[18]

Aside from some representation in Parliament, the Kurds generally fared much worse than the Shi'a throughout the 1968–1988 period. For example, only one token Kurd made it onto the RCC, and Kurds enjoyed no representation on the Party's Regional Command. Had Iraq functioned as a liberal democracy, the combined voting power of Shi'a and Kurds in Parliament would actually have enabled them to dominate the Sunni Arabs. There was never much likelihood of this occurring. On paper, the Parliament had a veritable plethora of powers; in practice, is was entirely subservient to the will of the RCC. In turn, the RCC was a creature of the Ba'ath Party, and the Ba'ath Party was the servant of Saddam Hussein. Similarly, while some Shi'a made it onto the RCC, and several attained cabinet rank, the key positions of power all remained resolutely in Sunni Arab hands. Thus the ministries of Interior and Defense, the officer corps of the Republican Guard, the vast majority of officers in the regular army, the various security services, and Saddam's closest circle of advisors remained securely in Sunni hands throughout the period.

While the political system as a whole became more representative of Iraq's diversity over the period, real decision-making power became significantly more concentrated. To speak of the dominance of Sunni Arabs is not strictly accurate. In reality, power was concentrated in the hands of Sunni Arabs hailing from Tikrit and its environs.[19] The ascendance of the "Tikriti mafia" within the Ba'ath Party, and consequently within the political structures of the state, was premised on the "blood is thicker than ideology" maxim shared by both Bakr and Saddam. In the violent, unpredictable world of Iraqi politics, tribal ties were deemed a stronger guarantee of loyalty than shared ideology. At times, the entire membership of the RCC hailed from Tikrit. Tikritis also dominated the officer corps of the army and the Republican Guard, and controlled the security services. As one associate of Saddam put it, "There is no real mystery about the way we run Iraq. We run it exactly as we used to run Tikrit."[20]

Beyond this, after about 1975, Saddam came to rely increasingly on kinship ties to staff the regime's most sensitive positions. By the end of the 1970s, Saddam's extended family ran the Party, and therefore the country. Saddam's cousin (and brother-in-law), Adnan Khairallah Talfah, was Minister of Defense; his half brother Barzan headed up the General Intelligence Apparatus

(*Mukhabarat*); another half brother, Watban, was governor of Tikrit; and cousin Sa'adun Shakr controlled the National Security Office (which had oversight powers over all the various security organizations). As one observer describes it, "It was a merger between the family and the party, with the former using the latter as a vehicle to control the country."[21]

## Governing Iraq

Many of the problems the Ba'ath initially faced—the Kurdish insurrection in the north, problems with Iran in the east, a resentful Shi'a population in the south, and a tradition of military coups—were inherited from previous regimes. The political turbulence of the first decade of the Iraqi Republic ensured that the prospects of liberal democracy emerging were essentially zero. Regime survival was the priority, and this required discipline, organization, and ruthlessness; political pluralism and civil liberties were of little concern. The Ba'ath Party was a product of this environment. Over the course of its first 20 years in power, the regime imposed stability on Iraq's political and social order, while creating the well-educated, professional middle class that most would consider essential for a functioning democracy. Simultaneously, though, the regime annihilated dissent, thereby eliminating the last vestiges of pluralism from Iraqi politics.

From the outset, the key to survival for the Ba'ath regime was to neutralize rival institutions. The top priority—avoiding a military coup—required the immediate "liquidation" of those army officers who had helped bring the Party to power in the first place. But beyond this, long-term survival required a fundamental redefinition of the nature of the relationship between the state and the military. In short, the military had to be brought back under civilian (Party) control. The goal was to create an "ideological army"—one whose ultimate loyalty was to the Party and Saddam, rather than its own officer corps. Promotion to the upper ranks of the army was thus governed not by merit, but by loyalty to the regime—and particularly, to Saddam. This task was rendered significantly easier by the fact that Tikritis had always been disproportionately represented in the army. Saddam took this one stage further, appointing those with whom he shared ties of blood to the highest ranks of the army. To act as the eyes and ears of the regime, Saddam established a system of military commissars, whereby loyal Party members, reporting directly to the Party's command, were attached to the armed forces at all levels. Members of the armed forces were soon only allowed to belong to the Ba'ath—membership of any other political party was deemed a crime punishable by death. Finally, to make sure the army truly understood who was in charge, periodic purges weeded out potential threats to the regime and personal rivals to Saddam. It is difficult to gauge how many of the numerous plot-inspired purges were grounded in fact, and how many were the result of convenient fiction. Many observers simply assume that either Saddam fabricated plots for purely political purposes (to remove enemies and rivals in the subsequent purge), or that the perpetual exposure of "conspiracies" against the regime during the 1970s demonstrates Saddam's increasing paranoia. On the other hand, it is easy to be paranoid when everyone really is out to get you.

As a counterweight to the army, Saddam reinstituted the Party's paramilitary militia force, renamed it the Popular Army, and transformed it into a genuinely mass organization. Over the course of the 1970s, the Popular Army was transformed from a barely organized rabble of thugs into an approximation of a legitimate fighting force with its own recruitment and training infrastructure, and a two-month-long indoctrination period for all members to ensure loyalty to the cause (i.e., Saddam). By 1980, membership in the Popular Army had risen to 250,000, and during the Iran-Iraq war it expanded still further to encompass about one million members.[22] In purely military terms, the Popular Army was no match for the regular armed forces; nonetheless, to mobilize and intimidate the masses, and to ward off the threat of military coup, the militia played a vital role in Saddam's regime.

Saddam also understood clearly the benefits of having a loyal buffer force between the regular armed forces and the regime. The Republican Guard—the last line of defense for the regime—was expanded, received the finest training and equipment the regime could offer, and was staffed with "reliable" elements—meaning Sunni Arabs hailing from the region around Tikrit.

Establishing tight Party control over the army was a question of regime survival. But the ambitions of the Ba'ath extended far beyond mere survival. The ultimate goal was to remake Iraqi society, in its entirety, in the Party's image. This was a striking departure from previous regimes. Under the monarchy and the first regimes of the Iraqi Republic, the overwhelming majority of the population remained largely untouched by politics at the center. Politics was an elite activity that had never penetrated the masses. This changed under the Ba'ath, and the Party's ideology and organizational structure became the main instrument to effect this transformation.[23]

The Ba'ath's (literally "renaissance") banner slogan—"Unity, Freedom, Socialism"—provides a fair indication of the content of Ba'ath ideology, while the ordering of the three terms accurately reflects their relative importance within this philosophy. Arab unity was always the primary concern. The term "freedom" carries a rather different connotation from the Western conception of individual liberty. Here, the term is used to denote both freedom *from* imperialism, and freedom *from* obstacles to self-realization (such as ignorance and poverty). The source of these obstacles, of course, is Western imperialism, which has imposed alien norms and values on the Arab nation, and kept it in a position of perpetual subservience and humiliation. The socialist dimension to Ba'athist thought was always the least developed theoretically—indeed, the term was not elevated to the same official status as "unity" and "freedom" until the 1960s. In practice, Ba'ath parties in power in Iraq and Syria, have stopped some way short of total state ownership of the means of production.

From this perspective, Ba'athist socialism resembled a more flexible, watered down version of communism. Critically, though, the Ba'ath were able to distinguish themselves from their powerful Communist enemies (most importantly, the Syrian Communist Party and the ICP) by their stress on nationalism.[24] The state-directed economy was a means of expressing *national* ownership over productive forces and harnessing economic power for *national* purposes. The Achilles heel of the Arab Communist parties was their perceived slavish devotion to the mother party in the Soviet Union. These parties could not simultaneously claim to be furthering the cause of Arab unity while obediently following directions from Moscow. The Ba'ath effectively outflanked the Communists because its message appealed to the dispossessed masses but was untainted by "foreign" influence.

The relationship between Islam and Arab nationalism in Ba'athist thought is complex and ambiguous. The Party's chief ideological architect was, after all, a Christian (Michel Aflaq). The Arab "nation" existed historically prior to the emergence of Islam; at the same time, Islam represents an integral component of the philosophical, moral and spiritual experience of the Arab nation. In Aflaq's formulation, Arabism is a body "whose Spirit is Islam."[25] Yet Aflaq never insisted on adherence to Islam as a prerequisite for "citizenship" in the Arab nation. In practice, this meant that the Ba'ath Parties in Syria and Iraq were secular in their exercise of governance.

Much of the success of Ba'athism derived from its capacity to appeal on multiple levels. Much like the writings of Marx, the dense, often obscure formulations of Aflaq were tailor-made for detailed textual analysis in elite intellectual circles. Indeed, the Party's initial membership was almost entirely composed of university teachers and students. At the same time, there was a brutal and elegant simplicity to Ba'athism that greatly facilitated its smooth transition down to lower levels of the intellectual food chain. On the positive side, there was the message of Arab rebirth; the Arab nation would rise again to recapture its former glories. On the negative, Ba'athism offered a compelling explanation for the failure of the Arabs to achieve the promise of pan-Arab unity: someone else was to blame. Naturally enough, the primary target of hostility was the West—initially the colonial powers (Britain and France), then subsequently the United States. In this respect, the Ba'ath Party simply tapped into a rich vein of animosity that had fueled Arab nationalism for decades. According to one analyst, one of the key tenets of Arab nationalism is that

> The West has in the recent past (and to many Arab nationalists still is striving to do so) impeded the Arabs from fulfilling their destiny. The West, as a sort of secular Satan, is not only identified as the target enemy of Arab nationalism because of the facts of history, but also because such an identification is necessary to the national movement.[26]

Arab nationalists assumed that the Arab world was culturally superior to the West, but reconciling this with the twentieth century reality of humiliating political, economic, and military inferiority required a scapegoat. Western imperialism is a popular contender—as is the hated state of Israel. "To the Arab, Israel is the personification of all that is western, a 'dagger' thrust into the heart of the Arab homeland."[27] The Ba'ath Party surfed the wave of militant Arab nationalism that swept the Arab world in the 1950s; it did not create this force.

The potential for Ba'athist ideology to transcend the sectarian and ethnic divide was strengthened by its economic appeal. A mild form of state-led socialism could help address the gross economic inequalities bequeathed by the monarchical regime. This had intrinsic appeal to the neglected (and mostly poor) Shi'a majority, as well as, potentially, to the Kurdish population of northern Iraq. It also blunted the message of the Ba'ath's main rival, the ICP. Iraqi Ba'athist ideology harnessed the power of Arab nationalism (both positive and negative aspects), coupling it with a new form of Iraqi nationalism and an appeal to the dispossessed majority. This was a potent formula.

Of course, the Ba'ath Party of Iraq never relied entirely on the popularity of its message to maintain power. Underpinning the edifice was a brutally effective coercive organization that was not slow to enforce obedience to the Party and eliminate dissent. Nonetheless, to assume that the success of the Ba'ath Party was due exclusively to its capacity to inflict organized violence on Iraqis is mistaken. Something about the Party's message resonated loudly among the people of Iraq.

The Ba'ath was organized along lines familiar to any student of Soviet history. It was essentially a replication of the basic structure of Communist parties the world over (including the ICP)—a complex cellular network, organized hierarchically according to the Leninist principle of "democratic centralism."[28] In theory, the Party was internally democratic in that the lower levels elected those immediately above them on the food chain, but in practice, Regional Command members were chosen by Saddam, then presented to the Congress for its rubber stamp of approval.

The Party structure coexisted, somewhat ambiguously, with the state's political institutions. Supreme decision-making power was vested in the Revolutionary Command Council, below which was the government (Prime Minister and Cabinet), and after 1980, the Parliament. In reality, this dual political structure was of little consequence. As the 1970s progressed, the Party and the state's political institutions effectively merged in terms of membership, and in essence, the Party's political structure absorbed the political institutions of the state.

In practice, the structure of the Ba'ath was tailor-made for dictatorship. It was also ideal for establishing total control over society. The Ba'ath Party was present in every village, in every factory, in every unit of the army, and in every school. Party membership was also structured hierarchically and tightly controlled. Becoming a full Party member required a painstaking process, taking between five and ten years of dedicated service to the Party, slowly moving up levels or ranks within the Party. The beauty of this arrangement was twofold. First, it provided a highly structured incentive system that required aspiring members continually to prove their loyalty and commitment. Second, it maintained the exclusivity of the Party's full membership while allowing the Party to draw on a huge cadre of supporters when the need arose. In this sense, the Ba'ath was a genuinely mass political movement. By 1988, full party members numbered perhaps 30,000 (roughly 0.2 percent of the total population), but the Party as a whole had reached 1.5 million supporters at various levels. This constituted nearly 10 percent of the entire Iraqi population, and provides a telling indication of the extent to which Iraq had become "Ba'athized" over the course of 20 years.

Realizing the need to inculcate Ba'ath values at an early age, steps were also taken to organize the youth of Iraq. As the Party's 1974 congress stated:

> The Party itself must exert great and urgent efforts to promote the activities of youth organizations. They must come to embrace a majority of our young people, boys and girls, and contribute actively to cultivating Pan-Arab and socialist principles among them, inspiring them with the vision and educating them in the ways that will allow them fully to participate in revolutionary construction, national defence and Pan-Arab tasks.[29]

Accordingly, children were organized into the Pioneers (between the ages of 6 and 10), the Vanguard (between 10 and 15), and the Youth Organization (between 15 and 20). In the words of one observer, "These are not the boy scouts; they contribute to the revolution and the Ba'ath party."[30]

To penetrate the hearts and minds of the young to an unprecedented degree, the Party initiated free compulsory education for the young and revamped the curriculum at all levels to promote "our Arab nation's basic aspirations and its aim for unity, liberty and socialism."[31] It also introduced a legal requirement that all teachers "be bound by the principles" of the Ba'ath Party. The Ba'ath's relentless drive to inculcate Party values into the population left little room for alternative political visions. A pretense at political pluralism was sustained via the National Progressive Front (which encompassed the ICP and various Kurdish groups), but once the ICP began openly voicing criticisms of Ba'athist policies, its days were numbered. From 1978 onward, ICP members were systematically hunted down, arrested, tortured, and executed. By 1979, the ICP leadership had either fled the country (mainly to Syria), or met a more terminal fate. Some level of political opposition was also voiced from the liberal end of the spectrum (mainly the intelligentsia and the professional classes), but this was never organized into a coherent political force. Rather than confront the regime directly, most liberal opponents simply voted with their feet by emigrating. By the onset of the 1980s, the Ba'ath had an effective monopoly over political ideas. While there was never much danger of Parliamentary elections (held in both 1980 and 1984) generating much in the way of opposition to Ba'athist rule, just to make sure, all candidates for election had first to be approved by the Ba'ath leadership to filter out unreliable elements. This practice did not differ greatly from the practices of previous regimes. Throughout Iraq's history, displays of democracy had been carefully stage-managed and opposition had been permitted only to the extent that it did not seriously threaten the established power structure. Where the Ba'ath regime did differ was in the scale of its ambitions. For the first time in Iraq's history, a concerted effort was undertaken to penetrate the entire population with a political message. Only time will tell the full psychological cost to the Iraqi people of this relentless invasion of hearts and minds.

## The Use of Violence

To analyze the use of violence as a political tool over a period that began with public hangings and ended with the use of chemical weapons in Kurdistan may appear somewhat superfluous. The Ba'ath regime under Saddam Hussein became synonymous with violence and terror in popular perception. But the relationship between Ba'athist rule and the use of violence was more complex than it first appears. Under previous regimes—especially that of Qassim—public violence was much more widespread. Whether it was ICP rampages in Mosul or Kirkuk, or the violent clashes of rival militia groups on the streets of Baghdad, this was a form of violence symptomatic of collapsing public order. This anarchic violence was largely eliminated under the Ba'ath Party. As the Party deepened its control over Iraqi society, so it imposed stability on a formerly chaotic system. In this respect, the Ba'ath Party presided over a more peaceful society than its predecessors. Of course, this stability came at a cost. The use of violence under Saddam became much better organized and more systematic. Violence became an instrument of state control rather than a symbol of the absence of state control. But it is important to put this in perspective. The primary targets of state-sponsored violence, whether in the form of imprisonment, torture, or execution, were opponents of the regime—naturally the Kurds, and certain sections of Shi'a society, ICP members, military officers, and Saddam's rivals in the Ba'ath Party hierarchy. The message was clear—those who opposed the regime would be dealt with in ruthless fashion. Perhaps not surprisingly, the large majority of the population chose not to oppose the regime, and were not directly exposed to its cruelty. Exposés of Saddam's Iraq that dwell on the gory details of torture techniques employed by the security services, or breathlessly inform us that "by the time Saddam came to power . . . it was estimated that the regime had perfected 107 different methods of torturing its enemies,"[32] rather miss the point. The use of torture among Middle Eastern regimes at the time was scarcely anomalous.[33] What distinguished the Ba'ath regime was not the number of torture techniques involved, but the potential reach of the state's apparatus of repression. The eyes and ears of the regime were literally everywhere. This was achieved partly through the deep penetration into society of the Party's structure, but also through a complex network of security organizations with overlapping jurisdictions. By the 1980s, there were at least five known security organizations in Iraq, employing over 200,000 operatives.[34] Each of these organizations engaged a huge network of informers to keep track of the population (and each other).

The regime's control was not achieved through the widespread, perpetual *infliction* of violence on its own people, but rather through the permanent and universal *threat* of violence. Resistance to the regime was futile. It would be detected, and it would be punished severely. In the words of one expert, this system was "highly effective in achieving one of its major objectives: promoting a sense of helplessness among the population."[35]

Perhaps more disturbing than the routine use of torture was the glorification of violence against minority groups, a tradition that stretched back to the Assyrian massacre in 1933 and the vicious pogrom against the Jews of Baghdad in 1941. Under the Ba'ath, the immediate target was the Jews. The public hangings of 14 accused conspirators in 1969 were important both because they illustrated the brutality of the Ba'ath regime and because they offered deep insights into the overall health of the Iraqi body politic as it entered its sixth decade. Neither public executions nor virulent anti-Zionism were unusual in the Middle East at the time, but what differed was the orgy of celebration that accompanied the grisly ritual, amounting to what one observer described as little more than "state-sponsored pornography."[36]

A public holiday was declared to celebrate the executions, and between 150,000 and 500,000 ordinary Iraqi citizens packed Liberation Square to witness the hangings and enjoy a "carnival-like atmosphere" as they ate picnics among the dangling bodies of the 14. Baghdad radio exhorted the Iraqi citizenry to "come and enjoy the feast."[37] Party officials regaled the throng with stirring speeches about the need for vigilance against Zionists, imperialists, and pretty much anyone else who threatened the sanctity of the revolution. The Minister of Guidance, Salah Umar al-Ali, was in fine form:

> Great people of Iraq! The Iraq of today shall no more tolerate any traitor, spy agent or fifth columnist! You foundling Israel, you imperialist Americans, and you Zionists, hear me! . . . We will hang all your spies, even if there are thousands of them . . . Great Iraqi people! This is only the beginning! The great and immortal squares of Iraq shall be filled up with the corpses of traitors and spies. Just wait![38]

The wait would not be long. This spectacle of mass audience participation was a grotesque bonding session between the Ba'ath and the people, designed to impart "legitimacy" to the new regime.[39] That the Ba'ath should seek and gain legitimacy through the glorification of public executions provides a telling indicator of the nature of participatory politics in Iraq circa 1969.

Aside from "enemies of the state," it was, as usual, the Kurds who bore the full brunt of the state's coercive forces. The Ba'ath regime adhered faithfully to the traditional template: a peace overture (probably insincere) to the Kurds (the 1970 March Manifesto); the gradual unraveling of the agreement when neither side proves capable of trusting the other (1970–1974); and ultimately, large-scale conflict in which Kurdish troops (*peshmergas*) were repeatedly assaulted, but never fully eliminated by the Iraqi army (1975). Subsequent to

1975, the regime's capacity to control events in the north was enhanced greatly by the traumatic split between the two major Kurdish factions—the Patriotic Union of Kurdistan (PUK) and the Kurdistan Democratic Party (KDP). Henceforth, depending on the nature of relations between the two Kurdish factions, the regime was often able to play off one side against the other. Such was the case in 1983, when divisions in the Kurdish ranks enabled Baghdad to negotiate a cease-fire with the PUK while simultaneously invading KDP-held territory. Between 5,000 and 8,000 male members of the KDP were rounded up by Iraqi security forces and were simply made to "disappear." According to Baghdad, they had been "severely punished and went to hell." But worse was to come. By 1987, toward the end of the Iran–Iraq war, the PUK and KDP were once more united in the Iraqi Kurdistan Front (IKF), and actively assisting the Iranians to open up a northern front against Iraqi forces. Saddam instructed his cousin, Ali Hassan al-Majid, to "take care" of the Kurds. To the enthusiastic al-Majid, this meant "burying them with bulldozers."[40] More accurately, it meant a sustained campaign of vicious retribution meted out to the entire Kurdish population. Over the course of 1987, and particularly from February 1988 onward, the infamous *Anfal* (literally, the spoils of war) campaign combined the systematic use of chemical weapons, the destruction of perhaps 4,000 Kurdish villages, and the forced relocation of up to 500,000 Kurds. In one gas attack alone (on the town of Halabja), over 5,000 Kurds (including women and children) perished in horrific circumstances. Since 1925, when the Geneva Protocol outlawed the use of poison gas on the battlefield, a dense web of international law has emerged governing codes of conduct during wartime. Over a period of about one and a half years, Iraq managed to violate almost every rule in the book. It was, however, brutally effective. In Massoud Barzani's words, "Everything has ended; the rebellion is over. We cannot fight chemical weapons with bare hands."[41]

Saddam's approach toward the Shi'a was altogether more subtle, and the violence inflicted much more selective. As has always been the case, the sectarian (Sunni–Shi'a) divide proved easier to bridge than the ethnic (Arab–Kurd) schism.[42] The major target of the regime's coercive forces was the religious leadership in the south. Between 1920 and the 1960s, Shi'a religious leaders had lain politically dormant. They had studiously withdrawn from active participation in the institutions of the state, and had also largely refrained from overt opposition. The emergence of *al-Da'wa* (the Call), a Shi'a fundamentalist organization/terrorist group dedicated to the promotion of Islamic revolution throughout the Middle East, changed this dynamic dramatically. The politicization of religion under the charismatic influence of leading cleric

Muhammed Baqir al-Sadr, was a serious threat to the secular Sunni Ba'ath regime. The crackdown on *al-Da'wa* began in 1974 with the execution of four members of the by-now banned political group. By 1977, however, a fundamental pillar of Ba'ath Party rule—the separation of religion from politics—was beginning to crack. Violent confrontations erupted in 1977 when the regime tried to impose its will on the Shi'a religious establishment by disrupting the annual *Ashura* religious procession between the two Shi'a holy cities of Najaf and Karbala. In the ensuing melee, 60 pilgrims were killed by police, and over 2,000 were arrested. A duly convened "special court" pronounced death sentences on 8 Shi'a clerics, and sentenced a further 15 to life imprisonment.

In the context of continuing unrest, the Islamic revolution in neighboring Iran and the emergence of a hardcore Shi'a fundamentalist regime under the leadership of Ayatollah Khomeini did little to calm troubled waters. Khomeini spewed venom against the detested secular Ba'athists, and poured money into militant Islamic groups operating inside Iraq—most notably, the *Mujahedin* (the Holy Warriors). *Al-Da'wa*, however, resisted Iranian influence and was thus untainted by foreign influence. Throughout 1979, Islamic groups stepped up their activities, engaging in low-level guerilla warfare against symbols of the regime—not just in the south, but also in the Shi'a-populated slums of Baghdad. Demonstrators in the south chanted pro-Khomeini slogans and called for Saddam's ouster. Perhaps unwisely, Sadr issued a *fatwa* (religious edict) against membership of the Ba'ath Party—a direct challenge to the regime. Matters reached a head in April 1980 when *al-Da'wa* members ambushed Deputy Prime Minister Tariq Aziz during a visit to Mustansiriya University in Baghdad. An assassination attempt with hand grenades only slightly wounded Aziz, but killed several students. During their funerals, an *al-Da'wa* hit squad attacked again, killing more people. Incensed, Saddam ordered a round-up of militants; hundreds were executed. Security forces were dispatched to Najaf to arrest Sadr and his sister Bint al Huda. They were carted off to Baghdad and executed—Sadr apparently by having nails driven through his head. In addition to widespread executions, nearly 40,000 "suspect" Iraqi Shi'a (those with any connection to Iran), were forcibly deported to Iran.

Overall, the first 20 years of Ba'athist rule relied heavily on violence—actual or threatened—as an instrument of political control. Evidence of the brutality of the Ba'ath regime under Saddam is ample. But two features of Saddam's rule need to be emphasized. First, the regime was confronted throughout the period by some genuinely serious threats to its survival; some of these threats were generated by the actions of the regime itself, but most were inherent in the fractured polity of Iraq. This explosive combination of multiple threats to regime survival, and a man who was plainly willing to use whatever levels of coercion were necessary to survive, inevitably led to large-scale bloodshed. Second, Saddam was a highly skilled political operator who understood clearly the efficacy of both punishment and reward, and who possessed an unerring instinct for deploying each at the appropriate time. Certainly, he wielded a big stick, but this alone cannot explain his survival, or his popularity with large swathes of the Iraqi population. Neither can it explain how Saddam, more so than any previous Iraqi leader, managed to forge a shared sense of identity among Iraq's Arab population. Sadly, this was an Iraqi identity that could not be stretched far enough to include the Kurds—and they suffered heavily as a consequence.

## National Unity

Ba'athist ideology, rooted as it was in militant pan-Arabism, initially seemed a singularly fragile and dangerous basis on which to construct a distinctive Iraqi identity. The Party's defining message had little appeal outside the Sunni heartland, and aroused suspicions among the Shi'a and understandable paranoia among Kurds. For the first two or so years of Ba'ath Party rule, the reckless pursuit of pan-Arab causes came close to precipitating the implosion of the new regime. At great economic cost, the Ba'ath retained over 25 percent of its army as an expeditionary force in Jordan, ready to resume hostilities against Israel. From the safe distance of Baghdad, the regime called upon all Arab nations to rise up once more against the detested "Zionist entity," and roundly insulted all Arab nations that failed to do so. Ideological coherence deserted the Party. While advocating the overthrow of Egyptian and Syrian leaders for their betrayal of the Arab cause, the same Iraqi politicians were simultaneously calling for a union between these two states and Iraq.

Had the Party been doggedly determined to remain true to its principles, the lifespan of the regime would no doubt have been short. The conflict between "Iraq first" versus Arab union—in essence a debate about the very identity of the Iraqi state—was still an open and potentially explosive issue. In the hands of a master manipulator like Saddam, the issue became a non-issue. Indeed, it was Saddam who first convinced the Ba'ath leadership of the need for the regime to turn inward and focus on Iraq's internal problems, rather than expend its energies on pushing the pan-Arab cause. By about 1974, a new, improved version of pan-Arabism was taking shape. This revised vision stressed the uniqueness of Iraq within the broader Arab world, and envisaged an extended period of internal consolidation, after which Iraq would emerge as the powerhouse of Arab union. A strong Iraq was necessary to spearhead Arab unity at some future (unspecified) date. This was an elegant reformulation that allowed the regime to champion the pan-Arab cause, while simultaneously focusing attention on the internal development of the Iraqi state. It was also less immediately threatening to both Shi'a and Kurds.

This gradual doctrinal shift was accompanied by a hugely ambitious project of social engineering, aimed at nothing less than the creation of an entirely new national identity for the people of Iraq. If the people were unable or unwilling to generate a sense of national identity for themselves, then the Ba'ath Party would have to create it for them. This required a shared history, accessible (at least potentially) to all of Iraq's various social groupings. The ancient glories of Mesopotamia ("the land between two rivers") provided fertile ground for the manufacture of the Iraqi "national myth." The history of Mesopotamia— stretching back some four and a half millennia—was pre-Islamic, even pre-Arab (thus not tainted by specific secular or ethnic associations), and was pregnant with social, economic, political, and cultural achievement.[43] Western civilization owes at least as much to Mesopotamia as it does to Greece, and it was this proud tradition that the Ba'ath regime sought to harness.

The approach was multi-dimensional. Throughout the 1970s the government dedicated huge sums of money to the excavation of the ancient city of Babylon, reconstructing it in its entirety from the ground up; cities and provinces were renamed—Mosul became Ninevah (the ancient Assyrian city), while al-Hilla province was renamed Babylon; Mesopotamian heroes began to appear on Iraqi coins and banknotes (Hammurabi, for example, graced the five-dinar bill); the Republican Guard acquired the "Hammurabi" and "Nebuchadnezzar" units; and even Iraqi cigarettes entered into the spirit of things. One could buy "Sumer Filters" with "Made in Mesopotamia" stamped on the packet.[44] This focus on Mesopotamia, with its galaxy of historical superstars, also provided endless possibilities for Saddam to fuel the cult of personality that began to envelop Iraq's great leader after the mid-1970s. Particularly after 1979, when the cult kicked into high gear, vast murals began to appear in major cities depicting Saddam in various historical guises—as Hammurabi (imparting justice to the people of Iraq), or as Nebuchadnezzar (delivering the Jews once more into captivity).

In addition to the elaborate efforts to construct a shared history for the Iraqi people, the regime also took great pains to forge a new contemporary cultural identity for Iraq. This relied on the concept of "unity-in-diversity," and advanced the proposition that Iraq's uniqueness as a nation stemmed precisely from its ethnic and sectarian diversity. Cultural differences were to be preserved and celebrated rather than denied or eliminated. As far as it went—and there was certainly never any suggestion that the celebration of diversity extended to the political realm—this was an enlightened policy, and it was pursued with vigor and enthusiasm by the Ba'ath regime. A vast new cultural bureaucracy was created. The General Directorate for Cinema and Theatre (established in 1969) was responsible for organizing festivals devoted to regional folklore; folklore museums were constructed throughout the country (predominantly in Kurdish- and Shi'a-populated areas); the Center for Popular Handicrafts and Industries was charged with the preservation of arts and crafts from Iraq's various regions; numerous folklore dance troupes were sponsored by the regime, including the Basra and Erbil (in Kurdistan) troupes, to tour the country; and the town of Nasiriyya in the Shi'a south was selected as the setting for the Festival of Popular Poets in 1969. The Iraqi Fashion House was established by law in 1970 and charged with suitably pretentious goals—"to preserve traditional attire from the various parts and communities of Iraq, and thus create a horizontal fusion, but also to 'protect and cultivate ancient Iraqi fashion,' and 'to raise the standard of design' of Iraqi textiles with 'designs inspired by the ancient Iraqi paintings,' thus establishing a vertical connection with Iraq's pre-Islamic past."[45] This was by no means a token effort. In 1982, during a time of war, the regime allocated $15 million for the construction of a huge permanent residence for the Fashion House.

Saddam himself seemed aware of the political significance of Iraq's new cultural curriculum. Referring to Kurdish autonomy, for example, he proclaimed in 1975 that

> when we discuss autonomy, we should not . . . transform the administrative structures of autonomy into a Chinese Wall dividing Iraq's Arabs and Kurds. For example, when we consider Iraqi folklore, there is nothing that requires us to talk endlessly about Kurdish folklore, and then Arab [folklore], and thirdly Turkomen [folklore] etc; rather, it should be depicted exclusively as Iraqi folklore . . . let us delete the words Arab and Kurds, and replace them with [the term] the Iraqi people.[46]

Coming from the leader of a Party doctrinally dedicated to militant pan-Arabism, this was extraordinary stuff. The fatal flaw, of course, was that the Kurds had no interest in being absorbed into the "Iraqi people"; moreover, as regimes in Baghdad demonstrated repeatedly, there was apparently a very fine line between deleting "the words Arab and Kurds," and deleting the Kurds themselves from Iraq by force.

Nonetheless, judged by historical standards, the Ba'ath Party's efforts to forge "unity-in-diversity" through the arts and culture should not be lightly dismissed. No previous regime in Iraq had offered anything close to a vision of national unity on this scale and pursued it with this degree of commitment. Similarly enlightened approaches—at least on the surface—were applied to the spheres of education, women's rights, and social welfare.

Saddam appears to have taken a personal and genuine interest in education. In 1977 he launched a Comprehensive National Campaign for Compulsory Education with the characteristically modest goal of eliminating illiteracy. An army of 62,000 teachers and bureaucrats was drafted to fulfill the goal, and it is estimated that by 1982, 2 million Iraqis had learned to read and write as a result.[47] So impressive was the achievement that Saddam was honored by UNESCO with the Kropeska award for his contribution to the worldwide elimination of illiteracy. Those who failed to enroll in the campaign were threatened with imprisonment. Only in Saddam's Iraq could illiteracy become a criminal offense.

Alongside massive improvements in education, the role of women in society underwent a radical transformation. Perhaps the most notable achievement in this sphere was the huge increase in the numbers of females receiving education. In 1970, only 34 percent of females received any sort of formal education; by 1980, this number had risen to 95 percent.[48] The expansion of the public sector also opened up new opportunities for women in the workplace. By the end of the 1970s, women comprised 46 percent of teachers, nearly 30 percent of doctors, and close to 50 percent of dentists.[49] A 1977 law opened the way for women to serve in the army—an achievement that took many Western countries at least another decade to accomplish. Relative to the position of women in the rest of the Arab world at the time (notably neighboring Kuwait and Saudi Arabia), Iraqi women resided in a different universe.

On one level, it is important to acknowledge the progressive achievements of the Ba'ath regime; on a deeper level, it would be naïve not to recognize the underlying political purpose. Throughout Iraq's brief history, education had been used for political purposes. Under the monarchy, the education system had been controlled by militant pan-Arabists and had been used to promote their cause. Under the Ba'ath, the goals were much more ambitious. Through tight state control over the curriculum and the teaching profession, the Party gained direct access to the raw material of young minds; these minds could then be molded en masse into the desired form. In this way, an entirely new Iraqi society could be formed—one that cohered around a common set of Ba'athist principles. Similarly, the drive to eliminate illiteracy

inevitably focused on the majority Shi'a population (the Shi'a being disproportionately illiterate at the time), enabling a governing Sunni regime to penetrate the minds of the lower-class Shi'a majority for the first time in Iraq's
history. But this was more than just a process of indoctrination through education. Education was used as a means of fracturing traditional ties of loyalty,
then replacing these with new ties that stretched directly from the individual
to the regime. Even the most fundamental bonds of family loyalty were not
sacrosanct. In Saddam's words,

> To prevent the father and mother dominating the household with backward-
> ness, we must make the small one radiate internally to expel it . . . The unity
> of the family must not be based on backward concepts, but on congruence
> with centralizing mores derived from the policies and traditions of the revo-
> lution in its construction of the new society. Whenever there is a conflict be-
> tween the unity of the family and these mores . . . it must be resolved in the
> favour of the new mores.[50]

Thus the goal of education was to inculcate within the young an allegiance to
the revolution and the Party that preempted allegiance to the family unit.

Some have argued that the liberation of women from the bonds of the pa-
triarchal family served a similar purpose—"if a new loyalty to the Leader, the
party, and the state is to form, women must be 'freed' from the loyalties that
traditionally bound them to their husbands and male kin."[51] Once again, the
shattering of traditional ties was a prerequisite for the emergence of deeper
ties of allegiance between the "liberated" (women) and the goals of the revolution (as defined by Saddam).

The psychological dimension of Ba'athist efforts to forge a new and unified national identity for the state of Iraq involved an ongoing process of destruction and creation. The population had first to be atomized via the
destruction of traditional ties of loyalty, then reassembled into a unified mass
with a glorious collective history and bound by shared ties of loyalty to the
Party, and, of course, the "Great Leader" himself. Increasingly over the course
of the 1968–1988 period, Ba'athist ideology ceased to have any discernable
content independent of Saddam; the Ba'athist vision became whatever Saddam
said it was. Under the guise of establishing ties of loyalty between the people
and the revolutionary principles of the Party, therefore, Saddam was effectively striving to create a society in which the fundamental bond was between
*himself* and individual Iraqi citizens. The logical outcome of this process was
the elevation of Saddam from his status as political leader to self-appointed
symbol of national unity. To carry this off successfully required Saddam to ap-

pear simultaneously as all things to all men; now as the honorable tribal leader bedecked in the regalia of the Bedouin; now as the devoted disciple of Islam, at prayer in the shrine cities; now as the mighty warrior, putting sword to the Persian, the Zionist, and the imperialist. As a consummate political actor, Saddam proved highly skilled at sustaining this colossal role-playing exercise. Where the great man himself (or one of his entourage of doubles) was not available for personal performances, vast murals depicting him in various guises peppered Iraq's urban landscape as a permanent reminder to the people of Iraq of where their fundamental ties of loyalty lay—or should lie. Iraq was becoming a personality cult of monstrous proportions.

The relentless drive for psychological unity was supplemented by material incentives. With the odd exception, the Shi'a majority was excluded from the heart of political power, but was incorporated into the vast machine of patronage that the state became over the course of the period. By the onset of the 1980s, government employees numbered in excess of one and a quarter million. Adding to this their dependents, members of the Popular Army, and of the various armed forces, it is estimated that the Iraqi state directly controlled the livelihood of a majority of the population. For the first time in the history of Iraq, a regime had established a state structure expansive enough to incorporate the Shi'a majority. Over the 1968–1988 period, the material well-being of the Shi'a majority improved significantly. Nor was this just a question of free refrigerators and TVs. By the end of the 1970s, the proportion of Shi'a enjoying access to education was roughly equivalent to that of Sunnis. In the purely Shi'a provinces of the south, there were more hospitals per capita than in the predominantly Sunni provinces of the north and center.[52] The Kurds fared less well, but even here there were improvements. By 1978, the proportion of children in Kurdish areas attending primary school was similar to other regions of Iraq, and there were actually more hospitals per capita for Kurds than for either Shi'a or Sunnis. Of course these quality-of-life improvements pale into insignificance relative to the magnitude of the violence inflicted on the Kurdish population over the period. Taken as a whole, the 1968–1988 period was a severe step backward in terms of integrating the Kurds into the state of Iraq.

To understand Saddam's Ba'athist regime, and thereby to appreciate the magnitude of the psychological damage it inflicted on the Iraqi people, it is necessary to move beyond simplistic formulations that focus solely on the use of violence. While state-sponsored violence was inflicted against the regime's opponents without hesitation, the regime also offered a large array of incentives for cooperation. A concerted effort was also made to forge a new national identity for Iraq—one that was inclusive rather than exclusive, and that placed the development of the Iraqi state rather than utopian pan-Arab schemes at the forefront of concern.

Gauging the success of Saddam's efforts to forge national unity from Iraq's diverse fragments is difficult. It is unlikely that many outside the Sunni heartland were convinced by the contrived attempt to forge a shared Mesopotamian history. Having said this, when the acid test came during the Iran–Iraq war, the Arab component of the Iraqi state cohered beyond all expectations to resist the invading Iranians. This need not indicate any loyalty on the part of the Shi'a to either the Ba'ath regime or even to the state of Iraq; it does suggest, however, that for the majority of Iraq's Shi'a Arabs, ties of ethnicity trumped shared sectarian identity. Conversely, the Kurds demonstrated repeatedly over the period that they were willing to side with anyone, regardless of nationality or ethnicity, to continue their struggle against the Iraqi state.

## CONCLUSION

The nature of the first 20 years of Ba'ath Party rule raises a number of critical concerns about the future of Iraq. First, it is important to stress the extent to which the Ba'ath regime was a product of its political environment. The Party succeeded in establishing and maintaining its grip on power at a time of severe and violent political anarchy. The logic of Ba'athist rule was premised on survival, and in the process of eliminating dissent and opposition, the Party established a brutal form of ordered society that contrasted strikingly with the turbulence of previous regimes. Order, it seems, can be imposed on Iraq, but only at a price.

Second, many of the techniques of governance employed by the regime and by Saddam were variations on traditional themes rather than novelties. Just as it had always been, Iraq was governed by Sunnis, with the Kurds and Shi'a relegated to supporting roles. Violence (and the threat of violence) was a key feature of Ba'athist rule—again, no great departure from previous practice. The use of patronage as a mechanism of governance was much more widespread and deep-rooted than previously, but the technique originated with the British rather than the Ba'ath. The British had also relied heavily on divide-and-conquer tactics to turn Iraq's disparate groups in on themselves, thus avoiding the emergence of a united opposition; Saddam played the same game—particularly in Iraqi Kurdistan—only with more success. In terms of political institutions, the Ba'ath drew heavily on the accumulated experience of prior regimes. Revolutionary command councils, revolutionary courts, the

Republican Guard, a "democratic" Parliament, paramilitary militias, even the cult of personality—all were developed under previous regimes, then adapted by the Ba'ath regime to suit the requirements of the time. In this respect, rule by the Ba'ath Party emphasized continuities rather than divergence with prior practice.

Third, to the extent that the Ba'ath regime did mark a break with traditional practices of governance, the results were not all negative. Clearly there was a difference in the degree to which the regime was able to penetrate down to the lowest levels of society. The huge expansion of the role of the state in the economy and the provision of public services, combined with the disciplined organizational structure of the Ba'ath Party, gave the Party a degree of control over the lives of ordinary citizens that had hitherto been unimaginable. On the positive side, the result was a well-educated, relatively affluent population inhabiting the most developed state in the Arab world. This was not a regime that ruled by violence alone. While it may seem inconceivable (or incomprehensible) to many, the Ba'ath Party, and Saddam in particular, enjoyed genuine, widespread popularity among ordinary Iraqis for most of the period.[53] Whether this was due to increasing standards of living, heavy indoctrination, or the regime's strident anti-Zionist, anti-imperialist, and pan-Arab rhetoric is unknowable. Probably it was some combination of all of these factors; but the fact is that Saddam came closer than anyone before him to establishing the recipe for the successful governance of the Iraqi state (minus the Kurdish north, of course).

The psychological price paid by the Iraqi people over the course of these 20 years will not be fully evident for some time to come. As totalitarian rule evolved into a gargantuan cult of personality, traditional societal bonds were deliberately shattered, to be replaced by direct ties from individuals to Saddam. This required a massive program of indoctrination that may take many years to undo.

Finally, this 20-year period effectively terminated any possibility of meaningful reconciliation between Kurds and Arabs. The problem was not just Kurdish resistance to central authority—this was scarcely a novelty—but the fact that when faced with a choice between Iraqi Arabs and Iranian Persians, the Kurds sided with the latter. This was a "betrayal" that has not been forgotten. From the Kurdish perspective, the legacies of the brutal Anfal campaign will be felt—psychologically and physically—for years to come. While Ba'athist rule did more than any previous regime to solidify the Arab component of the Iraqi state into a coherent national entity, the Kurdish component was brutalized, then cut adrift. Gone was any pretense at unity-in-diversity.

## CHAPTER FOUR

# 1988–2003:
# THE DESTRUCTION OF IRAQ

## INTRODUCTION

THE ATTITUDE OF MANY WESTERN POWERS to the Iran–Iraq war was neatly encapsulated in the immortal words of Henry Kissinger—"too bad they can't both lose."[1] In fact, by most reasonable criteria, both sides did lose; casualties for both states were in the hundreds of thousands, the economic costs were astronomical, both sides failed to accomplish their original war aims, and the war ended in territorial stalemate. Eight years of carnage had, in reality, produced nothing but pain for the two Gulf rivals. Naturally, this did not prevent Saddam from claiming the war as a historic victory for the Arab world over the "Persian hordes." But even as Iraqis enjoyed an eight-day party of celebration in the streets of Baghdad, and work began on the construction of Saddam's inevitably ostentatious victory monuments, it was evident that the war had inflicted serious damage on the social and economic fabric of Iraq.[2] Iraq had entered the war as one of the most stable, modern, and prosperous states in the Middle East; it emerged facing economic ruin. While not obvious at the time, this was the beginning of the end for Saddam Hussein. Iraq's invasion of Kuwait in 1990 was Saddam's response to his country's dire economic predicament induced by eight years of brutal warfare. Subsequently, a devastating military defeat by coalition forces in 1991 and over 12 years of stringent economic sanctions imposed by the United Nations destroyed the state of Iraq from the inside out. By March 2003, when Saddam once again defiantly confronted a massively superior coalition of the willing, he was presiding over a failed state—a state that no longer controlled large swathes of its own territory, and that could no longer meet even the most basic needs of its population. Over the course of the 1988–2003 period, Saddam (with the able assistance of the international community) managed to destroy almost all of the successful achievements of the preceding 20 years, and, in the process inflicted incalculable damage on the social, economic, and political integrity of Iraq. His legacy will be felt for decades to come.

## SOCIAL AND ECONOMIC PROBLEMS

The eight years of conflict against Iran had been expensive for Iraq. While Iran had largely avoided extensive borrowing from abroad (the fanatical Islamic regime had few supporters with money to spare), Iraq had incurred massive debts in order to sustain the war effort against its much larger neighbor. From the West and Japan, Iraqi debts stood at $25-$35 billion; from the Soviet Union, $10 billion; and from the Gulf states (mainly Saudi Arabia and Kuwait), $50-$55 billion. Thus Iraq's total foreign debt stood at something close to $100 billion. In part this money was used to shield the Iraqi people from the full effects of war—a deliberate policy of "keeping bellies full" in order to stave off internal unrest. By the mid-1980s, this policy was no longer sustainable, and over the course of the war, per capita income in Iraq declined by half from its 1980 level. Further, it was estimated that repairing Iraq's devastated infrastructure would require investments of up to $200 billion. The remainder of the borrowed money was used to construct the largest land army in the Middle East. By war's end, the Iraqi armed forces had increased in size to over a million. With no war to occupy his troops, Saddam was faced with a potentially serious threat to internal stability. As one observer notes, "He [Saddam] had a million man army with nothing to do . . . He would have to find something to keep them busy before they turned their thoughts to the presidential palace, the way armies do when they have time on their hands."[3]

The Iraqi economy was in no position to absorb a demobilized army of this magnitude, and at the same time, there were insufficient resources to maintain a million-man standing army. More dangerous still, the army's resilient defense of the Iraqi homeland during the latter years of the war had greatly increased the prestige and popularity of the military and created a new cadre of war heroes within the officer corps. The army had reemerged as a potential rival to Saddam's regime. The response was predictable—a coup attempt was exposed, and then one by one, prominent army officers were purged from the ranks. Victims included Saddam's cousin Adnan Khairallah Talfah, the popular and competent Minister of Defense, whose helicopter crashed in "unfortunate" circumstances in May 1989. Decapitating the military helped ward off an immediate threat to the regime, but did little to address the deeper problem of a crippled economy and a massive army of battle-hardened veterans with nothing constructive to keep them occupied.

Iraq's dire financial predicament also threatened one of the central pillars of Saddam's rule. The key to the durability of the Ba'athist regime had long been the skillful blend of stick and carrot—dissent was ruthlessly suppressed, but those who toed the Ba'athist line could expect to be richly rewarded for their loyalty. The distribution of patronage—essential to the smooth functioning of the system—required major financial resources, and these were no longer available in the aftermath of the war. In 1990, oil revenues comprised only $13 billion—a paltry sum given the magnitude of Iraq's debt and the price tag for the reconstruction of Iraq's infrastructure. The survival of the Ba'ath regime and of Saddam himself had relied upon delivering an ever-improving standard of material well-being to Iraq's population. By 1990, the coffers were empty.

## KUWAIT IN THE CROSSHAIRS

Relations between Iraq and Kuwait deteriorated rapidly in the aftermath of the Iran–Iraq war. Kuwait was adamant that Iraq's debt must be repaid; Iraq was equally convinced that, having spilt the "rivers of blood in defense of [Arab] nationalist sovereignty and nationalist dignity" the debt should be forgiven.[4] Efforts by Iraq to convince members of the Organization of Petroleum Exporting Countries (OPEC) to decrease oil production in order to drive up prices were undermined by the Kuwaitis, who persisted in exceeding their OPEC quota, and worse still, began to pump oil out of the Rumaila oil field—a huge reserve that straddles the Iraq–Kuwait border. By 1990, oil prices had slipped below the OPEC-agreed level of $18 a barrel; by June the same year, the price had fallen to $11 a barrel. For Iraq the calculation was straightforward; every dollar decline in the price of oil translated into a loss of $1 billion in annual revenues. Iraqi Foreign Minister Tariq Aziz reminded the Kuwaitis that they were treading on very thin ice, warning that "the Kuwaiti government's deliberate attempts to bring down the Iraqi economy is an aggression no smaller in its consequences than a military aggression."[5] By mid-July, U.S. satellites were detecting large numbers of Iraqi troops massing along the Kuwaiti border; but the U.S. reaction was subdued. On July 24, Margaret

Tutwiler, the State Department's spokeswoman, declared that "We do not have any defense treaties with Kuwait, and there are no special defense or security commitments to Kuwait."[6] Subsequently, the U.S. Ambassador to Iraq, April Glaspie, explained personally to Saddam that the U.S. had "no opinion on Arab–Arab conflicts, like your border disagreement with Kuwait." If not quite a "green light," a series of such statements coming out of Washington strongly implied that the U.S. would not intervene to defend Kuwait in the event of an attack by Iraq.[7] On July 31, Iraqi and Kuwaiti representatives met in Jeddah, Saudi Arabia in a final attempt to stave off war. The meeting ended in failure, and war became inevitable.

## The Invasion of Kuwait

On August 2, 1990, Iraqi troops crossed the border into Kuwait, and, meeting little in the way of serious resistance, had occupied the entire country by day's end. Kuwait was systematically stripped of anything of value; Kuwaiti men were beaten, tortured, and executed by Iraqi security services; and sexual assaults against Kuwaiti women were routine. The U.S. was swift to condemn the Iraqi invasion, acutely aware that the world's fourth-largest army was on the verge of securing the largest oil reserves in the world. Fearing that his country was next in line for the unwanted attentions of the rampant Iraqi armed forces, King Fahd of Saudi Arabia requested the support of the U.S. in defending his country. President George H. W. Bush was only too happy to oblige, dispatching 40,000 U.S. troops to guard Saudi's borders. Saddam responded by officially annexing Kuwait and declaring it the "nineteenth province of Iraq," and by mid-August, the battle lines were drawn.

Diplomatically, the U.S. wielded sticks and carrots to secure passage of United Nations Security Council Resolution 678 in November 1990, which authorized member states to use "all necessary means" to evict Iraq from Kuwait unless a withdrawal occurred before January 15, 1991. The U.S. assembled a coalition force of some 600,000, including troops from several Arab countries, to enforce the provisions of UNSCR 678. This force was numerically inferior to the Iraqi army, but was vastly superior in terms of technology, training, and equipment. Saddam's refusal to back down in the face of overwhelming odds has been interpreted by some as evidence of his propensity to engage in reckless gambles; more realistically, Saddam had painted himself into a corner. Domestically, withdrawal was not an option. To comply with the deadline would have meant losing face to such an extent in Iraq that the very survival of Saddam's regime would be placed in serious doubt. As one commentator put it, "withdrawal at this stage and under the conditions set by the coalition was tantamount to suicide for the Iraqi regime."[8]

## Operation Desert Storm

Two days after the expiration of the January 15 deadline, coalition forces launched Operation Desert Storm. The first stage of the operation, a ferocious, six-week aerial bombardment, destroyed much of Iraq's military (and civilian) infrastructure, wiping out most of the major achievements of the Ba'ath regime since the mid-1970s. The most intense air assault ever seen "thrust Baghdad and its 3.5 million inhabitants abruptly back into the third world."[9] In the wake of the air campaign, the coalition land invasion was in fact a rout of embarrassing proportions. Fighting was over in less than 48 hours and Kuwait was "free" once more. On February 28, 1991, President Bush declared a cease-fire, largely to avoid a continuation of the senseless slaughter of defenseless Iraqi troops in obvious retreat.

In the most obvious sense, Desert Storm was a crushing defeat for Iraq; in less than two months, coalition forces had obliterated Iraq's infrastructure and humiliated the largest land army in the region—and all at minimal cost in terms of coalition casualties. Saddam's chief of military intelligence, General Wafiq al-Samarra'i, was certainly under no illusions about the outcome of the conflict, stating, "I think this is the biggest defeat in history."[10] In another sense, however, this outcome was not entirely unfavorable for Saddam. He had, after all, survived. Moreover, most of the troops destroyed by the coalition forces were poorly trained, badly equipped Shi'a and Kurdish conscripts. Those not killed by the coalition onslaught surrendered in droves. Saddam's elite units (namely the Republican Guard) had emerged largely unscathed from the conflict—a serious strategic miscalculation on the part of the coalition, as it turned out. When faced with the most serious threat to his regime to date—simultaneous uprisings in the Kurdish north and the Shi'a south—it would be the Republican Guard that guaranteed regime survival.

## IRAQ IN REBELLION

On February 15, 13 days before the cease-fire was announced, President Bush made two speeches in the same day. Both called on "the Iraqi military and the Iraqi people to take matters into their own hands and force Saddam Hussein, the dictator, to step aside." These calls were aimed at inspiring a military coup against the regime, with the phrase "the Iraqi people" added as an afterthought, but were interpreted somewhat differently inside Iraq.[11] To the large numbers of Iraqi (mainly Shi'a) conscripts "chased like rats" out of Kuwait, and bitterly resentful at their betrayal by Saddam, the President's words seemed to indicate that a popular uprising would be actively supported by U.S. military forces.[12] As Iraq's bedraggled and humiliated troops streamed out of Kuwait into the towns and cities of southern Iraq, they found common cause in their resentment of the regime. The southern *intifada* (uprising) broke out on February 28 in the Sunni towns of Abu'l Khsib and Zubair 50 miles to the south of Basra, but soon spread like wildfire to the Shi'a strongholds of Basra, Najaf, and Karbala. This was not a coordinated rebellion, but rather a series of spontaneous and violent eruptions that never amounted to more than the sum of its parts. The targets of resentment were the symbols and personnel of the Ba'athist regime. Ba'ath officials were hunted down by packs of rebels, then publicly executed in brutal fashion by rampaging mobs. Regime symbols were either looted or trashed in what was fast becoming an anarchic orgy of wanton destruction and revenge killing. As one participant from Najaf recalls, "At first we were a little crazy . . . we believed even the traffic lights represented Saddam Hussein, so we wrecked them."[13] The major achievement of the *intifada* was to precipitate the collapse of law and order in the south, thereby creating a dangerous power vacuum. But devoid of leadership and any coherent sense of direction, it was unclear who would emerge to fill the vacuum.

The northern uprising was better organized. United under the banner of the Iraqi Kurdistan Front (IKF), the two major Kurdish political forces—the Patriotic Union of Kurdistan (PUK) and the Kurdistan Democratic Party (KDP)—imparted some coherence to the rebellion, and by March 19, southern Kurdistan was in Kurdish hands. At this point, with 16 of Iraq's 18 provinces in open revolt, Saddam's regime was in serious trouble. A timely U.S. intervention—perhaps in the form of air support for the rebels—would almost certainly have spelt the end of Saddam. But it was clear that regime change on the back of a grassroots revolution was not at all what the U.S. had in mind. The U.S. favored the more traditional Iraqi approach to regime change—an internal military coup that would leave the architecture of the regime in tact, but would replace Saddam with a more user-friendly dictator. As the rapidly unraveling situation in the south apparently demonstrated, the alternative to Saddam's style of law and order was no law and order. But the real fear for the U.S. was that radical Shi'a Islamic groups would step in to fill the void, thus transforming the entire complexion of the uprising.

Sure enough, the Iranian-backed Supreme Council for the Islamic Revolution in Iraq (SCIRI),[14] fortified by its own military forces (the *Badr* Brigade), seized its moment, issuing orders that "all Iraqi armed forces should submit to and obey SCIRI orders" and "no idea except the rightful Islamic ones should be disseminated."[15] SCIRI's attempt to gain control over the direction of the uprising was a potentially dangerous development. Not only did it threaten to infuse the situation with a Shi'a fundamentalist fervor that would be deeply threatening to Iraq's Sunni minority; it also increased Iranian influence over the unfolding course of events in Iraq. SCIRI's intervention was indeed decisive, but mainly because it doomed the uprising to failure. The prospect of a regime change that resulted in the replacement of Saddam by a Shi'a theocracy under Iranian sway was unappealing to many of the rebels, and totally unacceptable to the U.S. SCIRI's involvement fragmented the forces opposed to Saddam and effectively guaranteed that the U.S. would go out of its way *not* to assist the southern rebellion.

Faced with uprisings in the north and south, the Ba'ath Party and the central region of Iraq (the Sunni heartland) did not fall apart. Instead, these threats solidified support for the regime among the Sunni minority. The regime had been significantly weakened by coalition forces, but, critically, still remained stronger and more unified than its opponents. Any doubts about the intentions of U.S. troops occupying parts of the south were removed when intercepted phone calls revealed that the U.S. had denied a specific request for assistance from southern rebels. The American answer apparently was "We are not going to support you because you are Shi'a and are collaborating with Iran."[16] Thus reassured, Saddam dispatched his cousin and son-in-law, Hussein Kamel (the newly appointed Minister of Defense) and units of the Republican Guard southward to crush the rebellion. One by one, the major southern cities of Basra, Karbala, and Najaf fell to loyalist forces, and by mid-March, Saddam had regained control over the south.

The Kurds were next on the list. Equipped with helicopter gunships that the regime, inexplicably, had been allowed to keep as part of the surrender agreement with the coalition, regime forces, once again spearheaded by the Republican Guard, moved into rebel Kurdish areas. By the end of March, Kurdish forces had been driven out of the major cities and into the mountains bordering Iran and Turkey. The indiscriminate violence inflicted on the Kurds—*peshmerga* and civilians alike—precipitated a mass exodus from the cities, creating a humanitarian disaster of biblical dimensions. By the end of April, approximately one million Kurds were either freezing or starving to death on the Turkish border. In response, the UN issued a resolution demanding an end to the repression of citizens in Iraq and preventing Iraqi aircraft from operating north of the 36th parallel. A number of "safe havens" were created to protect the displaced Kurdish civilians, but these covered only a tiny portion of Iraqi Kurdistan, and did not include any of the major cities of the region. The Kurdish rebellion was clearly over, and the leadership of the IKF had little option but to seek an accommodation with the regime in order to curtail the humanitarian catastrophe unfolding in the Zagros mountains.

The second Gulf War and its immediate aftermath revealed both the strengths and weaknesses of Saddam's regime. When faced with a well-equipped, well-trained, and technologically advanced fighting force, Iraq's armed forces had disintegrated with alarming rapidity. Apparently, the bulk of the world's fourth-largest army simply had no interest in fighting and dying in defense of Saddam's regime. However, the coercive forces at the disposal of the regime—particularly the Republican Guard and the various security services—were infinitely more powerful internally than anything opposition forces could muster. In the end, the rebellions in the north and south had been crushed in the space of a week with consummate ease.

## CONFRONTATION WITH THE UN

The original UN sanctions package (SCR 661), passed in August 1991, had mandated UN member states to desist from engaging in economic transactions with Iraq. In effect this amounted to a blanket ban on all Iraqi imports and exports. UNSCR 687—known as "the mother of all resolutions" due to its length—permitted Iraq to import food and items of "essential civilian need"; held Iraq financially responsible for all damages inflicted on Kuwait; and required Iraq to accept, unconditionally, "the destruction, removal or rendering harmless, under international supervision" of all elements of its chemical and biological weapons programs, as well as ballistic missiles of greater than 150-kilometer range. Resolution 687 created a UN Special Commission (UNSCOM) to supervise the destruction, and charged the International Atomic Energy Agency (IAEA) with dismantling Iraq's nuclear weapons program. The lifting of economic sanctions against Iraq was made contingent on reports by UNSCOM and the IAEA that their missions had been successfully accomplished.

From the start, the UN's efforts were hamstrung by two basic problems. First, the various resolutions made Iraq financially responsible for funding UNSCOM and IAEA operations, as well as reparations payments to Kuwait. This funding could only come from Iraqi oil exports, which in turn required the active cooperation of Iraq. To Saddam, the provisions of 687 constituted a gross violation of Iraq's sovereignty and, more dangerously, a concrete testament to the weakness of the regime in the aftermath of the Gulf War. Essentially, Iraq was being required to foot the bill for national humiliation.

Second, Resolution 687 embodied a bargain, whereby Iraq's cooperation in the destruction of its weapons of mass destruction (WMD) programs would be rewarded by a lifting of the economic sanctions. However, as early as April 1991, President Bush made clear that the goal of UN sanctions (from the U.S. perspective) was not disarmament but regime change. In an April 16 press conference, Bush effectively rewrote 687, stating that, "we will continue the economic sanctions" until "Saddam Hussein is out of there."[17] Shortly thereafter, President Bush authorized the CIA to begin covert operations to "create the conditions for the removal of Saddam Hussein from power." This new policy was fleshed out on May 7 by Deputy National Security Advisor Robert Gates, who asserted, "All possible sanctions will be maintained until he [Saddam] is gone . . . Any easing of sanctions will be considered only when there is a new government."[18] The U.S.'s message to Saddam was clear—he had nothing to gain from cooperating in the destruction of his WMD capability. Under such circumstances, it is scarcely surprising that UNSCOM's efforts to fulfill its mandate degenerated swiftly into a lengthy and costly game of cat-and-mouse that was to occupy the attention of the international community for over a decade.

## The Game Begins

The "rules" of the game were established early on. UNSCOM and IAEA inspectors began arriving in Iraq in June 1991, and by late-June, had already uncovered evidence of Iraq's extensive and relatively sophisticated nuclear weapons program; the same month, Saddam convened a secret, high-level council of his closest advisors to plan the concealment of certain elements of Iraq's WMD programs. The plan was one of strategic concessions coupled with elaborate deception. Iraq would cooperate fully with inspectors in certain areas (nuclear and some chemical programs) while systematically concealing evidence relating to Iraq's advanced nerve agent and biological weapons programs. Meanwhile, plans to remove Saddam's regime from power began to pick up momentum.

In June 1992, the first meeting of the Iraqi National Congress (INC) convened in Vienna, Austria under the leadership of exiled Iraqi businessman Ahmed Chalabi. The INC was conceived of as an umbrella organization, uniting (at least nominally) Iraq's disparate opposition groups under a single banner. With the financial backing of the CIA, Chalabi's INC brought together the two major Kurdish parties—the PUK and KDP—the remains of the Iraqi Communist Party, various explicitly Islamic groups (including SCIRI), and an assortment of Iraqi exiles who had long opposed Saddam's rule. Affiliated with the INC was another group—the Iraqi National Accord (INA)—that comprised disgruntled ex-military officers and former Ba'athists. In contrast to the INC, which attempted to span Iraq's numerous factional divides, the INA, although headed by a secular Shi'a, Dr. Iyad Allawi, was a Sunni-dominated operation. The INC and INA offered significantly different solutions to the problem of regime change in Iraq. Aside from the affiliation of the two Kurdish parties, the INC lacked high-level contacts on the ground inside Iraq; Chalabi himself, having left Iraq in 1958, was virtually unknown. Their plan was to use Kurdish territory as a base from which to initiate a broad-based uprising against the regime, with the ultimate goal of replacing Saddam with a representative democratic order. The INA could claim contacts at the highest levels of Saddam's regime (including within the Republican Guard and the state security services), and their plan was to use these connections to stage a "silver bullet" solution—a bloodless coup that would replace one Sunni-dominated regime with another. Thus the INC and INA were pursuing different agendas from the outset, and their relationship was characterized by rivalry for the financial attentions of the CIA rather than by collaboration in pursuit of a common goal. The CIA was itself internally divided over the respective merits of the two approaches, though generally favored the INA option as the least messy, and the one most likely to succeed.[19] It was clear from the outset though that the exiled opposition to Saddam was anything but coherent or united.

## The Iraqi People Pay the Price

Between 1991 and 1996, Iraq suffered under one of the most comprehensive sanctions regimes ever inflicted on a country by the international community. Saddam's initial refusal to accept a UN "oil-for-food" deal (which would have allowed Iraq to export $1.6 billion worth of oil every 6 months to purchase essential civilian requirements) meant that, apart from the proceeds from small quantities of oil smuggled across the border into neighboring Jordan and Turkey, Iraq had no reliable source of income with which to purchase the imports of food and medical supplies necessary to sustain its population, let alone rebuild the country's shattered infrastructure. Among the "military" targets that had received the attention of coalition ordnance during the war were power stations, sewage treatment facilities, and water purification plants. These could not be repaired without importing spare parts from abroad. The real danger to the long-suffering Iraqi population was not, in the end, starvation (an equitable and highly efficient system of food rationing was introduced that enabled the government to provide over 50 percent of individuals' daily needs) but the combination of malnutrition, disease, and a collapsing health care system.

The precipitous descent of living standards for ordinary Iraqis to Sub-Saharan levels was a mixed blessing for Saddam. On the positive side, a people preoccupied with the daily business of survival was unlikely to pose a serious collective challenge to his regime. If anything, the introduction of food rationing increased rather than reduced the regime's control over its own people. "Good" citizens were rewarded with extra rations, while those who caused trouble could be denied food altogether. Moreover, the suffering of Iraq's most vulnerable—the very young and old—gifted Saddam with an invaluable propaganda tool in the war of words with the international community. Throughout Iraq, and across the Arab world, TV images of stunted Iraqi babies receiving minimal treatment in dilapidated hospitals generated outrage and resentment against the U.S. and Britain (the two most ardent advocates of the sanctions regime).

But the impact of sanctions also created potential dangers for Saddam. With close to 60 percent of Iraqis dependent on government salaries, Saddam needed to find some way to finance the institutions of state. Unable (or unwilling) to earn revenue from oil exports, the regime opted to open up the printing presses and pumped out dinars. The inevitable hyperinflation—prices rose an estimated 600 percent in the first six months after the war—effectively rendered the dinar worthless, and increasingly the population turned to barter to meet their needs. Government salaries were unable to keep pace with the rate of inflation, and as a result, the real income of state employees declined by 90 percent during the first year of sanctions. By 1993, the real value of government salaries had fallen to $5 a month. Saddam's regime, which had earned much of its legitimacy through its capacity to deliver an ever-better standard of living to ordinary Iraqis, was now presiding over an economic catastrophe. An important pillar of Saddam's rule was collapsing. Even more threatening to the stability of the regime was the realization in some parts of Iraq that the situation would not improve while Saddam remained in power. Formerly loyal Sunni tribes that had benefited hugely under Saddam's patronage now turned on their former provider. For example, in 1993, two military officers from the Juburi tribe, centered around the northern city of Mosul, were arrested and executed for plotting a coup. Unrest in other loyalist Sunni strongholds like Ramadi and Samarra had to be suppressed by force. These were Sunni tribal areas that had remained staunchly loyal to Saddam, even in the darkest days of 1991. Now, it appeared, they had had enough. The regime's support base was becoming precariously narrow. Saddam's response was to increase his reliance on members of his immediate and extended family—but even here, cracks were beginning to appear.

## Family Feud

To staff the most sensitive positions in his regime, Saddam increased his reliance on his immediate family—his two sons Uday and Qusay—and two branches of his extended family (the Bejat clan of the al-Bu Nasir tribe), the al-Majids and the Ibrahims. Among the al-Majids who enjoyed key positions within the regime was the infamous "hammer of the Kurds" and architect of the *Anfal* campaign, Ali Hassan al-Majid ("chemical" Ali), and Hussein Kamel and Saddam Kamel, who had married Saddam's daughters Raghda and Rana, respectively. The al-Majids were the family "enforcers"—those to whom Saddam turned when some serious brutality was required. In 1988, Ali Hassan had been at the forefront of brutalizing the Kurds; in 1991, the mantle had passed to Hussein Kamel, who helped crush the southern *intifada* with characteristic family ferocity. On the Ibrahim side of the family, Saddam's three half brothers Barzan, Watban, and Sabawi had all, at various stages, occupied prominent positions in Iraq's intelligence and security services. Together with Uday and Qusay, this was the core of Saddam's regime.

But it was not a happy family. Animosity between the two branches stretched back to 1983, when Saddam chose al-Majids above Ibrahims as marriage partners for his daughters, and had not improved by the 1990s. What from the outside looked like an increasingly tight-knit and coherent ruling clique was in fact a hotbed of festering familial rivalries. The extent of the divisions within the ruling family was graphically illustrated in August 1995 when a convoy of black Mercedes carrying Hussein Kamel, his younger brother Saddam Kamel, their wives (Saddam's daughters), and various members of the al-Majid family slipped across the border into Jordan.[20] Hussein Kamel, long a vital cog in Saddam's machinery of governance, had defected.[21] With him, he took important information relating to Iraq's elaborate program to conceal WMD from UNSCOM inspectors. Four days after arriving in Amman, Kamel appeared at a press conference and made clear that his ambitions extended far beyond a new life in Jordan. Declaring, "we are working to topple the regime," Kamel appealed to the core of Saddam's repressive apparatus—the security services, and the Republican and Special Republican Guard—to rise up and overthrow the regime. It was an appeal that, unsurprisingly, fell on deaf ears.[22] In the end, as a catalyst for regime change in Iraq, Kamel's defection was a non-event. It did reveal, however, that a seismic crack had opened up at the very heart of Saddam's regime. In this sense, the defection was potentially the most damaging blow Saddam had suffered since becoming president. Kamel's presence in Amman also allowed UNSCOM chief Rolf Ekeus to pick the brain of the man who had headed Iraq's WMD concealment program since its inception. During interviews, Kamel outlined how the concealment program had succeeded in deceiving UNSCOM for four years, and revealed details of Iraq's extensive biological weapons and VX nerve-agent programs.

Back in Baghdad, the regime moved into damage-limitation mode, claiming, somewhat implausibly, that Kamel had been solely responsible for concealing evidence of Iraq's WMD program, and had done so without the knowledge of the regime. Saddam also took steps to tighten his control over the regime. Kamel was stripped of all official positions and expelled from the Ba'ath Party. Judging Uday to be a political liability, Saddam chose his younger son Qusay to fill the vacancies left by the disgraced Kamel. One consequence of the defection, then, was to constrict further the circle of power surrounding Saddam. Extended family could no longer be trusted, leaving immediate family as the only reliable source of loyalty. Despite dangerous splits in Saddam's inner circle, two externally (CIA) inspired attempts to topple the regime both ended in failure during the mid-1990s, demonstrating that, in terms of his ability to control events inside Iraq, Saddam was still a force to be reckoned with.

## The INC Debacle

The first of the two CIA-backed efforts to force regime change in Iraq ended in disaster for all concerned (except Saddam). The plan, conceived by INC leader Chalabi, had been in the works for several years, and began to take concrete shape in 1994 as the CIA moved operatives en masse into the Kurdish-controlled town of Salahadin, a small mountain town 15 miles north of the Kurdish capital, Erbil. The plan involved an assault on Iraqi positions in the north spearheaded by the two Kurdish parties (KDP and PUK), with the intention of inspiring a military insurrection and a popular uprising against the regime. From the outset, the plan was beset with problems. Throughout 1994, the KDP and PUK were at each others' throats (see chapter 7), while the CIA was wracked with internal divisions over whether to support the ambitious INC plan or the silver bullet solution offered by the INA. The CIA's representative to Iraqi Kurdistan (known only as "Bob") assured Chalabi that the U.S. would provide military support once the assault was underway, a pledge that KDP leader Massoud Barzani (son of the late Mulla Mustafa) found difficult to believe (correctly, as it turned out). As the date for the implementation of the plan approached (early March, 1995), the INA convinced the CIA that any attack on Iraqi troops would be met by a devastating Iraqi counterattack, which would in turn require a serious military commitment on the part of the U.S. When the White House learned the details of the impending attack, National Security Advisor Tony Lake rapidly dispatched a cable to INC leaders, stating that "the United States would not support this operation militarily or in any other way."[23] At the eleventh hour, the U.S. withdrew its apparent support for Chalabi's plan. With the U.S. withdrawal, the KDP's Barzani refused to become embroiled in an escapade that had little chance of success and that might provoke an invasion of KDP-held territory by the Republican Guard. Hence, when the INC's 1,000-strong militia and PUK *peshmerga* forces launched their attack on Iraqi troops on March 4, 1995, it was without the support of the U.S. or the KDP. Predictably, the attack was a farce, and after the cities of Kirkuk and Mosul failed to rise up in support, and Saddam's army failed to mutiny, the entire operation fizzled out barely two weeks after it had started.

## The INA Debacle

The INA's coup attempt of 1996 was better organized than the INC's effort but the outcome was equally disastrous. Unlike the INC, the INA had excellent contacts within Saddam's regime that reached right to the innermost circles of power. Judging by the identities of those arrested in the aftermath of the coup's failure, these contacts included prominent officials in the Republican Guard, the Special Republican Guard, the *Mukhabarat*, the *Amn al-Khass* (Saddam's personal security service), and the General Security Service. Operating out of Amman, Jordan with the support of the CIA, the INA coup plot was planned for the third week in June 1996. Unfortunately for the participants, Saddam's intelligence agents learned of the attempt some six months before it was due to take place. Rather than pouncing immediately, the agents waited for the plot to reach fruition. The arrests began a day before the coup's scheduled date, and, in all, over 100 officers from various branches of Iraq's military and security apparatus were rounded up and executed.

## Saddam Cuts a Deal

The events of the mid-1990s revealed the inherent resilience of Saddam's regime in the face of internal threats, but they also illustrated the extent to which the loyalty of traditional support groups could no longer be taken for granted. On one hand, the regime had held firm in the face of two CIA-orchestrated efforts at regime change, and the defection of Hussein Kamel; on the other, the defection demonstrated that blood ties could no longer be taken as the ultimate guarantor of loyalty, and the INA coup attempt illustrated the extent to which the regime's broader support base had eroded since the uprisings of 1991. All the participants in the plot were drawn from the staunchly loyal tribes of the Sunni heartland and most occupied high-level positions within the regime's most sensitive institutions. Saddam's regime had survived because it was better organized and more unified than anything opposition forces could muster, but in reality, Saddam's traditional "stick and carrot" approach to governance was coming apart at the seams. The stick could still be wielded with some force, but, in the absence of a steady influx of oil revenues into state coffers, Saddam lacked the financial wherewithal to sustain a broader base of support. With this in mind, in 1996, Saddam finally accepted the UN's "oil-for-food" deal. The deal, embodied in UNSCR 986, allowed Iraq to export oil worth $2 billion every six months (this was later increased to $5.2 billion) and to use the proceeds to import products to meet essential civilian needs. A set percentage of the revenues were set aside to meet the cost of reparations to Kuwait and to sustain the Kurdish north (roughly 13 percent), and the list of permissible imports was to be tightly controlled by the Security Council. The UN's goal was to alleviate the worst of the suffering endured by Iraq's civilian population since 1991, while preventing the regime from using the proceeds of oil exports to purchase military equipment or WMD-related material. In practice, the U.S. and Britain used their positions as veto-wielding members of the Security Council to block all imports of so-called "dual-use" items (those with both civilian and military application) into Iraq. This meant that imports of many everyday items, such as chlorine, and, absurdly, pencils, were prohibited.[24] Moreover, most of the materials required to rebuild Iraq's shattered infrastructure fell under the dual-use classification. Thus, while the oil-for-food program alleviated the problem of food supplies, it did nothing to address the problem of Iraq's devastated civilian infrastructure.

Accepting the program required Saddam to swallow arguments about the violation of Iraq's sovereignty, but over the long-term enabled him to increase his hold on power. Prior to 1996, the regime had been spending at least $1 billion a year (from sources unknown) to keep government-run food stores stocked. This money could now be redirected to reinforcing the regime's patronage network, reequipping and restructuring selected military units, and financing the smuggling of weapons and associated technology. The program also afforded endless opportunities for corruption, both official and unofficial, facilitating the emergence of a new class of super-rich "entrepreneurs" who specialized in supplying the goods prohibited under the oil-for-food program. By the late-1990s, the black market was, by some distance, the most dynamic sector of the Iraqi economy. For a price, anything could be bought and sold on the streets of Baghdad. Unintentionally then, the UN sanctions regime had created a two-tiered society in Iraq—a new class of the seriously wealthy, either associated with, or tolerated by the regime, and the 99 percent of the Iraqi population that continued to exist in conditions of abject squalor. Notably absent was anything resembling a middle class. An important legacy of the UN sanctions regime was to eliminate precisely the class of people who might have provided the backbone of a moderate, democratically inclined political future for Iraq.

## UNSCOM vs Saddam: The Endgame

Saddam's acceptance of UNSCR 986 had done nothing to change the underlying dynamics of UNSCOM inspections in Iraq. The Clinton Administration's position on the relationship between sanctions and regime change did not differ from that of the previous Bush Administration. During a speech at Georgetown University in March 1997, Clinton's Secretary of State Madeline Albright explicitly rejected any link between the lifting of sanctions and Iraq's fulfillment of its disarmament obligations. Regime change became the law of the land with the passage of the Iraq Liberation Act by the U.S. Congress in October 1998. The Act authorized nearly $100 million in funding for opposition groups with the stated intent of removing Saddam from power. Devoid of any positive incentive to cooperate with UNSCOM inspectors and convinced (with good reason) that the inspections were a cover for the intelligence services of the U.S., U.K., and Israel to plan an assassination attempt against Saddam, Iraq's attitude toward continued inspections reached breaking point. The endgame was in sight. The final straw came when Australian Richard Butler (Rolf Ekeus' replacement) refused to certify that Iraq had destroyed its banned weapons. In response, Iraq refused any further cooperation with UNSCOM. UNSCOM inspectors were finally withdrawn from Iraq (never to return), and in mid-December 1998, U.S. and British forces launched "Operation Desert Fox"—an anemic 70-hour bombing campaign that achieved nothing of significance.

Operation Desert Fox was symptomatic of a White House that had simply run out of ideas about how to deal with Iraq. Seven years of the most stringent sanctions in world history had devastated the civilian population of Iraq (without affecting the material well-being of the ruling regime in the slightest), wiped out Iraq's middle class, sustained Iraq's civilian infrastructure in a state of chronic disrepair, yet done little to weaken Saddam's tenacious grip on power. By the end of Clinton's second term of office, the UN Security Council was in disarray, with permanent members China, Russia, and France now actively opposing a continuation of sanctions, and the U.S. and Britain doggedly ensuring their survival. The sanctions regime itself was crumbling fast as an increasingly large number of countries (including France and Russia) opted simply to ignore its provisions and do business with Iraq openly. Further, the effects of the sanctions on ordinary Iraqis were an ongoing PR disaster for the U.S. In particular, Madeline Albright's assertion that the deaths of 500,000 Iraqi children "was a price worth paying" for the containment of Saddam can have done little to enhance the U.S.'s reputation in the Arab world. Even Osama Bin Laden—certainly no great friend of the secular regime in Baghdad—cited America's "siege" of the people of Iraq as one of the three reasons for declaring *jihad* on America in 1998. What Clinton bequeathed to the incoming Bush Administration in January 2001, then, was not a coherent policy on Iraq, but an ugly mess of contradictions and failures that could not be sustained over the long term.[25]

## MARCH TOWARD WAR

By the time the newly elected Bush (junior) Administration assumed office in January 2001, the situation in Iraq had disappeared off the political radar screen. The new President had been elected on a "minimalist" foreign policy platform that sought to actively disengage America from commitments beyond her borders, and poured scorn on the Clintonian policy of "nation-building" in far-off places with unpronounceable names. Behind the scenes, a small group of so-called neoconservatives, many of whom had served under George Bush senior's administration, had rather different ideas about the appropriate role of American military power in the world. Dotted throughout the Administration, but concentrated in the Department of Defense, the neo-cons favored a pro-active (i.e., military) approach to the problem of rogue states such as Iraq and North Korea. Until September 11, 2001, these ideas had found plenty of disciples among the various right-wing think tanks in Washington D.C., but had failed to make an impact on the conduct of U.S. foreign policy.

The events of 9/11 changed this overnight. Within a day, Secretary of Defense Donald Rumsfeld was pressuring the President to include an attack on Iraq a part of the first wave of reprisals against those responsible.[26] Following

Secretary of State Colin Powell's advice, Bush opted to focus immediate attention on Afghanistan before turning to Iraq at a later date. The disagreement
over Iraq was one of timing, not of principle. It was to take another year and a
half for the Bush Administration's policy on Iraq to reach fruition—but the decision to invade Iraq had been taken long before March 20, 2003 when the
first bombs actually fell. Barely three weeks after the first bombs fell, Saddam's
regime had evaporated (as had Saddam himself) and the U.S.'s long-standing
policy of regime change in Iraq—a policy that dated back to 1991—had finally
been accomplished.

## LEGACIES OF SADDAM'S RULE, 1988–2003

### Sunni Dominance

The uprisings of 1991—particularly in the south—posed a direct threat to traditional Sunni dominance at the center, and provided a clear indication of the
narrowness of the regime's support base. But the southern rebellion mobilized
the Sunni center behind the regime. In the last analysis, when faced with the
loss of power and privilege, the Sunni-dominated instruments of coercion
(mainly the Republican Guard) did not hesitate to crush their Shi'a brethren
with the utmost brutality. The issue was not one of sectarian division—though
Saddam lost no opportunity to depict the revolt in terms of radical Shi'a fundamentalism—but about political power. Any major uprising within the predominantly Shi'a south threatened the existing status quo of power
distribution, and in 1991, the Sunni heartland favored the certainty of Saddam's regime to the uncertainty of a Shi'a-dominated revolution from below.
The southern *intifadah* also demonstrated that the Shi'a population of Iraq was
far from being a coherent, homogenous entity. It was precisely the lack of
leadership and common direction that doomed the rebellion to failure. Attempts by SCIRI to inject radical religious sentiment into the uprising were
largely resisted by the rebels. There can be little doubt, however, that Saddam
absorbed the lessons of 1991. The Ba'ath Party organization in the south—
staffed primarily by Shi'a, had disintegrated in short order. Ba'ath Party officials had either been publicly lynched, or had defected to the rebel side.
Following the tactics of the imperialist British some 70 years previously, Saddam sought accommodation with prominent tribal leaders in the south (some
of whom had fought on the side of the regime and against the rebels) and tried
to undermine the legitimacy of the Shi'a Islamist parties by co-opting key religious leaders of Iraqi descent. For example, Grand Ayatollah Abu al-Qasim al-

Khoei—the highest religious authority in Najaf—was persuaded to denounce the uprising publicly.[27]

Other, minor concessions were made to the Shi'a majority. For the first time in 22 years of Ba'athist rule, Saddam appointed a Shi'a Prime Minister, Sa'dun Hammadi, but of course real power remained, as ever, centralized in the hands of Saddam and the Tikriti Sunni elite.

The situation was somewhat different in the north. Recognizing that the most significant threat to the regime remained in the south and its possible linkage to Baghdad's large Shi'a population, Saddam could not afford to garrison adequately the Kurdish north. In fact, both sides were weak. Saddam had no option after the carnage of the Gulf War but to consolidate his military. The Kurdish parties had still not recovered from the devastation of the *Anfal* campaign (which had finished barely three years previously), and the people of Iraqi Kurdistan were traumatized by their exodus to the mountains. Saddam could not retake Kurdistan, but neither could the Kurds threaten the survival of the regime directly. Under the protection of the northern no-fly zone, and with a guaranteed source of income from the UN, the Kurds were no longer participants in the state of Iraq. With Kurdistan effectively removed from the political equation, the prospect of Kurds achieving any form of adequate representation in the institutions of central governance was eliminated. While some power devolved to Shi'a tribal leaders in the south, the Iraqi regime during the 1990s adhered faithfully to the venerable tradition of Sunni dominance. With the Shi'a south largely under control during the 1990s, and the Kurdish north beyond government control, the key question was whether the regime could maintain its grip over the Sunni heartland. The INA coup attempt of 1996, though unsuccessful in its execution, revealed that Saddam's traditional support base among the Sunni tribes of northwestern Iraq was no longer unambiguously loyal. Ultimately, the major threat to the survival of Saddam's Sunni-dominated regime during the 1990s was not from the Shi'a or the Kurds, but from fellow Sunnis.

## Governing Iraq

For the first time since the mid-1970s, Saddam was required to hold his regime together without the benefit of oil revenues or a major foreign war to rally the troops. Saddam survived for a further 15 years after the end of the Iran–Iraq War despite uprisings, coup attempts, and rebellions, and in the face of a brutal sanctions regime. In the end, it took the military might of history's most powerful fighting force to remove him from power. The end did not come from within, but was imposed from without. 1988 marked an important turning point in the nature of Saddam's regime. In previous years, regime survival had been a necessary prerequisite for the pursuit of more elevated goals, such as the development and modernization of the state of Iraq; after 1988, regime survival became an end in itself—to be pursued regardless of the damage inflicted on the social and political fabric of Iraq, or the psychological and physical cost to ordinary Iraqi civilians.

To survive the adversity of the 1990s and beyond, Saddam deployed a variety of governing strategies—some less successful than others. In the former category must be placed Saddam's brief flirtation with political liberalization, and his continued insistence on playing the Islamic card. Saddam's "democratic experiment" was as brief as it was unconvincing. The experiment was to embody such alien principles as freedom of speech, constitutional reform, and political pluralism. Iraqi newspapers were required to set aside a page for letters of complaint from readers at the head of which was a statement from Saddam himself, encouraging people to "write what you like without fear."[28] Foreign observers were invited to witness elections to Iraq's National Assembly in April 1989, a process that resulted in the Ba'ath Party actually losing seats in the Parliament. Perhaps because several prominent Ba'ath officials were defeated in the vote, the democratic experiment was abruptly terminated after the elections.

Saddam's commitment to Islam, about as convincing as his commitment to democracy, had begun in the late-1980s, but by the 1990s had become much more ostentatious. In 1990, for example, the words "Allah Akbar" (God is great)—the traditional Islamic rallying cry—were officially stitched onto the Iraqi flag. Saddam awarded himself a number of new honorific titles, including "Servant of God" and "Leader of All Muslims," and, in October 1990, announced solemnly to the people of Iraq that the Prophet Mohammed had began to appear to him in dreams to offer advice (apparently not very good) on military strategy. A variety of "Islamic" punishments were incorporated into the penal code by decree, such as amputation of the right hand for theft and decapitation for brothel owners. The sale of alcohol was prohibited in the Shi'a shrine cities of Najaf and Karbala—a ban that was soon extended to restaurants in the capital city itself. The most plausible explanation for this conscious attempt to burnish the regime's Islamic credentials is that it was an effort to capitalize on the significant upsurge in religious sentiment among ordinary Iraqis that took place during the 1990s. After two and a half decades of Ba'ath Party rule, during which almost every traditional social structure (including the family) had been systematically dismantled by indoctrination or coercion, the Iraqi people were increasingly seeking solace in religion.[29] It is difficult otherwise to understand the rationale underlying Saddam's decision in 1994 (when Iraq had no discernible source of income, and when the suffering of ordinary Iraqis was at its most intense) to announce plans for the construction of the world's largest mosque. "The Grand Saddam Mosque" was to feature a manmade lake the size of 70 football fields in the shape of the Arab world, dotted with islands in the image of Saddam's own thumbprint. The dome of the mosque was to be the largest and tallest in the Muslim world in order that Saddam could be "closer to God" than anyone else on earth.

Saddam as pious Muslim was always likely to be a difficult sales pitch given the avowedly secular ideology of the Ba'ath Party, but in truth, the Party's cardinal principles had long since ceased to have any meaningful influence over the policies of Saddam's regime. For example, it was difficult to reconcile the Party's core belief in Arab unity with the reality that Iraq was now almost entirely isolated from the rest of the Arab world. Several Arab countries had actually taken up arms against Iraq in 1991 (in response to Iraq's invasion of a fellow Arab country), and those that had not, such as Jordan, had, by 1995, finally turned their back on Saddam. Similarly, the "socialist" dimension of Ba'athist ideology bore little resemblance to the harsh new realities of economic life in Iraq during the 1990s. What emerged in Iraq during the course of the decade was a two-tiered economy.[30] The private economy, controlled by a small coterie of regime cronies and an emerging breed of "profiteers," focused on supplying the Iraqi market with the goods prohibited by sanctions. These ranged from cheap foreign cigarettes to missile guidance systems, and the profits to be made were immense. The public economy, inhabited by an increasingly impoverished workforce tied to minuscule government salaries and dependent for survival on government-rationed food, had essentially collapsed by 2003. All the major "socialist" achievements of the past—a free and comprehensive education system, a health care system comparable in quality with those of Western Europe, and a state-driven economy presided over by a well-paid, generally honest, and largely competent civil service—had been destroyed by the end of the period.

The increasing irrelevance of Ba'athist ideology was matched by a decline in the importance of the Party as an institution. While the Party continued to provide an institutional structure to the Iraqi state, and a convenient means by which to dispense reward and punishment, by the 1990s, the regime was no longer dependent on the Party's structure to sustain power. The Ba'ath had served its purpose in a political sense and Saddam increasingly employed his "own" structures such as the different paramilitary outfits.

The military continued to be a cause for concern. Throughout the 1990s, Saddam remained wary of the demoralization that had set into the masses of the armed forces since its unceremonious eviction from Kuwait, and was well aware that it could be mobilized in the name of Iraqi nationalism against him. Indeed, it was on the Republican Guard that Washington's greatest hopes of a coup were pinned.[31] The praetorian Special Republican Guard (SRG) was reportedly formed in early 1992 with the task of protecting the President and providing a swift and decisive military response to an internal coup attempt. Its task was somewhat different than that of regular army forces or the Republican Guard (RG). The sole purpose of the 30,000-strong SRG was to protect Saddam and the highest echelons of the regime. Along with the Special Security Organization (the *Jihaz al-Amn al-Khas*, or SSO) the SRG recruited directly from Saddam's own tribe, the al-Bu Nasir, and other loyalist Sunni tribes from the Tikrit region. Often, the recruits were poorly educated youths who were taken from their deprived lives and pandered to excess by the regime. The combination of patronage and intense indoctrination created a force that was fiercely loyal to Saddam. The SSO and the Presidential Protection Unit (the *Himaya al-Rais*, aka *Himaya*) were controlled and staffed by Saddam's immediate family and tribe members of the al-Bu Nasir. These groups contained highly educated and motivated individuals whose very survival was dependent upon the continuing prosperity of Saddam.[32] The creation of forces such as the SRG no doubt strengthened the regime internally, but the very fact that Saddam *needed* to create such forces was an indication of weakness. The RG had originally served as a buffer force between the regular armed forces and the regime, with the goal of preventing a military coup—now, apparently, Saddam needed a further force to protect him from his own buffer force. Given the evidence of the INA's 1996 coup attempt (in which the bulk of the plotters were RG officers), Saddam's belief that the RG could no longer be trusted was probably justified—after all, this was the only military force with the capability to unseat his regime. Because of this, the RG was prohibited from entering the capital city. However, in neutralizing the threat of the RG, Saddam effectively rendered his only capable military force impotent when faced with an external threat. During the 2003 war, the logical strategy, from a purely military perspective, would have been to withdraw RG divisions into the heart of Baghdad, blowing the bridges over the Tigris behind them. As it turned out, the regime left its RG divisions outside the capital city and at the mercy of a ferocious coalition air onslaught. Either by this point the Iraqi command and control system had completely broken down, or this was a conscious decision on the part of Saddam, driven by the fear that the RG would use its entry into Baghdad as an opportunity to overthrow the regime.

The restructuring of the military into a force that would defend the regime from internal threats was only the most public and noticeable of Saddam's efforts to reconsolidate power in the difficult years of the mid-1990s. Saddam's survival strategy was not simply based upon the final defense of his regime. As far as Saddam was concerned, the SRG and SSO were effectively proactive deterrents, and if their protective expertise was ever required in a purely physical sense, his days were surely numbered. Saddam needed to ensure that his security was embedded within Iraq's, and for this, he needed to secure the loyalty of the tribes. Prior to the ascendancy of the Ba'ath Party, the tribes of Iraq were already in a process of decline in terms of their political organization and influence.[33] The years of agrarian reforms and the assertion of progressively more centralized government robbed the tribes of their economic base and their political role. Powerful tribal federations such as the Muntafiq in the south were in the process of breaking up and state authorities took over many of the social functions previously fulfilled by the tribe.[34] However, just as the Ba'ath Party had learned about how to control the street from the ICP, they also learned a great deal from the lessons of tribal authority. First, and perhaps least effectively, an attempt was made to construct a form of national tribalism, with Saddam Hussein at its center. This process saw Saddam's own "tribe" becoming synonymous with institutions of government, and gave his legitimacy a tribal edge, which appealed to other supportive tribes through its de facto recognition of their own authority structures. The culmination of this strategy could be seen with the formation of the highest security organizations of the state, the SSO and SRG. Second, the Ba'ath implemented a policy of military tribalism, by which Saddam exploited intertribal tensions, particularly amongst the Kurds, to reinforce his regime. The Barzani tribe, which led half of the Kurdish movement, was strong in a local sense, but its predominance brought with it the antipathy of other Kurdish tribes that were only too willing to support Saddam in return for favors bestowed. The tribes of the Zebari, Herki, Surchi, Baradosti, and Doski were recruited as ready-made mercenaries throughout the 1970s, and remained a component of Saddam's Battalions of National Defense (*Afwaj al-Difa' al-Watani*) right up until 2003, when the Zebari defected over to the Barzanis. Tribes patronized by Saddam became extremely wealthy, and tribal Aghas were able to provide for their lowly kinsmen generously. The calculation for such tribes was purely pragmatic; by embracing Saddam's regime, a tribal chief could ensure that his people prospered; by embracing "Kurdistan," their future was highly insecure.[35]

The most important element of Saddam's "neo-tribalist" approach to governance was the co-option of southern tribal leaders. When faced with the uprising in 1991, the Ba'ath Party had capitulated with alarming ease. It could no longer be relied upon to police the south. The tribal groupings of the south never deferred to the Shi'a religious establishment (as tribesmen generally are not motivated by religious concerns), and remained apathetic toward the so-called Sunni–Shi'a split. Hence their loyalty could be bought—even by a regime dominated by Sunni Tikritis. In the aftermath of the 1991 uprising, Saddam adopted a conscious policy of delegating power from the center to certain (selected) tribes. In contrast to "Saddam as pious Muslim," "Saddam as tribal chieftain" was a role that came naturally. After all, Saddam himself had run Iraq as a glorified tribe for years. Nonetheless, this approach marked a significant deviation from standard Ba'athist philosophy, which had traditionally viewed the tribes and their associated values and leadership structures as a source of "backwardness" and an obstacle to be overcome in the modernization of Iraq. Now Saddam was reactivating tribalism, not just as a political force, but also as a system of values. Tribal traditions were incorporated into the "Iraqi myth" alongside Arabism and Mesopotamian history and culture.

Hence in 1992, Saddam, outfitted in traditional Bedouin robes, hosted tribal chiefs from the south in Baghdad. One by one the chiefs swore an oath of loyalty to the "Sheikh of Sheikhs" (Saddam). In return, the powerful tribes were accorded a new respect from the regime, lauded in the Iraqi media as the epitome of traditional Iraqi values, and given leeway to act as Saddam's agents in affairs of local law and order. Tribes were even allowed to form private militia armies equipped by the regime with light arms, and, in some cases, howitzers and rocket-propelled grenades. The tangible results of this policy were evident in March 2003 when coalition forces were marching through the south. The "civilians" identified by the Western media as providing some of the sternest resistance were, in all probability, members of tribal militias rather than disguised regular army forces.

Given the paucity of resources available to the regime to police the south, this devolution of power to the tribes was a necessary but risky step. Saddam's natural inclination had always been to concentrate rather than disperse power. Now he was consciously creating and arming private armies in the south to perform the functions that his regime could no longer adequately perform. This was a clear admission of regime weakness. Moreover, the tribes were now authorized to perform a judicial function. In areas policed by the tribes, tribal norms of justice prevailed; in all other areas, justice was meted out according to the state's legal code. Iraq's two-tiered economic system was now supplemented by a two-tiered judicial system. Where the two came into conflict, more often than not, tribal justice prevailed. The most notorious example of the ascendance of tribal law involved the fate of defector Hussein Kamel (see above). After seeking political asylum in Jordan, calling for a military coup against Saddam, and revealing the most intimate secrets of Iraq's WMD concealment program, Kamel displayed a truly staggering lack of political judgment by agreeing to return to Iraq. Upon crossing the border, the two Kamels were separated from their wives (Saddam's daughters) and forced to sign divorce papers. The following day, the male members of the family, ensconced in a Baghdad villa, were besieged by a 40-strong gang of armed youths, and were all killed during the course of a fierce, 13-hour gun battle. This was a ritualistic "honor" slaying. The assailants were all members of the Kamel's *khams*—a five-generation kinship unit in which all male members were required to avenge violations of the unit's honor. In effect, the Kamel's had been eliminated by their own extended family. Obviously, the revenge killings violated the state's legal code, but far from seeking punishment for the perpetrators, Saddam justified the killings as part of a "purification" process, akin to amputating an "ailing finger" from the tribal "hand."[36] Two of the assailants killed during the course of the assault were subsequently accorded heroes' funerals, attended by senior regime dignitaries. Seemingly, tribal norms of justice had transcended the law of the land.[37] Saddam's reliance on tribal structures to govern was a return to past practices. By the 1990s, Saddam had apparently learned from the British experience. As Iraq's former colonial overlords had astutely surmised, governing through existing social structures on the ground, while not without cost, was infinitely easier than imposing a unified governing regime on Iraq's fractious population.

## The Use of Violence

Even though Saddam had been grievously weakened by the cumulative effects of the Iran–Iraq War and the Gulf War, it would still have taken a brave (or foolish) individual or group to stand against him in 1991. Although thoroughly defeated on the battlefield by the forces of the coalition, Saddam still retained enough loyalist military power and the ability to employ extreme coercion that, in a state characterized by social and political fragmentation, he retained his overall predominance from the center.

The use of violence to quell the uprisings of the south was on a particularly grand and inhuman scale. Columns of refugees leaving Karbala and Najaf were doused with kerosene poured from helicopters, then set alight with tracer bullets. Basra suffered over a thousand deaths as the Republican Guard recaptured Iraq's second city. Over a hundred of Ayatollah al-Khoei's followers simply disappeared, and one can only speculate at the number of casualties inflicted by Ali Hassan al-Majid ("Chemical Ali") as he brought his unique version of justice to the south.[38] It is worth noting, however, that the *intifada* itself was characterized by severe violence and brutality. The treatment meted out to unfortunate Ba'ath Party officials was every bit as gruesome as anything the regime inflicted on the rebels. In all, the rebels "tortured, decapitated and dismembered" hundreds of people. As has so often been the case throughout Iraq's history, an uprising in response to the violence and brutality of a central regime was itself characterized by extremes of violence and brutality.

As well as controlling the rebellious potential of the Shi'a and any other anti-regime groups, the regime also had to contend with the ramifications of rapidly deteriorating economic and social conditions. With sanctions seriously affecting the day-to-day life of ordinary Iraqis by the mid-1990s, civil crime, corruption, and disorder rose correspondingly. For the regime, this rise in unlawful behavior and public disorder was a threat to the stability of the country. The response was predictable. The regime developed the most gruesome methods of punishment for criminal offences of the smallest proportions. For theft of items worth over $15, the unlucky criminal would be sentenced to having their right hand amputated. To distinguish the dangerous villains from unfortunate war heroes who had lost limbs in defense of Iraq, the criminals would also be branded with a large letter X on their forehead. If a convicted felon who had already suffered an amputation were caught stealing again, a further limb would be removed. Death sentences were automatically imposed for felons who were members of the military or the administration—a significantly large element of the population.[39]

The randomized terrorization of the Iraqi people was maintained throughout the 1990s. The *Fedayeen Saddam*—formed in the mid-1990s, and headed by Uday Hussein—gained notoriety as the thugs of the regime. The primary purpose of the *Fedayeen* indeed was to "control" the Iraqi population, a task that was, more often than not, accomplished via random acts of violence, including summary executions, against those whom the regime had identified as potential subversives. As part of Saddam's concerted effort to portray himself as a devout Muslim, the *Fedayeen* were tasked to deal with prostitution. In their own inimitable fashion, the *Fedayeen* in October 2000 arrested dozens of women on charges of prostitution and beheaded them in public places without trial. Men associated with their activities were similarly decapitated.

In contrast to the violence inflicted by the Ba'ath in previous decades, the violence of the 1990s was more random, much less controlled, and much more public. In past years, infractions of the "rules" had certainly been addressed with impressive brutality—but the rules themselves were fairly clear-cut. Do not criticize the President, and do not challenge the regime. By the 1990s, the regime was changing the rules on a daily basis. Opposition to the regime was still a capital offense, but so too now were all manner of "crimes" against Islamic values (or, more precisely, Saddam's version of Islamic values). The brutalization of the unfortunate Iraqi population reached its zenith as gangs of *Fedayeen* roamed the streets dispensing summary, often arbitrary punishment for minor violations of laws that often did not exist. This reversion to a form of violence designed to terrorize, rather than just intimidate, was symptomatic of a deeply unhealthy political order.

## National Unity

In 1991, the Iraqi state was effectively divided into an Arab state with a rump Kurdish "entity." The Kurdish de facto state was separate in political and economic terms, and operated under its own governmental and judicial structure, with parliamentary provisions and a military force independent of Baghdad. This split in the administrative arrangement of the Iraqi state is arguably the most significant event in the country's modern history. For the first time, the Kurds now truly had the opportunity to administer their own region. Admittedly, the Kurdish parties had been given a task of truly staggering proportions, yet the next ten years would ultimately prove that the Kurds could construct a self-governing entity, albeit in a characteristically volatile Kurdish way.

With the Kurdish north effectively beyond the coercive reach of the regime, Saddam no longer had sovereignty over a sizable portion of Iraq's territory. Throughout Iraq's brief history, a succession of rulers had attempted to create a unified entity out of a patchwork of competing (often conflicting) identities. None had successfully developed a formula that could transform the state of Iraq into something more than the sum of its various territorially contiguous parts. After 1991, the state of Iraq—for all practical purposes—ceased to exist even on this minimal, territorial level.

With respect to the Arab-dominated portion of the state, the period after 1988 was a mixed picture in terms of national unity; some forces undoubtedly helped foster unity, while other (more powerful) forces favored the further fragmentation of Iraqi society. The unity displayed by Arab Iraqis during the first Gulf War, in which Shi'a and Sunni had fought side-by-side in the trenches against the invading Iranian hordes, clearly signified something. Whether this was shared loyalty to the regime (highly unlikely), a sense of Iraqi nationalism, or an expression of shared Arab ethnicity is difficult to say for certain. Whatever the nature of this unifying force, it was clearly fragile. The southern uprising that occurred barely three years after the end of this impressive display of Arab unity was a rude awakening. To interpret the *intifada* as an event driven by sectarian (Shi'a versus Sunni) hatred is to simplify a complex occurrence. This was not the opening stage of an Iraqi war of religion. Yet the very fact that the vast majority of the participants in the uprising were Shi'a, while the coercive forces that were mobilized to suppress it were overwhelmingly Sunnis, reveals an important truth about the sectarian divide in Iraq. The core problems are historical and political, not doctrinal. Iraq has always been governed by Sunnis, and the Shi'a have always been governed. In times of war, Sunni regimes have always made the major decisions, a Sunni officer corps has always commanded troops on the battlefield, and the Shi'a (or Kurds) have always provided the cannon fodder. The war in Kuwait did not depart significantly from the basic historical pattern. A plausible interpretation of the *intifada*, then, is that it represented an explosion of pent-up animosity directed not just at the governing Sunni regime of the time (though hostility toward Saddam was clearly quite intense) but at the traditional hierarchy of power in Iraq since its creation as a state.

Despite the evidence of the *intifada* that Arab unity was not as robust as it had seemed after Iraq's "victory" against Iran, there were forces at work during the 1990s that helped solidify Iraq in the face of adversity. Most notably, the sanctions regime inflicted a shared misery on the Iraqi people and enabled Saddam to harness and channel the consequent resentment away from his regime. Regardless of who was actually to blame for the continued suffering of the Iraqi people, the tightly controlled state media in Iraq was never likely to dwell on the nuances of the diplomatic game. Daily propaganda lambasting the U.S. and Britain (both of whom were resolute in their opposition to the lifting of sanctions) was beamed into Iraqi houses, leaving no doubt in most minds as to who was responsible for the "siege" of Iraq. If anything, the sanctions helped rather than hindered Saddam's survival. Ever the consummate manipulator of men and events, Saddam revelled in the cat-and-mouse game with UNSCOM inspectors. As noted above, Saddam had nothing to gain by cooperating with inspections, but much to gain by manufacturing confrontations. Throughout the 1990s, but especially in 1998, Saddam engineered successive crises with UNSCOM that enabled him to appear as the brave defender of Iraq's sovereignty and honor. Despite being a political pariah among the leaders of Arab states in the region, Saddam evolved into something of a cult hero among the Arab masses. This low-risk, "rally around the flag" strategy can only have helped boost the standing of the regime at a time when there was precious little else for ordinary Iraqis to cheer about.

Beyond this "unity in misery" aspect, the prevailing trend over the period was overwhelmingly negative in terms of national unity. Iraq's regular army, long a source of Iraqi pride and one of the few institutions that bound Iraq's various populations together into a single entity (albeit a Sunni-dominated entity), was almost entirely destroyed as a credible force during the 1990s. The resources available to the regime were channeled almost exclusively to existing "elite" institutions, such as the RG, or to newly created forces, such as the even more elite SRG. In terms of conditions, training, and equipment, the regular army became a shadow of its former self. This was a deliberate policy on the part of Saddam. The army had performed with distinction against Iran, and was therefore a threat to his regime. The effect of this policy on the standing of the army was all too evident in 2003, when half-starving conscripts confronted America's "wall of steel" armed only with rifles and tanks of Soviet 1950s vintage. In 1991, the regular army's war against coalition forces became an (understandable) exercise in mass surrender; judging by the lack of dead bodies in 2003, the second war against America became an exercise in mass desertion. No doubt the army can be re-equipped, but it will take a long time for the prestige of the army to recover from these two humiliations.

Other symbols of national unity were also dealt devastating blows after 1988. The state—as provider of public services rather than instrument of coercion—essentially collapsed during the 1990s. Iraq's once-proud education and health care systems were crippled by the effects of sanctions. In previous decades, these had been sources of national pride, and had helped bind together the population through shared experiences. In its guise as Iraq's major employer, the state limped on, but only just. Whereas previously Iraq's bureaucrats, doctors, dentists, and teachers had lived comfortable middle-class lives, by the end of the 1990s, those who had not deserted the country, were left scraping an existence on a monthly wage of less than $5. The creation of a viable, growing middle class in Iraq had been one of the Ba'ath Party's most impressive achievements—and Iraq's best hope of transcending traditional ethnic and sectarian divisions. By the end of the period, the middle class had ceased to exist. Instead, Iraq was divided into two classes: the very wealthy, and the very poor. As one Iraqi government official observed in 1999, "Two decades of war, deprivation, and the indifference of the world have destroyed the social fabric. Now everyone thinks of himself."[40] Whereas previously Saddam had consciously sought to "atomize" the Iraqi population as the necessary first stage in the creation of a new, improved social order, now the "atomization" of the people was pursued as a survival strategy. An atomized population was easier for the regime to control. This was clearly evident in the presidential "elections" of 1995 and October 2002. The outcome in both cases—over 99 percent of people voted for the continuance of Saddam as President on a near universal turnout—was never in doubt. But while most of the Western media chose to focus on the farcical nature of this exercise in popular democracy, the real point—that the regime (even as late as October 2002) could still mobilize virtually the entire population to do anything (however farcical)—was widely ignored. The 99.96 percent "Yes" vote achieved in 2002 may not have been a reliable indicator of the popularity of Saddam, but it *was* a testament to the power of Saddam's psychological hold over his own people. The Iraqi people were on "automatic pilot"—when the regime commanded, they obeyed without question, not necessarily out of love or respect, but because any capacity for independent thought or action (at least in public) had been relentlessly beaten out of them by decades of Ba'athist rule.[41] The alternative explanation—that Saddam still enjoyed widespread popularity, even as late as 2002, after having led his country to the abyss—is perhaps equally disturbing. The reconstruction of Iraq's physical infrastructure will take years to achieve, but the psychological reconstruction of a brutalized society will take far longer.

The political reconstruction of Iraq will also be that much more difficult as a consequence of the last decade or so of Saddam's rule. Political fragmentation rather than unity was the predominant trend. By devolving power to tribal chiefs, Saddam created a network of mini "fiefdoms" within which the authority of the chief was largely unquestioned by central authorities. Governing through tribal structures enhanced the stability of Saddam's regime during difficult days, and Saddam even claimed (with some justification) that the tribes were a source of sectarian unity rather than division in Iraq. Many tribes spanned the sectarian divide. For example, Saddam's own al-Bu Nasir tribe had a Sunni branch, centered around Tikrit, and a smaller Shi'a branch in the vicinity of Najaf. However, Saddam's neo-tribalist policy also opened up new avenues for division. Providing light arms and artillery to the tribes transformed many tribal disputes into full-scale military confrontations. During one such dispute involving several tribes from the region around Kut, howitzers were used, leaving 266 dead and 422 wounded. As the regime's mouthpiece *Babil* noted, "the tribes were given the weapons to fight the United States . . . not to fight among themselves."[42]

The removal of Saddam's regime has left a significant power vacuum in Iraq. The tribes constitute some of the only remaining coherent social structures, and will therefore undoubtedly play a major role as powerbrokers in their respective regions. Given that many tribes have their own private (and quite well-armed) militia forces, the potential for violent intertribal power struggles is high. In the absence of a strong central authority to hold the whole together, tribal structures are unlikely to provide a reliable foundation for the stable political development of Iraq, and the prospect of the tribes willingly embracing liberal democracy and the rule of law is remote indeed.

Alongside a revival in the fortunes of the tribes, the 1990s also witnessed a significant resurgence in religious sentiment among the Shi'a, inspired largely by the charismatic figure of Ayatollah Muhammed Sadiq al-Sadr. As the regime's carefully vetted appointee to replace Najaf's Ayatollah al-Khoei, al-Sadr was expected to defer to the regime, but instead pursued an independent line from the start. His sermons, attended by thousands of devotees, became increasingly critical of Saddam's regime during the course of the 1990s, and, more importantly, al-Sadr successfully forged a huge network of followers that united diverse Shi'a groupings within its framework. Clearly, al-Sadr was becoming a threat to the regime, and paid the price in 1999 when he was assassinated (together with his two sons) a stone's throw from the Holy Shrine of Imam Ali in Najaf. There seems little doubt that this was a regime-sponsored assassination; certainly large segments of the Shi'a community believed this to be the case, and sizable anti-regime demonstrations erupted in several Iraqi cities. Saddam marshalled his instruments of coercion, dispatching the *Fedayeen*, Special Security Units, and the Republican Guard to restore order. Under the guidance of Chemical Ali, the city of Nasiriya was subjected to a military blockade, then indiscriminately bombarded using heavy artillery. Most disturbing for the regime was the outraged response from the Shi'a sections of Baghdad. Angry anti-Saddam demonstrations broke out on the day al-Sadr's death was announced and had to be violently suppressed by the SRG and *Fedayeen*. In all, 25 protestors were killed and 50 others wounded. Saddam's effort to surf the wave of the Shi'a religious revival by co-opting Islam as a force to sustain his regime had evidently failed. Al-Sadr had succeeded in constructing a power base from which to criticize the regime, and had, therefore, reactivated religion as a political force. Any religious leader who can build on the legacy of al-Sadr and harness the power of religion unleashed during the 1990s will play a major role in Iraq's political future. The numbers alone speak volumes. In 1999, over 2 million Shi'a pilgrims traveled to Karbala to celebrate Hussein's martyrdom; by 2001, this number had risen to 2.4 million (roughly 20 percent of Iraq's entire Shi'a population).[43] Saddam and the Ba'ath had spent most of their 30 years in power using whatever means necessary—whether coercion, co-option, or bribery—to avoid the emergence of Shi'a Islam as a powerful political force in Iraq. But by the time his regime collapsed in April 2003, this is precisely the potential he had created.

## CONCLUSION

The 1988–2003 period saw the end of the Saddam era. By May 2003, Saddam was no longer President of Iraq, and the country began the long and dangerous road toward political, social, and economic regeneration. The magnitude of the task confronting those who seek to rebuild Iraq cannot be understood without reference to the 35 years of Ba'athist rule. This period left a highly traumatized and divided society—not the most conducive environment in which to implant any sort of sustainable democratic structure. Furthermore, the period heightened the internal divisions within Iraqi society by sharpening the ethnic Arab–Kurdish divide, and by strengthening Sunni domination at the center. The (re)emergence of further groupings—such as tribes and religious leaders in the south—will also prove to be influential in the future Iraq. Saddam's legacy has been to leave a society riddled with booby traps for any organization attempting to promote a sustainable cohesive Iraqi state governed by democratic institutions.

Perhaps most important, the period witnessed the commencement of the partition of Iraq. The establishment and institutionalization of a Kurdish state in all but name has shown that Iraqis are not alien to the concept of democracy. But in its current manifestation, the structure of the Iraqi state is not conducive to the development of democracy (to put it mildly). The fact that Iraqi Kurdistan has been independent since 1991 and operating separately from Baghdad has created structural problems that would make it painful for Kurdistan to return to its pre-1991 position. The dominant language is now Kurdish—Kurdish children have been brought up without having to learn Arabic. The Kurdish education system is now equipped with "national" universities in each major city, and the Kurdish administrations have established their own standing military forces. Even if Iraqi Kurdistan was "given back to Baghdad," it is entirely likely that the animosity toward Baghdad by the Kurds would be far greater than has ever been witnessed even at the height of the Kurdish Revolution in the 1960s. The Kurds have tasted freedom and will want to keep it.

However, this weakening of the territorial integrity of Iraq is matched on the opposite side by the strengthening of key Sunni groups. Tribes other than those of the Tikrit region are now powerful and have been empowered by Saddam. Furthermore, those tribes disenfranchised by Saddam will certainly re-emerge after his presence has been eliminated and attempt to reclaim their lost position. Iraq without Saddam promises a society at war with itself, as the restraining and terrifying arm of Saddam is removed and the spoils of the Iraqi state are up for grabs. Saddam was a product of the Iraqi state, but the Iraqi state in turn was fundamentally transformed by the sheer power of his personality. His enduring legacy to the U.S. and Britain is to leave behind him a state that by 2003 may have become ungovernable in his absence.

## CHAPTER FIVE

# THE SHI'A

## INTRODUCTION

THE ESTABLISHMENT OF A TRULY REPRESENTATIVE democracy in Iraq would result in a Shi'a-dominated state. In numerical terms, the Shi'a number approximately 14 million people, a majority (60 percent) of the Iraqi population (including the Kurds). This assumes, of course, that the Shi'a population would act as a cohesive voting bloc in any democratic election. But historically, the Shi'a have seldom been a cohesive entity, enabling successive Sunni-dominated regimes in Baghdad to exploit (through a variety of means) natural divisions among the Shi'a community to preclude the emergence of a unified Shi'a opposition, thereby maintaining the Sunni stranglehold over power. The Shi'a have traditionally been grossly underrepresented within the decision-making offices of the Iraqi state. Furthermore, they have suffered from the systematic targeting and repressive activities of the central government, which have included mass and summary executions and the devastation of vast areas of marshland in the south of Iraq. Motivated by a fear of the latent power of the Shi'a masses and fueled by the concerns of Saudi Arabia and other Gulf states regarding the supposed spread of Iranian political influence through their Shi'a Arab brothers, Saddam pursued a ruthless policy of persecution, oppressing the Shi'a Arabs throughout his period in power and particularly after 1988.

This policy of preserving the power of minority Sunni governments and excluding the Shi'a from access to power has been prevalent in the short history of Iraq and is a recurring theme of Middle East Arab history. To understand why the Shi'a are a politically marginalized group in the Arab Middle

East and in Iraq, it is necessary to delve into the recesses of Islamic history as far back as the formative moments of the religion. However, while historical influences and the legacy of the traditional disassociation of Shi'ism with the affairs of state still have an impact upon the political psyche of devout Shi'a, modernity has again altered the mass political outlook of many. The prevalence of many Shi'a urban centers in Iraq, the support given by Iran to Shi'a organizations, and the atrocities committed against the people of southern Iraq by Saddam's regime in particular have politicized the Shi'a to a level that may prove impossible to ignore in the post-Saddam Iraq.

Further complicating the issue of the Shi'a position in Iraq is the fact that they consider themselves to be Iraqi nationalists. While different manifestations of Shi'a political forces have targeted successive Iraqi governments, the Shi'a masses on the whole have no qualms about accepting and supporting the validity of the Iraqi state. Indeed, it is this problem of representation *in* the Iraqi state that makes the Shi'a issue so different, and potentially more problematic to resolve, when compared to that of the Kurds. The Kurds ultimately strive for autonomy and control of their own territory, and have little interest in issues relating to Iraqi nationalism. The Shi'a, conversely, *are* Iraqi nationalists. Shi'a tribes were heavily involved in the 1920 revolt against the British, for example, and the majority supported the Iraqi state against Iran in the Iran-Iraq War of 1980–1988. This latter fact, at a time when the political reach of Shi'ism was at its most extensive after the impact of the Islamic revolution in neighboring Iran, is often quoted as an example of the successful integration of the Shi'a into the Iraqi state and cited as proof of the inherent falseness of the supposed communal divide between the Sunni and Shi'a.

Yet in at least two important respects, this sectarian divide is very real. First, on a political level, the "narrative" of the Iraqi state has been dictated by the Sunni minority since the inception of the state itself. A succession of strongly pan-Arabist, largely secular, Sunni-dominated governments have attempted to mold the identity of the Iraqi state around themes, most of which (virulent pan-Arabism, and avowed secularism, for example) have only a limited appeal to the Shi'a majority. Unlike the ethnic Kurdish/Arab divide, the Sunni/Shi'a divide does not revolve around the basic legitimacy of Iraq as a territorial entity, but concerns the *identity* of the state itself. In particular, the appropriate political role of religious leaders, and the extent to which Iraq should be governed as an Islamic state, are issues that will certainly create tension across the sectarian divide. Second, and more important, politically minded Shi'a consider that the inadequate representation of Shi'a in the Iraqi political system is *the* fundamental problem facing Iraq.[1] Those who downplay the significance of the sectarian divide must also accept that, while the Shi'a community is an integral part of the Iraqi state structure, the Shi'a have never been integrated throughout the decision-making echelons of the Iraqi government.[2] Perhaps even more so than the problem of the Kurds, it is the issue of Shi'a representation in the Iraqi state that will be the focus of attention in the months and years to come.

## WHO ARE THE SHI'A?

Unlike labels such as "Kurd" or "Arab" which denote a particular ethnic/cultural identity, Shi'ism and Shi'a are neither sociological, political, nor cultural classifications.[3] The terms denote a particular set of Islamic beliefs that are distinguishable from other beliefs, including those of the Sunni. With this is mind, "the Shi'a of the Middle East" are as homogenous an entity as "the Protestants of North America" making meaningful generalizations somewhat difficult to formulate.

Shi'ism and the Shi'a are more often than not associated with the Islamic Republic of Iran, particularly by the Western media. Images of Ayatollahs identifying the U.S. as "the Great Satan," the selected scenes of Shi'a beating and whipping themselves during their religious ceremonies, and the association by the U.S. government of Iranian complicity with international terrorist organizations have tainted the image of the Shi'a in the eyes of Western audiences. Furthermore, the Shi'a are often assumed to be Iranian, when in fact many Shi'a are Arab, and are loyal to their Arab homelands rather than to Iran.

However, to raise the case of Arab Shi'a political representation in the Sunni-dominated Arab world is to raise an issue that most governments would prefer to ignore.[4] The nature of the Sunni/Shi'a relationship in the Arab states of the Middle East has a history almost as old as Islam itself, and it relates to an unresolved dispute that has become an institutionalized reality in the Middle East. Events over a millennium ago that saw the Sunnis emerge triumphant over the Shi'a established the political dominance of the Sunni in the Arab Middle East that is so evident today. Attempts to now resolve its political manifestations would, in effect, threaten the current regional status quo and alter the political landscape of the Middle East out of all recognition.[5] In post-Saddam Iraq, with the Shi'a now flexing their newly found political muscles, the fears of the Sunni-dominated regimes of the Gulf in particular are being realized and, if Iraq is to turn into a Shi'a-dominated state, the domino effect within the rest of the Middle East will be difficult to avoid. It is therefore essential to describe how the Sunni achieved their position of dominance over the Shi'a by investigating the origin of the schism.

## ORIGINS OF THE SUNNI/SHI'A DIVIDE

Soon after the foundation of Islam by the Prophet Muhammad in the early seventh century, the religion suffered a major schism over the issue of succession of leadership over the Muslim community. Following the death of the Prophet Muhammad in A.D. 632, political differences emerged regarding how his succession was to be determined. One group favored the election of a caliph by a selection of notable leaders. The second group favored the direct appointment of the Prophet's son-in-law, Ali ibn Abi Talib, as caliph. From this, Ali's followers were known as *Shi'at Ali* (supporters of Ali), simplified to *al-Shi'ah*.[6] They maintained that Ali had the closest ties by blood and marriage to the Prophet. The Shi'a further contended that only those persons who were from the immediate family and line of Muhammad (the *Ahl al-Bayt*, the "people of the house") could rightfully become caliph. However, Ali's quest to lead the Muslims was repeatedly blocked. Even over a millennium ago, it would appear that issues pertaining to the succession of political leaders in the region, later to become Iraq, were already characterized by ruthless and bloody competition. The first caliph was Abu Bakr, followed by Umar, and then Uthman. Ali finally secured the position in A.D. 656, only to be murdered five years later. The caliphate then passed to Muawiya ibn Abi Sufyan, a figure despised by the Shi'a due to his earlier opposition to the Prophet Muhammad. Instead, the Shi'a focused their political hopes on the sons of Ali and Fatima (Muhammad's daughter), Hassan and Hussein. Hassan, revered as the "Second Imam" by the Shi'a,[7] was forced into retirement by Muawiya in Medina, before being poisoned by the cunning caliph.

In 680, Muawiya died, only to be succeeded by his tyrannical and somewhat immoral son Yazid. With the house of Muawiya in a state of weakened transition, the Shi'a of Kufa recognized the opportunity to restore the *Ahl al-Bayt* to its position of leadership and sent messages to Hussein, who resided in Mecca, to head a Shi'a revolt and claim the caliphate for the Shi'a. Hussein never reached Kufa. Instead, he and his small band of followers were intercepted at Karbala, in present day Iraq, by Yazid's forces. Hussein was killed and his household marched to Yazid's seat of power in Damascus and into captivity.[8] From this point on, the Shi'a have continuously been the underdogs in the affairs of state in the region, with the Sunni dominating successive governments from Damascus, and then from Baghdad.

But the Shi'a movement was not eradicated by the defeat at the Battle of Karbala. Instead, the feelings of injustice and enmity toward the Sunni caliphs were only heightened. With the death of Hussein at Karbala, Iraq assumed its status as the birthplace of Shi'ism.[9] Combined with the belief that the Sunni caliphs were corrupt and immoral, the majority of the Muslims of southern Iraq converted to Shi'ism, particularly in the 18th and 19th centuries. The resting places of Ali, Hussein, and 4 of the other 12 Imams are in the holy cities of Iraq—Najaf (where Ali is buried), Karbala (Hussein's resting place), Kazmiya (near Baghdad), and Samarra, making Iraq the undisputed focal point of the Shi'a world.

The story of the Battle of Karbala and the slaying of Hussein became a rallying point for the Shi'a, and the succession was maintained with Hussein's son and subsequent family members. The line of the Imams, according to the "Twelver" denomination of Shi'ism, number twelve since the death of Muhammad. The Shi'a believe that the "Twelfth Imam" (Muhammad al-Mahdi), in 874, was taken by God and concealed in order to prevent his murder. Twelver theologians contend that the Imam is alive and will return as the *Mahdi*—the one guided by God—who will bring about the final judgement.[10] Ultimate authority for the Shi'a therefore remains with the Hidden Imam. In his temporary absence, the leadership of the Shi'a community was the responsibility of the *ulama* (the learned ones, sometimes referred to as mullahs). An *alim* (singular of *ulama*) who is recognized by the *ulama* as significantly learned bears the title of *mujtahid*, denoting his capability to engage in *ijtihad*, the exercise in applying Islamic law to specific issues. The position, which fuses religious authority with political power, is difficult to attain, and so Shi'a believers follow prominent *mujtahidin* as reference figures for imitation, or *marja' al-taqlid*. Currently, the most prominent Iraqi *marja'* is Ayatollah Abu al-Qasim al-Khoei, followed by Grand Ayatollah Ali Sistani of Najaf.[11] Politically, this emulation of prominent figures is highly important, as Shi'a individuals are free to follow the teachings of any *marja'*, irrespective of geographical location. The effect of this is to create a vibrant and active society, which has many poles of spiritual authority. However, in political terms, it has resulted in a fragmented and diffuse structure, which does not promote the formation of a unified Shi'a polity. This multipolar aspect of the Shi'a is a key feature of their society.

The exclusion from power and influence from earthly administrative organizations (such as governments) is therefore a defining feature of Shi'a history, and even goes some way to defining a major attribute of Shi'ism itself. Shi'ism developed into a sect of the oppressed, of the disenfranchised, modeled upon the exclusion of Hussein and the domination of the Sunni caliphs. A paradox therefore exists between Shi'a apolitical theology and the quest of the politicized Shi'a to gain power in the countries in which they reside, including Iraq. Politically motivated Shi'a aspire to control and influence governments, yet their religion is founded upon their initial exclusion from government, and their empathy with the oppressed Imams of over a thousand years ago. The solution of the Iranian Ayatollahs led by Ayatollah Khomeini to the problem of securing political legitimacy for Shi'a religious leaders was to deputize the *ulama* to take over the religious functions of the Hidden Imam, which by association also meant heading the sociopolitical life of the state.[12] Conversely, in Iraq, the political identity of the Shi'a has not managed to resolve this internal problem and appears schizophrenic, in the sense that the forces of modernity encourage the Shi'a masses to seize the levers of governmental power, while the traditional religious establishment is reluctant to assume an explicitly political role. It would take a figure of considerable presence and intellectual ability to reconcile these seemingly opposing dynamics in the Iraqi Shi'a psyche.

If we consider the Iraqi Shi'a separately from the Shi'a of Iran, their numbers within the Middle East are impressive. The population of Iraqi Shi'a is larger than the native populations of the Gulf Cooperation Council (GCC) combined. The next largest grouping of Arab Shi'a is in Lebanon, but these number only about a tenth of the number of those in Iraq.[13] The Iraqi Shi'a are therefore an important political group in the Middle East, yet perhaps more so than any other people in the region, their identity has been misunderstood (at times intentionally) and their ambitions demonized. It is therefore a useful exercise to build an approximate picture of the Iraqi Shi'a in terms of their communal identity and political outlook.

## THE DEVELOPMENT OF POLITICAL SHI'ISM IN IRAQ

To analyze and assess the development, history, and dynamics of the Iraqi Shi'a position in a Sunni-dominated state is a complex task. Shi'a political organization is fluid in its character, reflecting the multipolar nature of Shi'a religious authority. Whereas the Kurds were united (even during their periodic squabbles) by a notion of Kurdish nationalism, no such comparable rallying cause exists to serve as a focal point to unify the Shi'a politically. After all, they are Arab and have no particular issue concerning the legitimacy of the Iraqi state *per se*. In addition, the Iraqi Shi'a religious establishment has an aversion to involvement in the secular political realm, thereby separating the primary locus of religious identity from the leadership of militant political activity conducted in the name of the Shi'a.

Historically, Sunni regimes have maintained their political dominance by keeping the Shi'a weak and divided. A variety of techniques—co-option, rewards, and punishment—have been employed to preclude the emergence of a coherent, unified Shi'a opposition force capable of challenging Sunni dominance. The key to this strategy has been to prevent the politicization of the Iraqi Shi'a religious establishment (the *hawza*), and, thereby, to maintain its political isolation from the Iraqi Shi'a masses. The fear of successive Sunni regimes, and particularly of Saddam's regime, was neither the *hawza* itself, nor the masses of Iraqi Shi'a, but the potential for both together to initiate mass political activity against Baghdad. While neither the *hawza* nor the secular Shi'a masses were a threat to Sunni dominance while they were divided, it was a different matter when a figure or organization bridged the gap and succeeded in politicizing the *hawza* and spiritualizing the masses. The most significant of these figures was Ayatollah Muhammad Baqir al-Sadr (1935–1980), the inspirational *marja'* whose allying of the sacred with the political via the popular *Hizb al-Da'wa al-Islamiyya* (The Party of the Islamic Call—*al-Da'wa*) was to present a serious challenge to the legitimacy of the ruling Ba'ath regime.[14] Just as analyses of Kurdish politics must begin with an assessment of Mulla Mustafa Barzani and the Kurdistan Democratic Party, to understand the dynamics of contemporary Shi'ism in Iraq it is necessary to trace the development of the oldest of the Shi'a political parties—*al-Da'wa*—and its principle ideologue, Ayatollah Muhammad Baqir al-Sadr.[15]

## The Formation of *Hizb al-Da'wa Islamiyya*

The emergence of militant political Shi'ism can be traced to the instability prevalent in Iraq in the aftermath of the demise of the monarchy in 1958.[16] The first and arguably most important of the Shi'a political movements was *al-Da'wa*, established in the late 1950s in Najaf. The first leader of the new Iraqi Republic—Abdel Karim Qassim—relied heavily on the organizational prowess of the Iraqi Communist Party (ICP) to eliminate his opponents, and to infiltrate the religious establishment of the cities of Najaf and Karbala. Faced with the emergence of "godless" political powers, the Shi'a religious establishment, led by Grand Ayatollah Muhsin al-Hakim, was prompted into action and supported the establishment of a Shi'a entity capable of confronting this secular encroachment upon the Shi'a population. The organization that would translate the political concerns of the religious establishment into political action amongst the masses would be *al-Da'wa*.[17]

Opinion was divided within the Shi'a *hawza* between the traditionalists, who wanted to maintain a clear separation between the religious and political domains, and the activists who sought to redress the balance of power within the Sunni-dominated state. The latter advocated Shi'a political involvement and established the *Jama'at al-Ulama* (Society of Religious Scholars) in Najaf to act as an interface between the Shi'a religious establishment and different socioeconomic groups.[18] The power of the Shi'a *hawza* and the influence it could have on national politics became abundantly clear when Grand Ayatollah Muhsin al-Hakim issued a *fatwa* (religious decree) that forbade Muslims from joining the ICP, which in turn forced Qassim to abandon his alliance with the Communists. Still, a more worldly direction was needed from the Shi'a establishment to identify political and economic solutions for the problems of society. Muhammad Baqir al-Sadr was an important figure in tackling this problem. During this period, Sadr was a young scholar working with the *Jama'at al-Ulama* as an editor of its publications. He was responsible for outlining many aspects of the components of an Islamic government, culminating in the publication of *Falsafatuna* (Our Philosophy) in 1959, criticizing communism. This work was then followed by *Iqtisaduna* (Our Economics) in 1961, which introduced a theory of Islamic economics and attacked the economic theories of both communism and capitalism. The works were well received by the Shi'a audience, and succeeded in further depleting the morale of the Communists.[19]

The first Ba'athist coup of 1963, followed by the Arif governments between 1964 and 1968, saw political Shi'ism solidify its gains, allowing *al-Da'wa* to expand.[20] The new regime felt indebted to the actions of the Shi'a establishment for discrediting and weakening the position of the ICP, thereby forcing Qassim into an increasingly vulnerable position. Indeed, the Shi'a *hawza* appeared to be as zealous as their Ba'athist counterparts in rooting out suspected Communists in the aftermath of the coup of 1963. But the seeds of tension were already apparent. As *al-Da'wa* expanded its membership and political influence among the Shi'a masses, and new religious centers and libraries were established across the country, so it became that much more threatening to the socialist, pan-Arab, secular Ba'athist regime that seized power in 1968.

## Toward Oppression

The new government, with Saddam Hussein as Vice-President, became almost immediately embroiled in an increasingly acrimonious squabble with Iran that was to have disastrous consequences for Iraq's Shi'a.[21] When Ayatollah al-Hakim refused to condemn the Shah of Iran when requested to by Iraqi President Ahmed Hassan al-Bakr, the fate of the Shi'a was set. Faced with a religious establishment that was motivated, popular, and ideologically opposed to the secular socialist doctrine of the Ba'ath, the regime set out to eliminate systematically the political forces of the Shi'a, and particularly the influence of the *hawza*. Religious schools and colleges were closed, and their publications removed from circulation. Ayatollah al-Hakim's son was arrested and tortured, and prominent Shi'a figures were eliminated by the regime. Recitation of the Koran on television and radio was stopped, and Islamic instruction removed from the school curriculum.[22]

Up until this point, *al-Da'wa* and Sadr had not been singled out for special attention by the Ba'athist regime, which had instead focused its efforts upon the *hawza* in Najaf and the foreign (mainly Iranian) nationals whose loyalty to Baghdad was in doubt. This was to change following the peaceful death of Ayatollah al-Hakim in June 1970 and his succession by Ayatollah Abu al-Qasim al-Khoei. In this supreme position, the new Ayatollah chose to adopt the position favored by the Iraqi *hawza* and remained aloof from the political fray. It was left to Sadr, who now filled the position of heir apparent to Khoei and who himself became Ayatollah al-Sadr, to provide leadership for the forces of political Shi'ism in Iraq.[23]

Sadr found himself benefiting from the middle ground of Shi'a political sentiment. Ayatollah Khomeini, by this point in exile in Najaf after being expelled from Iran by the Shah in 1964 (first to Turkey, and then he traveled to Iraq in 1965), was at the extreme of political Shi'ism, advocating clerical rule. Ayatollah al-Khoei was at the other, attempting to focus Shi'a sentiment toward the more sacred, rather than the secular. Sadr was somewhere in the middle and, as an Arab, he became the focal point for the Iraqi Shi'a. With the notoriety of *al-Da'wa* increasing, it was only a matter of time before it attracted the coercive attention of the Ba'ath regime. From 1972, suspected party members were imprisoned and tortured by the regime, with some being executed. Iranians were routinely expelled and not allowed to undertake the pilgrimage to Najaf and Karbala, depriving the Iraqi Shi'a religious establishment of much-needed financial input. Alongside these coercive measures, the Ba'ath regime promoted an extensive social welfare system. Health insurance was introduced, and electricity provided to deprived villages.[24] The Shi'a of Iraq were effectively divided and weakened by a government skilled in the art of manipulating its opponents' weaknesses in order to strengthen its own position.

The action that set the standard for the subjugation of the Shi'a in the Ba'athist Iraqi state came in early 1977. The regime banned the annual religious ceremonies commemorating the martyrdom of Imam Hussein. However, as many as 30,000 Shi'a gathered to make their pilgrimage between Najaf and Karbala, with anti-Ba'athist banners and slogans making the political feeling against the regime obvious. Faced with such dissent, the regime mobilized the military against the pilgrims. The resultant riots in Karbala and subsequent executions of prominent demonstrators created two dynamics—both of which were to have a profound influence on the Shi'a. First, the demonstration and what was to be known as the *Safar Intifada* were planned, and benefited from the organizational skills of the clerics of Najaf. Ayatollah al-Sadr and *al-Da'wa* were at the forefront of those individuals and groups that the Ba'ath regime suspected as being the primary instigators of politically motivated Shi'ism. From 1977 onward, both Sadr and *al-Da'wa* became the primary targets of the Ba'ath regime. Second, the harsh actions of the regime created a split within the Ba'ath leadership itself. Saddam ensured that so-called moderates were removed from office, thereby allowing future Ba'athist policy toward the Shi'a to progress in an increasingly more coercive manner. Ba'athism was pushed as the dominant ideology in Iraq, and Shi'a institutions were heavily targeted by the regime.

Faced with this upsurge in state-sponsored violence, and buoyed by the success of Ayatollah Khomeini's Islamic Revolution in Iran in 1979, the leaders of the Iraqi Islamic movement, including Sadr, chose to promote violent confrontation with the Ba'ath regime. In doing so, Ayatollah al-Sadr sealed his fate. Sadr was imprisoned from June 1979 until March 1980. During this period, the imprisoned Sadr encouraged his followers to stand against the Ba'ath regime. The rise in tension was further fueled by the government's continued policy of repression and execution, with 3,000 being arrested in mid-1979 alone. Under the noses of his captors, Sadr continued to work against Saddam's government and appealed via tape-recorded messages to all Muslims in Iraq, whether Shi'a or Sunni, Arab, Kurd or Turcoman, to unite and secure an Islamic state through violent means. In what was to become known as Sadr's "last message," his focus on violence and the unity of Muslims against the Ba'ath is clearly evident: "It is necessary to assume a fighting position . . . I have spent this existence for the sake of Shi'i and Sunni equally in that I defended the message that united them and the creed that embraced them in a body."[25]

Militant Islamic groups, including *al-Da'wa*, found themselves inundated with recruits willing to sacrifice their lives rather than continuing to live under the repression of the Ba'ath regime. Other organizations also blossomed under the reinvigorated militancy, including the *Jund al-Imam* (Soldiers of the Imam) and the *Munazzamat al-'Amal al-Islami* (Islamic Task Organization).[26]

The *Munazzamat* was an attempt to focus on political activity at the community level. Headed by Ayatollah Muhammad Taqi al-Mudarissi, it is important to note that the *Munazzamat* was a Karbala-based organization, emphasizing the different and divided geographical focal points of Shi'ism in Iraq. *Al-Da'wa*'s base, meanwhile, was Najaf and this inability to promote solidarity amongst the political leadership stunted the growth of the Iraqi Shi'a Islamist movement.[27] The expansion of militant Islamist groups, fueled by the Islamic Republic of Iran, was accompanied by increasingly daring and violent actions targeted against Saddam's regime. By mid-1979, *mujahidin* were undertaking attacks in Baghdad itself, and Saddam himself was targeted in August. The religious establishment, led by the Society of Religious Scholars in Najaf, gave its support to militancy, issuing a *fatwa* in October encouraging the fight against the Ba'ath. By the end of 1979, *al-Da'wa* had established its own military brigade named *Shahid al-Sadr* (Martyr al-Sadr) Force.

Heightened Islamic militancy was met with increased brutality by Saddam. In March 1980, 96 members of *al-Da'wa* were executed, and membership in the party was made a capital offense. In April, over 30,000 Shi'as were expelled to Iran, and, on April 8, Ayatollah al-Sadr and his sister, Bint al-Huda, were executed. The death of Sadr had a profound impact upon the Islamic movement in Iraq. Losing their spiritual leader, the movement disintegrated, as the bridge between the revolutionaries and the religious establishment was broken. The regime continued with its repression and expulsion of Iraqi Shi'a to Iran and, in September 1980, Iraq invaded Iran, commencing a bloody 8-year war during which Saddam demonized the Shi'a threat posed to the entire Middle East. Faced with these events, the politicized Shi'a of Iraq followed either one of two paths. With many expelled and the leadership now dependent upon Iranian support, a significant number evacuated to Iran to regroup and continue their struggle against the regime.[28] Many others, however, chose to remain in Iraq, waiting until the opportunity to challenge the regime again emerged. The division is apparent today. Those who went to Iran have matured in a political sense, but, alienated from the Shi'a grassroots of Iraq, they are more often seen by their Iraqi brothers as acting as proxies for the government of Iran.

## The Formation of the Supreme Council for Islamic Revolution in Iraq (al-Majlis al-A'la li'l-Thawra al-Islamiyya fi'l-'Iraq)

SCIRI was formed on November 17, 1982 in Tehran. It was, and remains, essentially an Iranian creation, and is perceived as such in Iraq. The organization emerged as a result of efforts by the Iranian government to unite the fragmented

Iraqi Islamist movements.[29] The SCIRI umbrella included remnants of *al-Da'wa* and *Munazzamat* that had escaped from Iraq, and some prominent independents. However, the relationship between the SCIRI leadership, headed by Ayatollah Muhammad Baqir al-Hakim, and the various component entities proved to be strained as *al-Da'wa* in particular did not appreciate the involvement of Iran in its affairs. The component groups therefore maintained their independence and had access to their own resources and manpower. They could also withdraw whenever they wished. The leader of SCIRI remained Ayatollah Muhammad Baqir al-Hakim of Najaf until his assassination in August 2003. He was succeeded as leader by his younger brother, Ayatollah Abdel Aziz al-Hakim. However, the leadership continues to rely heavily upon those figures taught by Ayatollah Muhammad Baqir al-Sadr in the 1950s.

The driving force behind the formation of SCIRI was to a great extent the Iran–Iraq War. The intention was that the SCIRI leadership could form a transitional government if Iran captured areas of southern Iraq, including Basra.[30] Until this time came, SCIRI focused on coordinating opposition to the Ba'ath regime. Saddam responded with characteristic violence. Ninety members of Hakim's family were arrested in May 1983, with six leading members being executed in front of their relatives. Of the remainder, only five were eventually released.[31]

The Islamic opposition persisted, however. As an umbrella, SCIRI could claim the support of a wide range of Islamist groups within Iraq and also claim to unify Iraq's diverse Islamic opposition. However, SCIRI was also acting as an independent party in its own right, and, just as the Iraqi National Congress (INC) was to develop in the 1990s, SCIRI was at once a composite umbrella and a unitary entity. By 1983, SCIRI had established its own military force, located in the northernmost reaches of Iraqi Kurdistan at Haji Omran, under the protection of the Iranian army. Named the *Badr* Brigade, the outfit presented a troublesome if not militarily significant problem for the Iraqi government. However, the fact remained that the "party" SCIRI, rather than the umbrella, was dominated by the Iranian government. The *Badr* Brigade was commanded by Iranian *Pasdaran* (Revolutionary Guards), and took its orders from Hakim only after they had been routed through the appropriate Iranian filters. Indeed, by the 1990s and the resurgence of the Iraqi opposition, Hakim could not even visit "his" *Badr* Brigade without first obtaining the approval of Tehran.[32] SCIRI therefore developed a three-way identity. It was first of all an umbrella. However, as such, it was only as strong as its constituent parts allowed it to be. Second, it was a military outfit in the form of the *Badr* Brigade. Lastly, SCIRI was the political vehicle for the ambitions of the immediate circle of Ayatollah al-Hakim.

Even though the Islamist opposition to Saddam had been effectively fragmented after the execution of Ayatollah al-Sadr, the instability created by the Iran–Iraq War facilitated the continuation of militant opposition to the Ba'ath regime. *Al-Da'wa* cells continued their armed attacks against the regime, and Saddam himself was targeted in Mosul in April 1987. The Shi'a ghetto of *Al-Thawra* in Baghdad became a no-go area for government forces as covert *al-Da'wa* activity proved to be particularly effective in what was to become its Baghdad stronghold. SCIRI's *Badr* Brigade grew and, by 1988, had been reorganized into infantry, artillery, armored, and guerrilla divisions.[33] Still, the repression of the regime remained savage in the face of heightened Islamic militancy. Iraqi sources indicate that between 5,000 and 10,000 Islamists had been killed by the mid-1980s.[34]

## The Southern Intifada of 1991

As with the Kurds, the Shi'a opposition to Saddam was reinvigorated by the mistimed invasion of Kuwait in 1990. However, the Shi'a movement had been weakened as the bridge between the *hawza* (still in Najaf and Karbala under the leadership of Ayatollah al-Khoei) and society had been broken with the execution of Ayatollah al-Sadr. Without a charismatic figure to nurture and harness the revolutionary potential of the Shi'a masses while drawing the *hawza* into the political realm, the Shi'a Islamic movement in Iraq was relatively easy for Saddam to subjugate.

The popular uprising that took place in the south against Saddam in 1991 was a spontaneous event, unprovoked by the political parties. Unlike the later Kurdish Uprising, the main Islamic parties failed to successfully involve themselves in the unfolding rebellion, and rebelling Shi'a ultimately fell under the control of the more traditional Shi'a institutions of the religious establishment, symbolized by Grand Ayatollah al-Khoei. The fragmented nature of Shi'a civil society was obvious to all with the collapse of the uprising. The increased politicization of Shi'a militant parties caused by the Iran–Iraq War gave them a misguided belief in the strength of their own revolutionary appeal. Organizations such as SCIRI (and *al-Da'wa*, to a lesser extent) were, in the eyes of many Iraqis, tainted by their association with Iran. After eight long and brutal years of war during which the overwhelming majority of Iraqi Arabs, regardless of sectarian identity, had rallied to resist the Iranian onslaught, there was little enthusiasm among ordinary Shi'a for an Iranian-sponsored insurrection against Saddam's regime. The Shi'a political groups opposed to Saddam had made the fatal but understandable mistake of collaborating with Tehran—thus losing domestic legitimacy. This was particularly the case with SCIRI and Ayatollah Muhammad Baqir al-Hakim, whose regular antiregime broadcasts from Tehran during the Iran–Iraq war had done little more than strengthen Saddam's grip on Shi'a society by portraying SCIRI as a puppet of Iran. Saddam's appeal was based upon the oldest of human conditions—the desire to protect territory. His rallying cry relied on a simple but powerful message: Iraq's borders must be defended against a foreign Iranian aggressor. In this scheme of things, radical Shi'ism could be portrayed as a dangerous and traitorous fifth column—threatening the security of the Iraqi motherland. Saddam portrayed the Iraqi Arabs as defending the Arab world against the masses of the Iranians, and recalled heroic figures of the past such as Nebuchadnezzar, who had invaded Palestine, and Salahadin al-Ayubi, who had fought the Crusaders.[35] SCIRI's attempt to claim leadership over the southern *intifada* played straight into the hands of the regime, enabling Saddam to portray the uprising as an Iranian-backed threat to the integrity of the Iraqi Arab state. This helped to solidify the Sunni heartland behind the regime, took the steam out of the uprising, and, critically, virtually guaranteed that the U.S. would not intervene on behalf of the rebels. The *intifada* was crushed with exceptional brutality in short order. The precise number of Shi'a dead will perhaps never be known, but based on the excavation of mass graves after the war in 2003, this number must be in the tens of thousands.

At the height of the 1991 uprisings against Saddam, the regime controlled only 3 of Iraq's 18 provinces. This was as close as Saddam's regime had ever come to being eliminated, and the lessons were not lost on Saddam. The Ba'ath Party organization in the south had disintegrated with alarming rapidity. Therefore, to police the south, Saddam resurrected the standard practice of the British by co-opting and empowering the tribes. Simultaneously, the regime moved to destroy what remained of the radical Shi'a militias operating out of the southern marshlands.

## The Destruction of the Marsh Arabs

The marshlands of the south once covered an area of approximately 20,000 square kilometers around the confluence of the Tigris and Euphrates rivers in southern Iraq.[36] The marshes supported the *Ma'dan* people, who numbered several hundred thousand inhabitants of primarily Shi'a orientation, and also covered one of the richest oil deposits in the country at the Majnun and West Qurna fields, with a proven 40–50 billion barrels of oil between them.[37] The traditional way of life of the indigenous *Ma'dan* was based upon the conditions of their habitat, with occupations including fishing, subsistence cultivation, reed gathering, and associated crafts. The numbers of Marsh Arabs were already in natural decline by the 1980s due to the attraction of the urban environment, which encouraged the migration of the young and more educated parts of society. However, the area had already been targeted for development by the government as far back as the early 1950s with the "Third River Project," which sought to drain the marshes and turn the land over to agriculture. The progress of the project was halted by the Iran–Iraq War in 1980. However, when Iranian forces captured the Majnun Islands, Saddam ordered the recommencement of the drainage of the marshes and a subsequent ferocious military assault against the Iranians utilizing chemical weapons, which ultimately reclaimed Majnun in 1988.

The recapture of the area and the ending of the war with Iran did not herald the return of peace and tranquillity to the marshes. Instead, the Iraqi government had identified the marshes as being a center of subversive activity, providing refuge to SCIRI's *Badr* Brigade and *al-Da'wa* militia, in addition to allowing Iranian infiltration across the difficult-to-police marshland border of the *al-Huwaizah* marshes. Just as Saddam eradicated the Iranian threat coming from Halabja and taught the Kurds a lesson that would physically and psychologically scar them for generations, so he would later apply the same tactics to the south.

After the defeat of the southern uprising, Saddam's forces returned to the already devastated marshes. Guilty by association, the indigenous *Ma'dan* bore the brunt of the initial tactics of military occupation, followed by wholesale drainage of their marsh environment.[38] No weapon was too small in the fight to secure the marshes. Artillery, air assault, napalm and a shoot-to-kill policy were all reminiscent of the slaughter of the Kurds during the *Anfal* Campaign, and were undertaken with equal sadistic vigor and determination. Tens of thousands of the *Ma'dan* fled to Iran, leaving behind many to be executed by the regime. The number of people displaced by these activities is estimated to be between 100,000 and 190,000, with an unknown number executed or remaining missing. The vaunted economic strategy of reclaiming the marshes to enhance agriculture proved to be false. The drained areas show little evidence of successful land reclamation, and the UN special rapporteur starkly noted the "indisputable evidence of widespread destruction and human suffering."[39]

## THE RESURGENCE OF SHI'A COMMUNAL IDENTITY

During the 1990s, the issue of the Shi'a in Iraq fell off the radar screen of the international community. Occasional concern was uttered regarding the fate of the Marsh Arabs, but this was often focused more at an environmental level than on the greater human tragedy that had occurred. This lack of interest was testament to Saddam's ability to consolidate his power after the uprisings and either subjugate his dissenters or co-opt them. Such co-optation was not necessarily forced. Saddam manipulated his weak position with masterful skill and managed to lay the blame for the devastated Iraqi economy and the poverty of the south squarely on the shoulders of the U.S. and its allies. No longer were Saddam's military excursions to blame for the deprivation of the Iraqi people; instead, it was UN sanctions and the policies of the U.S. that were responsible for the devastation of the Iraqi people and their untold suffering. At the same time, the government set about destroying civil institutions in the south that had survived previous assaults, including organizations and bodies not associated with the religious establishment, which could be used to promote a more aggressive Shi'a identity among the masses. The policy backfired as, in their place, prominent clerics expanded their religious networks of support and charitable institutions.[40] The growth in popularity of religious affiliation and the strengthening of communal identity during this period was remarkable, and was even encouraged by the regime. Saddam identified himself with his Shi'a countrymen, performed pilgrimages to Shi'a shrines, and falsified his family lineage to include Shi'a historical figures as far back as Imam Hussein himself. The message was clear—Saddam was playing the Shi'a card and attempting to co-opt its huge potential in his favor. The security forces of the regime continued with covert (and, at times, not so covert) targeting of political groups, and, under this repression, *al-Da'wa* was forced to operate clandestinely, while the *hawza* seemed to be content to maintain and practice its core belief of the division between religion and politics.[41]

While such tactics were successful in the short term, Saddam remained all too aware that an alliance of the *hawza* with the masses would be potentially devastating for his weakened regime, and his sensitivity toward any figure who could bridge the gap between religion and politics remained keen. This keenness became strikingly evident in 1999. The leading Shi'a cleric in the late 1990s was Ayatollah Muhammad Sadiq al-Sadr. Another member of the al-Sadr family and cousin of the late Ayatollah Muhammad Baqir al-Sadr, Ayatollah Sadiq al-Sadr was a government-appointed cleric who initially appeared to act according to the wishes of the regime. However, with the increased popularity of Shi'ism, Sadiq al-Sadr moved into the most threatening position of bridging the gap between the *hawza* and the masses and began preaching against the Ba'ath party.[42] For the first time since 1980, the Shi'a had a leader who had a mass following and the ability to politicize the *hawza* and spiritualize the masses. Recognizing the threat, Saddam acted swiftly; Ayatollah Sadiq al-Sadr was assassinated in Najaf in 1999, along with his two eldest sons, leaving his youngest son, Muqtada, as heir to the political legacy of *al-Sadr al-Thani* (the Second Sadr). Since 1999, the leading cleric in Iraq has been Grand Ayatollah Ali Sistani of Najaf. Of Iranian origin but of Najaf clerical background, Ayatollah Sistani returned to his theological roots and preached the separation of religion and politics. However, Ayatollah Sadiq al-Sadr had succeeded in reinvigorating and politicizing Shi'a sectarian identity. By 2001, the pilgrimage to the Shrine of Hussein at Karbala reached 2.4 million (approximately 10 percent of the Iraqi population, and over 20 percent of the Shi'a population).[43] It would only be a matter of time before the newly motivated Shi'a community would flex its populist muscles and realize the inequity of their existence in the Iraqi state.

## THE SHI'A IN POST-SADDAM IRAQ

In the runup to the military actions that removed Saddam from power in 2003, the press officers of the White House used the subjugation of the Shi'a as a powerful propaganda tool to demonize Saddam. The rather naïve belief following from this was that, once liberated from an evil regime, the Shi'a would choose to fit neatly into a new secular government in which all of Iraq's ethnic and religious groups would be represented.[44] However, with Saddam's removal, it would appear that the political strength of the Shi'a religious establishment was grossly underestimated in the prewar planning stage.[45] Deputy Defense Secretary Paul Wolfowitz illustrated this tendency clearly when, in early March 2003, he described Iraqis as being "secular" and "overwhelmingly Shi'a." He also dismissed as unproblematic the existence of Shi'ism's most sacred shrines on Iraqi territory.[46] Wolfowitz blatantly failed to appreciate the power of the religious organizations, and seemed to be oblivious to the importance of the shrine cities of Karbala and Najaf. Juan Cole, a professor specializing on the Shi'a, mockingly noted that "the neo-conservative fantasy of Iraq is now meeting the real Iraq, on the ground, in the shrine cities as well as in the smaller, mostly Shiite towns in the south of the country."[47]

It was perhaps to be expected that another member of the Sadr family would rise to the challenge of bridging religion and politics. Since the assassination of Ayatollah Muhammad Sadiq al-Sadr in 1999, his son Muqtada al-Sadr went underground. Over the next three years, Muqtada continued with covert attempts to organize Shi'a militia and succeeded in establishing and enhancing his following in the Saddam City area of Baghdad. Muqtada's movement (*Jimaat al-Sadr al-Thani*) began legitimizing his youthful authority (he is approximately 30 years old) by insisting that only the directives of his deceased father were legitimate, and the clerics of Iranian origin (presumably including his father's replacement, Grand Ayatollah Ali Sistani) had no legitimate authority over Iraqi Shi'a.[48] Muqtada changed the name of Saddam City to *Medinat al-Sadr* (Sadr City), and this deprived neighborhood of at least 2 million people of mainly Shi'a background became his power base.

Muqtada then set about removing potential opponents. These included Abdul Majid al-Khoei—perhaps the only notable Shi'a figure who enjoyed the support of Western governments. He was acquainted with Tony Blair, and seemed set to play a prominent role in the reconstruction of Iraq.[49] The son of the late Grand Ayatollah Abu al-Qasim al-Khoei, he was brought into Iraq on April 3 by U.S. forces, keen to bring the southern cities under some form of pro-U.S. control. In his quest to unite Shi'a groups in Najaf, al-Khoei was stabbed at least 30 times and "his remains were dragged across the city, leaving a trail of blood on the streets."[50]

The involvement of Muqtada in the killing of al-Khoei is generally assumed, and even if his followers did not do it, he later used the killing to intensify the pressure he was applying against Sistani, whom he viewed as being complicit with the atrocities of Saddam's regime by refusing to take a political role against him. Muqtada also threatened Ayatollah Said al-Hakim, the nephew of Ayatollah Muhammad Baqir al-Hakim, leader of SCIRI.

Whether Muqtada will go from strength to strength, or whether the more established parties such as SCIRI and *al-Da'wa* become the inheritors of the mantle of leadership first worn by Muhammad Baqir al-Sadr nearly 25 years ago, it would seem unlikely that this newly emergent Shi'a identity in Iraq, conscious of its potential political muscle in a post-Saddam political environment, will again be placed in a position of subservience under a future regime dominated by Sunnis. This balance of power between the Sunnis and Shi'a promises to be problematic to resolve.

## THE SHI'A: KEY ISSUES

### Legacy of Discrimination

While there are some who question the intensity, or even the existence, of a sectarian divide in Iraq, the reality is that Iraq has operated an informal system of political *apartheid* since its creation in the 1920s. In certain areas, the financial and commercial worlds for example, there have been no barriers to Shi'a advancement, but in terms of access to political power, the Shi'a have been almost entirely excluded. Regime change, when it has occurred, has simply resulted in the replacement of one Sunni group with another. Similarly, the upper echelons of the armed forces and the various security services have always been Sunni-dominated. This is not to imply that Iraq is wracked by sectarian hostility, but to emphasize the point that decades (in fact, centuries) of official discrimination have helped to create a distinctive identity for the Iraqi Shi'a as an oppressed people. As the June 2002 "Declaration of the Shi'a of Iraq" puts it, "the continuing isolation of the Shi'a from any meaningful exercise of power has contributed, in the modern period, to the transformation of the Iraqi Shi'a into a recognizable social entity," and further, that "the crystallization of the Shi'a as a distinct group owes far more to the policies of discrimination and retribution than to any specifically sectarian or religious considerations."[51] Such statements imply that the sectarian divide is defined less by differences in religious interpretation and more by an oppressor/oppressed relationship. It is a political divide that falls along sectarian lines. The removal of Saddam's regime will inevitably transform this traditional distribution of political power, as it seems highly unlikely that the Shi'a will once again accept a subservient role in a future Iraqi government. But the stakes are higher than they first appear. Along with control of the levers of power comes control over Iraq's vast oil reserves and the opportunity to define the "identity" of the Iraqi state. To date, the identity of Iraq, such as it is, has been determined by Sunni Arabs. Thus, Iraq has been strongly pan-Arab and secular. This will almost certainly change if the Shi'a come to dominate the politics of Iraq. This seismic shift in the hierarchy of power will create friction around the issue of who gets to define the nature of the Iraqi state, rather than around any inherent religious differences.

## What Unifies the Shi'a?

It may well be that the only sense in which the Shi'a form a coherent entity is through a shared experience as victims of systematic discrimination. Beyond this, few forces have mobilized the Shi'a behind a common cause. Historically, political organizations that emphasize wealth redistribution—such as the Iraqi Communist Party—have appealed to the Shi'a masses, as indeed did Saddam's Ba'ath Party during its "socialist" phase in the 1970s. The Shi'a have always held together in the face of external threats, such as that presented by the British in 1920 and by the Iranians in the 1980s. Indeed, the Arab component of the Iraqi state has traditionally been at its most unified when confronted by hostile foreign forces. This does not bode well for a long-term U.S. military occupation.

Potentially the most pervasive unifying force, however, is religion. An unfortunate legacy of Saddam's rule was that he created precisely that which he set out to crush—namely, politicized religion. At the same time, Saddam succeeded in eradicating almost all other forms of social structure. The removal of his regime has created a serious power vacuum in Iraq, which is being filled by any force with the authority to provide a semblance of order and rudimentary social services to a desperate population. Increasingly, it appears, organized religion is filling the vacuum. Inevitably then, religion will play a major political role in the future of the Iraqi state because it is one of the very few social structures remaining that has the capacity to mobilize the Shi'a masses.

## The Major Players

Among religious leaders in Iraq, there is likely to be a sustained struggle for influence over the Shi'a population. A key battle will be between indigenous Iraqi clerics and those tainted by Iranian association. Among the latter is Abdel Aziz al-Hakim, leader of SCIRI. While SCIRI has the financial backing of Iran, and its own armed forces, grassroots support for SCIRI in Iraq is probably limited. Thus SCIRI 's role is likely to be restricted to that of "spoiler." It may well seek to mobilize support around strident anti-Americanism, thereby becoming a lightning rod for Shi'a resentment against continued U.S. occupation. Muqtada al-Sadr remains the figure most likely to mobilize the masses, but for what purpose remains to be seen. In addition to the religious establishment, tribal leaders will inevitably play an important role in a post-Saddam Iraq. Saddam's empowerment of tribal structures reversed decades of waning influence for tribal leaders. They are unlikely to relinquish this power without a struggle. Once again, in the absence of an overarching coercive force capable of administering law and order, this function has been assumed by those in a position to provide security at a local level—namely, the tribes. The longer the period between the end of the war and the investiture of a new central government, the more deeply entrenched tribal authority will become.

## CONCLUSION

In general terms, the Shi'a in Iraq are Iraqi first and Shi'a second. Their ethnicity as Arabs is perhaps the defining feature of the Shi'a, along with their acceptance and association with the Iraqi state. To propose that the "Shi'a south" is fundamentally distinct from the "Sunni center" is to ignore the human linkages that exist between the two regions. Intercommunal ties, particularly under the reign of Saddam, have been enhanced to the point that it is difficult for even some Arabs to identify whether they are Shi'a or Sunni. Saddam's policy of not classifying Islamic sects within the national census further contributed to this ambiguity.

However, the resurgence of Shi'a sectarian identity and the potential linkage between the *hawza* and the masses suggests that the future political landscape of Iraq must change. While it may be a futile task to identify Shi'a and Sunni as distinct entities in Iraq, one issue continually returns to haunt the designers of a new Iraq, particularly in a constitutional sense. The Iraqi government and the most important institutions of administration have remained, on the whole, a Shi'a-free zone. The levers of power have always been controlled by those Sunnis deemed appropriate by whichever regime was in power. Of course, the occasional Shi'a would find his way in, but one only has to look at the backgrounds of successive Iraqi governments to realize that the Shi'a were a grossly underrepresented group of people, no matter how their involvement is measured. This is set to change.

## CHAPTER SIX

# THE SUNNIS

## INTRODUCTION

TO VIEW IRAQI SOCIETY AS STARKLY DIVIDED into three internally coherent and mutually hostile groups is admittedly an oversimplification of a complex reality. Yet it has some obvious truths, driven by the dominance of the state by the Sunnis Arabs. As the historical record clearly indicates, the power hierarchy in Iraq has been dominated by different groupings of Sunni elites since the inception of the Iraqi state. Saddam Hussein, himself a Sunni, did not invent this system but certainly perpetuated it. With the Ba'athists in power from 1968, again dominated by Sunnis, the pattern was repeated. It is therefore not an oversimplification of reality to state that this pattern is one of the unfailing facts about Iraqi politics, at least until the demise of Saddam, and perhaps after.[1]

However, it is indeed a simplistic notion that Iraqi society is made up of three discrete blocks: the Kurdish north, Sunni Arab center, and Shi'a Arab south. One only has to remember the basic overlap of Kurdish Sunnis, Sunni Arabs, Arab Shi'a, and Shi'a Kurds to realize that Iraqi society is kaleidoscopic in its complexity. But while acknowledging this complexity, one of the key questions to ask of any political system is a simple one: Who rules? Perhaps the most enduring feature of the politics of modern Iraq is rule by Sunni Arabs. More importantly, Sunni dominance has clearly transcended social class. Under the monarchy, governance was dominated by the Sunni middle and upper classes; under the Republic, by lower-middle-class Sunnis; and under the Ba'ath regime, by Sunnis (mainly Tikritis) from the bottom tier of society. The trend seems to be clear—class changes, but Sunni dominance remains constant. No single regime in the tortured history of Iraq, regardless of its underlying social basis, has done anything other than perpetuate Sunni dominance.

## EQUALITY OF SUFFERING

Are the Sunnis, therefore, a privileged sect that have a preordained right to treat the Iraqi state as their own? History would certainly appear to support the contention that "Sunni Arabs" and "Iraqi government" are at least associated closely if not fully synonymous. However, it would be a mistake to group the Sunnis as one homogenous block. As much as every other group in Iraq, they are heavily fragmented, with internal divides often being characterized more by violence than cooperation. Futhermore, the domination of the state has often been the result of competition within the Sunni, rather than between the Sunni and Shi'a. Until the removal of Saddam, ensuring predominance over the Shi'a and the Kurds was a bloody sideshow to the main game going on among the Sunnis themselves. While there is no denying that the Kurds and the Shi'a have suffered greatly under the regime of Saddam, it is also the case that the Sunni Arabs have suffered perhaps just as much, and possibly in a far more destructively traumatic manner in the longer term. To support this argument, we need to consider the nature of the threat posed by the Kurds and politicized Shi'a to Saddam, or to any Iraqi regime for that matter. Their threats were always orientated toward changing the status quo of the whole of Iraq—whether through Kurdish separatism in the north, or pressure for Shi'a representation in Iraqi institutions of government—but rarely focused primarily on the personal rule of Saddam. Of course, had the Shi'a in particular been successful in their aims, the result would have been the swift and probably very bloody demise of Saddam; but it would not have been "personal." It was also a relatively easy task for Saddam to ensure that neither the Kurdish separatists nor the politicized Shi'a were successful by his well-tried and polished policies of patronage and terror, and by appealing to the "Sunni masses" to support the regime as it stood against the threat of radical Islamism (as happened in 1991). Furthermore, the lack of geographical contiguity between the Kurds and the Shi'a, and the absence of a unifying ideology or political aim between them (apart from a certain antipathy toward Saddam, which was rarely constant, particularly as the Kurds were in and out of alliances with him), ensured that the opposition forces of the Kurds and the Shi'a never acted in a coordinated manner against the regime.[2]

As with most dictators, for Saddam, the most credible and genuine threat to his continuous rule and physical well-being came from the inside—both from the ranks of his own supporters, and from those empowered by the institutions of state, security, and civil society around him. Saddam staffed positions of importance from supportive sections of the population. The upper echelons of the Ba'ath Party, the officers corps, the special security apparatus (including the SSO and the SRG), and the circles of patronized businessmen and individuals that surrounded the institutions of governance and administration within Iraq were all Sunni-dominated. Saddam's preference for Tikritis, and his reliance on other key tribes (especially the Douri, Jubbar, and Ubayd) was designed to ensure that the regime was staffed by loyal Sunni foot soldiers.[3] However, there were limits, and the greatest threat to Saddam's continued rule was always from those he had empowered in order to bolster the loyalty of the regime to himself. No one else had the opportunity to gain access to the bare minimum required for revolution (organization and weapons), nor the access to the institutions of government, as did the Sunni Arabs. It is for this reason that, under Saddam, the oppression of the Sunni Arabs of the center was perhaps as great and as widespread (and in many ways far more sinister) as that instigated against the Kurds and the Shi'a. Whenever military purges occurred, the greater proportion of deaths would be of Sunni Arab officers. Political purges followed a similar pattern, and whenever particular tribes were targeted by Saddam, they were nearly always Sunni tribes from Baghdad and its environs. Being closer to the regime than any other segment of society, the Sunni Arabs were as much the victims of Saddam's brutality as any other group in Iraq. However, the fact remains that they historically associate themselves with governing Iraq.

Key questions remain unanswered. If U.S. plans for a democratic Iraq are to be implemented in this post-Saddam environment, would the Sunni Arabs, who have lived in a state dominated by a Sunni ruling elite since the formation of Iraq (and enjoyed a similar situation during the Ottoman Empire), be prepared to accept a democratic Iraqi government dominated by the Shi'a? One only has to look toward the way Saddam successfully mobilized Sunni Arab "center" sentiment in 1991 when faced with a possible Shi'a uprising. It was the fear of Shi'a dominance in government (and its associated fundamentalist Islamist coloring) that galvanized the Sunnis behind Saddam, thus saving the regime and brutally oppressing the Shi'a and Kurds in the process. Would the secularized Sunnis be prepared to accept a regime they perceived to be theocratic in its tendencies and colored by Shi'a religious doctrine? The fear of the Shi'a ayatollahs gaining control in the uprisings of 1991 was enough to turn Sunni Arab support back to a massively weakened Saddam as the only figure capable of protecting their interests, allowing him to once again preserve Sunni and Tikriti dominance in the state.

The events of 1991 clearly illustrate the dangers of underestimating the significance of the sectarian divide when considering the future stability of Iraq. While the southern uprising was, in reality, a popular uprising by Iraqis, comprising Sunni, Shi'a, elements of the military, and disaffected Ba'athists, Saddam was able to capitalize on the *perception* of the uprising as Shi'a-dominated to mobilize Sunni support. These perceptions remain an extremely powerful force in the future development of the Iraqi state. In order to ascertain the position of the Sunni Arabs in Iraq, it is essential first to identify what, if anything, identifies a Sunni Arab within the Iraqi state.

## WHAT MAKES A SUNNI?

The association of Sunnis with the central organs of power in Iraq has been a constant since the period immediately following the death of the Prophet Muhammed and the crisis of succession. In other words, Sunnis have either administered or ruled the territory that is now Iraq for the last 1,500 years. The reigns of the Abbasid Caliphs were centered on Baghdad, and the associated bureaucrats, administrators, and governors were effectively selected from and molded in the Sunni heartland of central Iraq. The association of Sunnis with governance and Shi'a with disenfranchisement later became an institutionalized feature of the political psyche of the population. Furthermore, the structural divide that exists in Sunni Islam between sectarian affairs and religious authority has meant that Iraqi Sunnis have had few qualms about dominating the levers of power in the state. The Shi'a meanwhile, have constantly struggled to reconcile their seemingly intractable problem of subservience to apolitical religious authorities while attempting to gain control of the earthly political realm.

Although Sunnis are in a minority in Iraq, they are in a majority in the Arab (and Muslim) world. This has resulted in strong Arab nationalist links developing between Baghdad and other regional Arab capitals, and has given Sunni hegemony in Iraq unrivalled legitimacy in the eyes of regional neighbors. The association of the Iraqi Sunnis with Arab nationalism, secular politics, and the dominance of institutions of governance were manifested in its final, powerful form in the regime of Saddam Hussein; the character of the

Ba'ath Party and of Saddam's regime was very much a product of, and a natural successor to, previous administrations.

## The Identification of Sunnis with the Iraqi Kingdom

The ascension of the Sunni Arabs within the modern Iraqi state can be traced to the formation of Iraq in the 1920s. Sunnis were in the minority from the outset. Baghdad lay in the heartland of the Sunni Arabs. The Mosul *vilayet* (province) was to the north, and populated primarily by Kurds, Turcomans, and Assyrians, with significant Arab populations. As such, the principal ties of the Mosul *vilayet* stretched north and east to Turkey and Syria. The province of Basra to the south was inherently Shi'a in outlook and its strongest ties were traditionally with Persia to the east and with the trading settlements in the Persian Gulf.[4]

Within Iraq as a whole, 56 percent of the population were Shi'a, 36 percent were Sunni, and 8 percent were non-Muslim (mainly Christian). In addition, around a quarter of the Iraqi population was Kurdish. National unity was therefore somewhat lacking from the outset. The Kurds sought autonomy, the Shi'a preferred direct British rule in order to forestall Sunni dominance (which they remembered with trepidation from the manner in which the Sunnis retained their hold on power during the Ottoman period), and the Sunnis were openly opposed to creating a state in which they would be a numerical minority.[5]

King Faisal I therefore began his reign from a position of numerical weakness, ostensibly representing the Iraqi "nation" but in reality being the focal point of the minority Sunnis. The pattern of governance established under Faisal's regime was to become the blueprint for all successor regimes. Faisal's Sunni Arab supporters, the Sharifians, were elevated to positions of authority in order to bolster the legitimacy of the regime.[6] The Sharifians remained loyal to Faisal because they shared the greater notions of pan-Arabism, itself a Sunni-driven concept, and because they had no other power base within the Iraqi state. Furthermore, the Sharifian officers were almost wholly localized around the environs of Baghdad, due mainly to the fact that Baghdad housed one of the few military preparatory schools.[7] Militarized, educated, and elitist, but a minority in the new Iraq, their source of power became the state apparatus itself. As Malik Mufti notes: "Unconnected to the urban and rural elites and therefore with no stake in protecting their interests, the Sharifians realized that their only hope for social advancement lay in the expansion of Faisal's central state apparatus."[8]

However, even though Sharifians were found in every corner of Faisal's regime, the new monarch attempted a sincere and energetic policy of Iraqi nation-building. He realized that any state incorporating the diverse peoples of the three Ottoman *vilayets* of Mosul, Baghdad, and Basra would need to have representatives of all component groups in government. His immediate and pressing concern regarded the conciliation of the Shi'a with the Iraqi state. Recognizing that "the taxes are on the Shi'i, death is on the Shi'i, and the posts are for the Sunni," Faisal pursued a policy of attempting to associate the Shi'a with the state.[9] However, his preoccupation with notions of pan-Arabism, and his reliance on the unwavering support of the Sharifians, meant that the Iraqi state retained its inherent Sunni coloring, and the intrusion of Arab nationalist Sunnis into all levels of the administration marked a critical step in the Sunnization and Arabization of the state institutions and political culture of Iraq.[10]

## The Identification of Sunnis with the Iraqi Republic

Little was to change after the removal of the monarchy in 1958. Although General Abdel Karim Qassim was keen to portray his "Iraqi" side—of having both Kurdish and Arab blood-ties—the Free Officers movement was clearly pan-Arabist and ideologically comparable to the Sharifians of the *ancien régime*, having passed through the same military schools and originating from the same regions and the same lower middle class.[11] If the composition of the movement is considered, the overwhelming majority of the governing Central Committee was Sunni Arab, with only two Shi'a and no Kurds.[12] The Iraqi Communist Party (ICP), an organization that was as much dominated by Shi'a as by Sunnis and enjoyed strong Kurdish support, was a true threat to the position of the Sunni elite in Iraq. Its subsequent removal as a political force had as much to do with its anti–pan-Arab sentiment as any other motivation. The enduring nature of Iraq's vertical divisions proved to be insurmountable for a class-based organization to overcome, primarily due to the obstructions of the ruling Sunnis.

By the late 1950s, Iraqi society was in a state of economic and social flux, due primarily to the impact of increasing oil revenues. The social mobility that ensued from this influx of revenue saw the composition of the politically active classes similarly change. Previously, Iraq had been dominated by the middle-class urban intelligentsia, and particularly those hailing from Baghdad and Mosul. Now, with heightened social mobility, the rural population migrated into the expanding urban areas. This influx included large numbers of Tikritis from the Sunni heartland between Mosul and Baghdad. Through growing connections and the appeal of military service, Tikritis were already well established in the ranks of the armed forces when the monarchy was toppled.[13] In effect, the rural, more tribally minded Sunnis had now come to the cities. This factor was important to the subsequent political history of Iraq. When the Ba'ath party came to power a second time in 1968, it purged the officers' corps of any vestige of left-wing (communist) or pro-Syrian sentiment. Perhaps the only group left untouched was the rural Sunnis. This factor, combined with the Tikriti origin of President Bakr, set the tone for the future orientation of the Ba'ath party, the government, and the state.[14]

For Saddam, the Ba'ath party was merely the means by which he, and his Tikriti and associated cohorts, could exercise their power over Iraqi society. It was an effective tool by which to consolidate power. It also gave a propaganda edge as it allowed the regime to incorporate Shi'a and Kurdish elements into its ranks at the low to middle levels of the party, without ever allowing them entry into the inner circles of the regime where meaningful power was concentrated. Real power was increasingly focussed upon Saddam's own immediate clan (from the al-Bu Nasir) and individuals from other supportive groups. The Ba'ath Party provided a notion of political representation, but could not threaten Saddam directly. In this, Saddam had learned well the dangers of having organizations such as the ICP too close to the center, where they could wreak havoc with any regime that had not yet consolidated its power (as the ICP had done with Qassim).

In consolidating his power upon becoming president in 1979, but also beforehand as the "Czar of Internal Security" under President Bakr, Saddam began by protecting himself in the most effective way possible—"from the top." Recruiting from young Tikritis, and mainly from the al-Bu Nasir, he formed the *Himaya*, the personal presidential bodyguard whose sole responsibility was to ensure the physical safety of the president but, in reality, of Vice-President Saddam Hussein. Ensconced in his own personal security network, Saddam flooded the internal security apparatus of the Party and the state with his own tribesmen and loyalists, mainly from the towns of Tikrit, al-Dur, Beiji, and Uja. The Israeli scholar Amatzia Baram insightfully notes that, if placed at the right nodes of security and government, a small number of dedicated loyalists could have a disproportionate influence upon the security of the regime.[15]

In many ways, the Ba'ath Party was a stalking horse for Saddam's ambition—it allowed him to gain access to the highest levels of government, and became an institutional mechanism through which Iraqi society could be consolidated and harnessed politically behind him. Regime consolidation was achieved by a devastatingly pervasive Party structure (modelled on that of the

ICP), patronage flowing from oil revenues, and the tying of Ba'athist slogans with already prominent and popularly accepted Sunni ideals of Arabism, socialism, and nationalism. Its secular pan-Arabist ideology and overt focus on egalitarianism and the redistribution of wealth were identical to political sentiments shared by the Sunni masses under the monarchy and under the republic before the Ba'ath took power.[16] It was therefore a relatively straightforward exercise in political engineering to target the Ba'ath Party's message to mainstream Sunni political views (and, arguably, some secular Shi'a opinion), and to ensure that the Party became the primary means of social, political, and economic advancement within Iraq. The structure of the Party emphasized this role, with its cells penetrating society down to the neighborhood level, and with its influence penetrating much deeper into the hearts and minds of the population.

Alongside this pervasive political structure running throughout society, the regime highjacked a further feature of the Iraqi political scene: trades' unions (again made popular by the ICP), which mobilized the population along occupational lines. Rather than functioning as instruments of civil society, they became simply another means by which the Ba'ath could exercise social control, with membership of the unions dependent upon acceptance by the Ba'ath. A similar policy was successfully implemented with regard to the military and the civil bureaucracy. Ideologically, the Ba'ath Party essentially trotted out the slogans that had always appealed to the Sunni heartland in the past. But the Party had also become the institutional "glue" that held Iraqi society together, and the only mechanism by which advancement could be achieved. For the whole of Iraq, adherence to Ba'athist slogans became a necessary prerequisite for social mobility and, arguably, even normal existence. With its inherently "top-down" mechanisms and its built-in requirement of allegiance to the ideals of the Party (which became synonymous with "the state" and "Iraq" and, ultimately, embodied in the figure of Saddam himself), the regime had spectacularly harnessed the energetic political forces primarily of the Sunni, but also, to a certain degree, of the Shi'a, and tied them to the legitimacy and authority of the ruling elite of Sunni loyalists answerable to their godfather, Saddam Hussein.

## THE SUNNIS IN SADDAM'S REGIME

In many ways, Saddam reinvented Iraq if not in his own image, then certainly to serve his own image. Key to his survival and the legitimacy of his regime was the Arab Sunni heartland of Iraq, or at least those portions of it deemed loyal to him. Those deemed disloyal would be removed in merciless purges as the years progressed. The large-scale and systematic abuse of the Sunnis by Saddam's government has been one of the consistently overlooked facts in the modern history of Iraq. The intelligentsia of the Ba'ath were effectively removed as Saddam assumed the presidency. In their absence, the Party became dominated by the provincial Sunnis, all totally loyal to Saddam, and disinterested in furthering any ideological or political belief beyond that which came from the leader.

With this move, Saddam had effectively tribalized the political leadership of Iraq, both in terms of actual tribal outfits receiving patronage in the form of government positions, financial inducements, and the benefits of being associated with the regime, but also in the interpersonal relationships that constituted the political culture of the institutions of state. Saddam had introduced his own people into positions of authority and security; but perhaps more importantly, he created a "tribe" out of the institutions of state. To act in a manner judged hostile to the state—with regard to political allegiance—would incur the medieval tribal wrath that Saddam had now cultured and empowered. Saddam was a Sunni; his tribe was Sunni; therefore, his government institutions would be staffed primarily by Sunnis. Indeed, within the Ba'athist ideology, there was little room to even acknowledge that Iraq was home to clear sectarian divides. According to Ba'athist doctrine, one's national identification should not be determined by one's religion or sect.[17] However, the Ba'ath Party ensured by its very structure that neither Shi'a nor Kurdish representatives would be actively socially empowered to the point where they enjoyed a proportionate say in the activities of the central government. The Ba'ath's nationalist tendency and strategy to embrace Iraq's kaleidoscopic multicultural society was fine as long as the institutions of state remained politically controlled by the Sunnis themselves, increasingly represented by the Tikritis.

## THE POSITION OF THE TIKRITIS
## AND ASSOCIATED SUNNI TRIBES

Saddam's own involvement with the rise of the Tikritis in the Iraqi state can be clearly seen by comparing the composition of the first Ba'athist government of 1963 (in which Saddam had little to do with staffing) and the second Ba'athist government of 1968, in which Saddam had significant power as President Bakr's deputy. While the members of the first government were all Sunnis, they were split between those from Baghdad and those from Tikrit. The composition of the second government made it quite clear that the Tikritis now held the upper hand within the regime, which was now dominated by the lower classes, rather than the middle classes.[18] This was not by accident. Again, Saddam had learned that the threat to the regime ultimately did not come from the Shi'a as Sunnis could be relied upon to unite against the threat of Shi'a rebellion (as in 1991). As far as Saddam was concerned, the major threat came from the Sunnis themselves, and so his primary goal was to protect his own immediate circle against the possibility of being overthrown by Sunnis from within.

Initially, Saddam was perceived as something of an upstart by the traditional ruling Sunni classes—an uneducated, violent rural thug with no military training. His natural Sunni detractors could be expected to hail from the cities and from the military. He therefore made sure that forces from these sections of Iraq would find it impossible to generate political momentum to threaten him. His survival instinct went even further than simply not trusting the more privileged Sunnis, however. With hindsight, it is quite apparent that he did not even trust his own family members, and one would have to again congratulate him on his instinctive judgment. Therefore, even his closest relations were subjected to the same regime of patronage and coercion as the Iraqi state as a whole, and the survival of Saddam over the years is covered with the blood of his own relatives as he curtailed the potential ambitions of those near to him.

For Saddam, this meant playing a balancing act between the three wings of his immediate family—"the brothers," "the cousins," and "the maternal cousins." The rise and fall of each of these branches illustrates quite clearly that Saddam managed his families affairs in such a manner that even those closest to him existed in a state of perpetual uncertainty and fear.[19] A well-documented feature of this strategy was Saddam's creation of multiple security agencies with overlapping jurisdictions. The single most important security body established was the Special Security Organization (*Jihaz al-Amn al-Khas*, or SSO). As the ultimate protection body of the President, it was staffed primarily with Tikritis from the al-Bu Nasir, and was commanded by Saddam's younger (but more influential) son Qusay.[20] Similarly, the presidential bodyguard (*Himaya*) was the preserve of the closest members of Saddam's tribe and family. Within the General Intelligence (the *Mukhabarat*), Tikritis were also predominant, and through this office made sure that they pervaded the activities of all other governmental and military offices. In the military, the key units of the Special Republican Guard and Republican Guard were traditionally headed by Tikritis and performed the role of protecting the regime against a Sunni coup attempt or insurrection from the Shi'a.[21] The Israeli analyst of Iraqi politics Amatzia Baram estimated that no less than 50 percent of the divisional commanders of the Republican Guard were always Tikritis, Nasiris, or Duris and, quoting a dissident Republican Guard colonel, estimated that by the end of the 1990s over 80 per cent of its officers came from the Tikrit region.

These official structures of security and authority were supplemented by the establishment of informal militia groups including the *Fedayeen Saddam* under the command of Saddam's eldest (and highly volatile) son, Uday. The *Fedayeen* were much derided during the build up to the U.S.-led invasion of Iraq in 2003, yet their training and performance in the field, as they mounted successive and, at times, suicidal attacks against far superior coalition forces, indicated that their allegiance to the regime was perhaps matched equally by their commitment on the battlefield. In the civilian government, the trend was again for Sunni military officers to be appointed even to positions within the Shi'a south. For example, Lieutenant General Mohammad Fayzi al-Haza (a member of the al-Bu Nasir) was governor of Amara until 2000. The governor of Baghdad was Lt. Gen. Sabir al-Duri, and Lt. Gen. Ibrahim Hamash al-Tikriti was governor of Basra.[22] Thus, Saddam placed Tikritis and Sunni loyalists where they mattered most—in the security apparatus of the state, within the key military formations, and in the main institutions of civilian control. The Iraqi government under Saddam was no different on paper than its predecessors in that Sunni dominance remained an overriding characteristic of the state. However, Saddam had merged tribalism with this dominance and weakened the role of the Sunni middle classes by empowering the rural tribes of his homeland of Tikrit.

However, the assumption that the Tikritis (or even the Sunnis) were synonymous with the Ba'ath Party is an exaggeration, and indicates a serious problem in the future if an attempt to rid Iraq of the influence of Saddam is targeted primarily at ridding the country of the Ba'ath Party. Unlike the armed forces and the security apparatus, the Ba'ath Party has been less clearly dominated by Tikritis. At the highest level of the Party (the Regional Leadership), perhaps half of the positions were staffed by Tikritis or Duris, although before the uprisings of 1991, the proportion was much lower.[23] Lower down the Party, the composition of its offices reflected the sectarian makeup of the dominant society. Therefore, at the lower and middle levels, Shi'a members tended to predominate, although overall policy direction was dictated from above. At the highest level, it was Saddam who controlled the Ba'ath, rather than the Ba'ath controlling Saddam, particularly after the purge of the Party that occurred immediately after he assumed the presidency in 1979. In commenting on the weakness of the Ba'ath party, Ofra Bengio notes that "the Ba'ath party has since [1979] been

inexorably neutralized, even castrated, losing its independence and autonomy as a decision-making body as well as its ability to check the president's
power."[24]

The prevalence of the Tikritis within contemporary Iraqi politics is well
documented; however, what is less well recognized is the fact that, with the ascendancy of certain Tikriti families and tribes came the jealousy and antipathy
of other Sunni tribes. Again, the threat posed to Saddam by the Shi'a was a
constant, but remained a potential threat against the whole of Sunni Iraq
rather than toward him directly. But, the internal Sunni threat was personal
and aimed at Saddam. As Amatzia Baram tellingly notes, Saddam's strategy of
tribalizing the political structure of Iraq and placing heightened importance
upon certain powerful tribes cut both ways.[25] The presence of persons in the
most capable military units and most sensitive political positions who had (at
least potentially) stronger ties of loyalty to their own tribe than to Saddam
personally gave them both the power and the opportunity to attempt to overthrow the regime. One of the most notable examples of the Sunni threat came
in the early 1970s. The *Jawa'ina* tribe of the town of Haditha, northwest of
Baghdad, has been a prominent group throughout the history of modern Iraq,
and is part of the Tikriti region (and therefore supposedly part of the Tikriti
support base of Saddam). Saddam's execution of prominent *Jawa'ina* members,
including the air force General Hussein Hiyawi, resulted in the *Jawa'ina* becoming at least partially antipathetic toward the regime.[26] A further example
occurred in January 1990, when Saddam's security forces foiled a coup attempt
led by the powerful *Jubbur* tribe. Dozens of *Jubburi* Republican Guard officers
were executed, and the surviving, terrified *Jubburi* officials were sent to places
where they could pose no further threat to the regime.[27] Even small localized
revolts were enough to ensure Saddam's wrath. The execution of Major General Mohammad Mazlum al-Dulaymi provoked a local revolt of a small part of
the *Dulaym* tribal federation, yet it was crushed ruthlessly as an example to
other Sunni tribes. Saddam was particularly riled by the rebelling *Jubburi* as
they had enjoyed a prominent position within the regime.[28] Baram even suggests that Saddam could not trust his own tribe, the al-Bu Nasir, and cites the
arrest of Saddam's kinsman Lt. Gen. Hamid Sha'ban as indicative of the double-edged sword Saddam created.[29]

## THE SUNNIS SINCE THE DEMISE OF SADDAM

In the aftermath of Saddam's removal from power, Western media coverage
has focused almost entirely on the status of Shi'a and Kurds. Images of Shi'a

religious leaders with flowing robes and beards alongside turban-clad Kurds have been commonplace. However, manifestations of any Sunni political activity were more noticeable by their absence. From being the time-honored preserve of selected Sunni cliques, the Iraqi state is set for a traumatic upheaval. Perhaps the Sunni have accepted the destruction of Saddam's regime as being the death knell of Sunni hegemony in Iraq. Any form of democratic governance that emerges will necessarily reduce the political influence of the numerically inferior Sunnis. Thus the Sunnis have more to lose than most if the U.S.'s bold experiment in democratization succeeds, and therefore have a powerful incentive to ensure that it fails. The Sunni Baghdad–Mosul–Rutba heartland triangle is proving to be the most unruly and dangerous area of the country for U.S. troops. Indeed, great swathes of this area have little if any U.S. presence as it is effectively a "no-go" area for patrols of limited firepower. If the riots and public displays of disobedience against U.S. occupation in Fallujah are any indication of popular opinion, the Sunni heartland has evolved into the primary locus of armed resistance to the continued U.S. presence in Iraq.

Sunni sensitivity remains greatly heightened in the north of the country around Mosul and Kirkuk. The Kurdish occupation of the dangerously unstable city of Kirkuk, and the subsequent election of a Kurdish mayor, did little to assuage Sunni fears that the Kurdish desire to annex Kirkuk as a Kurdish regional capital has diminished. Arab–Kurdish competition in the city remains bloody and fierce, with the U.S. seemingly incapable of establishing peace and stability. Perhaps tensions are even greater in that bastion of Sunni Arab sentiment Mosul. The sight of Barzani's KDP *peshmerga* roaming the streets of the Arab city did little to soothe Sunni concerns and fears.

The most telling days occured when the U.S. administrator for Iraq, Paul Bremer, attempted to implement the much-vaunted de-Ba'athification policy. Using post–World War II Nazi Germany as a rather incongruous model, the plan was to "de-Ba'athify" Iraq in a manner similar to the "de-Nazification" of Germany. The immense numbers associated with this process, combined with the inherent Sunni association of the majority of targets, served to further antagonize the Sunnis. In such an environment of external involvement in the affairs of the state (whether from the U.S. or regional powers), attempted Shi'a dominance of governmental institutions and Kurdish strides toward autonomy and securing Kirkuk, one should have expected that most consistent aspect of Iraq's political history to reemerge—the political and military organization of the Sunni population into a force capable of seizing and securing power and subordinating all other groups. The inherent fragmentary weakness of the

Shi'a remains evident for all to see. The Kurds continue to focus on autonomy but remain seriously internally divided. The Sunni have traditionally been the most politically coherent and organized section of Iraqi society, and there is little to suggest that they will roll over and allow their inheritance to be taken from them and handed to non-Arab Kurds or supposedly pro-Iran Shi'a fundamentalists.

## THE SUNNI: KEY ISSUES

### Legacy of Domination and the Future Role in Iraq

The Sunnis have ruled over the territory that is now Iraq for centuries. In this sense, they are the "natural" rulers of Iraq. But a truly representative democratic government in Iraq, where political power accurately reflects population size, would see the Sunnis reduced to a position of political subservience not just in relation to the Shi'a but also with respect to the Kurds. The most strongly "Arab" part of this majority Arab state will find this difficult to swallow—especially in sensitive cities such as Mosul. Yet this is precisely what will happen if the U.S. succeeds in creating a representative democracy. Sunni Arabs will be expected, virtually overnight, to accede to a process that relegates them to the bottom of the political heap. With the loss of political power, the Sunnis will also lose the power to define and shape the identity of the Iraqi state. Both the Kurds and the Shi'a have much to gain from the dismantling of the existing power hierarchy in Iraq. Only the Sunni have much to lose. Thus, Sunni Arabs have every incentive not to let the U.S. succeed in its mission. The best option at this point for Sunnis is to play the Iraqi nationalism card; to form the core of an organized resistance force dedicated to eliminating the U.S. presence in Iraq. The Kurds have every reason to hope U.S. troops remain in Iraq; the Shi'a lack organizational coherence (unless a charismatic religious leader can provide this), leaving the Sunnis as the most likely source of organized resistance in a post-Saddam Iraq.

In the aftermath of Saddam's removal, the Sunnis have no figure of political authority capable of representing them as a communal group to the Coalition Provisional Authority (CPA) of Bremer. Attempts by Shaikh Zayid (leader of the UAE) in mid-2003 to promote some form of Sunni political leadership by supporting the octogenarian Adnan Pachachi, or the leader of the monarchists, Sharif Ali Bin Al-Hussein, illustrate the lack of political organization amongst the Sunnis in Iraq itself. When faced with the powerful political machinery of the Kurds, and the popular if unwieldy strength of the Shi'a (vocal in their newly found freedom of speech) the Sunnis are very much the underrepresented component of Iraqi society. It is an issue that is perhaps more destabilizing than the current crop of coalition administrators realizes, and the Sunni backlash against occupation and their degraded position in the state could be even more bloody and devastating than it already has been.

## CONCLUSION

The Sunnis, like all other groups in Iraq, were kept in line by a delicately crafted and changeable policy of patronage and coercion, and the closer any group was to the center of power, the more extreme this policy became. As a group the Sunni have often been overlooked by commentators who choose to focus on the more obvious plight of the Kurds and the Shi'a.

However, the position of the Sunnis in Iraq has to be acknowledged as they have been a driving force in the administration of the region, even before the formation of Iraq, for several hundred years. Their regional linkage with other Arab states will also present the architects of a future Iraq with a structural reality that may prove difficult to overcome, particularly if such architects attempt to alter the political coloring of the Iraqi state by introducing representative Kurdish and Shi'a elements into government. Arguably, if Iraq is to be maintained as a territorially integrated unit with government emanating from Baghdad, and no provision is made for the devolution of power to different regions or the partition of the state, it would seem that Iraq must resume its normal state—Sunni dominance with the most stable system of government being dictatorship. Saddam may have been removed only to be replaced by another dictator who also happens to be a Sunni.

## CHAPTER SEVEN

# THE KURDS

## INTRODUCTION

THE HISTORICAL PLIGHT OF THE IRAQI KURDS provides a constant reminder of the artificial nature of the Iraqi state, and the most emotive indicator of the structural problems that have haunted Iraq since its formation. The Iraqi Kurds may be seen in two ways. The first and most common way is to view the Kurds as victims, both of the central government and neighboring powers. The second, almost opposing, position is to see them as an *agent provocateur*, acting as proxy forces for states opposed to the incumbent Iraqi regime.[1] In both cases, it is the fact that Kurds are marginalized geographically and politically within the Iraqi state that has resulted in them being simultaneously victim and provocateur.

At the core of the marginalization of the Kurds in Iraq is the simple fact that they identify themselves primarily as being "Kurdish" and then, maybe, "Iraqi" and certainly not "Arab." Arguably, Kurdish nationalism has been an underrated phenomenon in understanding the tortured development of Iraq. This issue of being a non-Arab people in a state that has been dominated by a succession of strongly Arab nationalist regimes has meant that the Kurds have remained a provincial force, concerned politically with achieving localized autonomy and militarily with gaining control of localities in which Kurds constitute a majority.[2] Because of this non-Arab identity and the provincial focus of Kurdish political aspirations, Kurds rarely have had access to positions of influence within the Arab, Sunni-dominated central government. Furthermore, the Kurds as 25 percent of the Iraqi population have never enjoyed beneficial representation proportionate to their size, but instead have suffered levels of oppression and coercion unacceptable in any moral and ethical sense.

The human cost of keeping the Kurds in the Iraqi state has been horrific. As Kurds sought higher degrees of autonomy, the central government responded with increasingly harsh repressive measures to ensure that the territorial integrity of Iraq was preserved and the authority of the central government over such strategic locations as Kirkuk (with the associated oil fields) was maintained. Indeed, the consciously discriminatory policy of Arabization—whereby non-Arabs (including Kurds, Turcomans, and Assyrians) inhabiting areas of strategic sensitivity or economic importance such as Kirkuk were removed and replaced with Arab settlers—has a history stretching back to a time when Iraq was still under British mandate in the 1920s.[3] In these early formative years of Iraq's history, the British-backed Iraqi government brought in large numbers of Arab workers to satisfy the expanding oil industry of Kirkuk, in addition to settling the area with several large nomadic Arab tribes in the 1930s. Virulent Arabization appeared with the ascendancy of the first Ba'athist government in 1963, and the regime targeted Kurdish national sentiment with brutal ferocity. One event, notable for its terrifying degree of calculation, saw the newly appointed Ba'ath party military commander of Suleimaniyah, General (*Za'eem*) Sadiq Mustafa, execute nearly 100 people in June 1963 who were deemed "Kurdish successes," i.e., the best athletes, the most renowned artists, the most respected teachers. All were potential targets for elimination.[4] Such excesses were not peculiar to the first Ba'athist government. Under Saddam's regime, the Arabization strategy of previous regimes was expanded and intensified. At times, the term "ethnic cleansing" seems a more apt description of what the strategy had become and the Kurds bore the brunt of his actions. Such repression was known to neighboring states and Western powers, but just as it was a straightforward task to arm the Kurds against Saddam, it was similarly not a problem to desert them and leave them to the mercy of a vengeful regime.

This legacy of betrayal culminated in its most grievous and graphic form with the infamous *Anfal* campaign, which witnessed Saddam deploying chemical weapons against civilian Kurds, resulting in several hundred thousand Kurds dead or still missing.[5] Occurring directly after the *Anfal* campaign, though no less grotesque, the destruction of the town of Halabja in March 1988 was just one of the many occasions on which the Kurds suffered the full wrath of the central government. After Kurdish fighters and Iranian forces captured the strategically located town nestled in low hills 70 kilometers southeast of Suleimaniyah, Saddam responded with a murderous mixture of chemical and conventional weapons delivered by artillery and aircraft against the town.

Within the space of minutes, at least 5,000 people lay dead, killed by the devastating effect of cocktails of chemical weapons and nerve agents. If this was not calamitous enough, the long-term impact of this attack is still being felt in the now-populated Halabja, with occurrences of congenital birth defects remaining distinctly high.[6] Weapons supplied by Western nations were used, and Western governments knew of these crimes against humanity, yet no official objections were raised. Sadly, this has been the standard pattern of the West's dealings with the Kurds. When it was deemed advantageous to support the Iraqi government, as in 1988 during its war with Iran, the plight of the Kurds was conveniently ignored. When the Iraqi government was later considered to be a pariah after the 1990 invasion of Kuwait, the Kurdish predicament was exploited to support Western objectives.[7] With such historical precedents the fear is that, with Saddam no longer in power, the Kurds have outlived their political usefulness to the occupying powers. As the dominant mantra of U.S. and U.K. occupation appears to be maintaining the territorial integrity of Iraq and empowering a central government in Baghdad (with no provisions as yet made for the continued existence of Kurdish de facto rule in the north), there are few indications that the cycle of repression will be broken.[8]

Still, times are now perhaps different than in previous years when the West flirted with Kurdish nationalism. The managed partition of Iraq effectively began in 1991 with the evacuation of Iraqi government officials from the north and the subsequent formation of the Kurdish de facto state. For over a decade, the Kurds have governed their own region; held a multiparty democratic election and several rounds of local elections; developed increasingly sophisticated institutions of government embracing legislative, executive, and judicial functions; and dealt with the international community as representatives of their own region independent of Baghdad. Since 1991, Iraqi Kurdistan has been a zone in transition, and one which was arguably steadily improving. From being a repressed, unrepresented people dominated by a strong central government, the Kurds have had the temerity to make a reasonable success out of what is a state in all but name. From the first tentative steps toward independence taken in the wake of the 1990–1991 Gulf War, the Kurds have made momentous progress toward achieving their goal of self-determination—thereby heralding the demise of unitary Iraq.

Perhaps they have been too successful. A problem obviously now exists as to how Iraqi Kurdistan can be cleanly reintegrated into the Iraqi state, while satisfying the autonomous aspirations of the Kurdish parties and people. Indeed, in the runup to the removal of Saddam, Iraqi opposition parties (including Kurds) along with the U.S. administration, had seemingly swallowed political science textbooks, as policy speeches and positional statements became littered with references to "federalism," "democracy," "devolution," and "consociation," all bandied about in an attempt to assure the Kurds that everyone had their interests at heart and that some degree of Kurdish autonomy was acceptable after Saddam's removal. However, it is one thing to espouse high-minded principles in order to create a unified front, but another to implement them on the ground of an Iraq in turmoil. Notions of maintaining Kurdistan within the recognized territorial limits of Iraq, as forwarded by the U.S., the Iraqi opposition, and the Kurds themselves, focus on the decentralization of central state authority and the devolution of power to the Kurds. However, this pattern of a weakened central government devolving power to the Kurds has occurred previously in the history of Iraq, and always been reversed when the central authority has gained enough strength to reexert its authority over the periphery. There is little to suggest that Kurdish conceptions of autonomy correspond with the levels of autonomy the U.S., or any power which ultimately emerges in Baghdad, would be prepared to grant. History, it appears, threatens to repeat itself, with the Kurds once more being seen as provocateur, as they will undoubtedly struggle to maintain their gains, and then as victims, as their autonomy and aspirations are sacrificed in order to secure the authority of a new Iraqi government.

If the Kurds are the perennial victims of the instabilities of Iraq and are now the vanguard of the forces of partition, it is necessary to identify exactly how and why the Kurds are "different" and thereby fail to fit into the construct of the Iraqi state. In addition to acknowledging the ethnic, linguistic, and cultural differences that set Kurds apart from Arabs, key moments in the painful history of the Kurds need to be addressed in order to understand the trauma that has tainted the Kurdish experience in Iraq. Since 1991, the unthinkable and supposedly unworkable has become a reality: an increasingly impressive "nation-state," dominated by one of the three main components of Iraqi society has emerged in the north of "sovereign" Iraq. Iraqi Kurdistan possesses almost all of the attributes—clearly demarcated territory, a functioning governmental system, and a monopoly over the legitimate use of coercive force—commonly associated with the concept of statehood.[9] Arguably, the partition of Iraq began over a decade ago with the creation of a separate state in the north.

## WHO ARE THE KURDS?

The Kurds are an ancient Indo-European people, ethnically distinct from their Arab, Turkic, and Iranian neighbors. They speak their own language (Kurdish, with several dialects) and have a proud cultural tradition distinct from that of their neighbors.[10] Descended from the Medes (a people mentioned in the Old Testament of the Bible), the Kurds live in the landlocked mountains and high plateaus of the Zagros, Taurus, and Pontiac ranges astride the current and artificial borders of Iraq, Iran, Turkey, and Syria. The inability of neighboring powers to access the high mountain regions enabled the Kurds to preserve their unique culture and way of life. But the curse historically has been the presence of oil under the plains to the south of the mountains; oil has attracted intrusions in the past and continues to be a geopolitical focus today.

The majority of Kurds (at least 75 percent) are Sunni Muslims (the majority religion in the Middle East). Approximately 15 percent are Shi'a Muslims, (the dominant religion of Iran), with the remaining 10 percent following a variety of ancient religions including Yezidi-ism (a syncretistic religion) and ancient Zoroastrian-based creeds. These religions predate the monotheistic religions of Judaism, Christianity, and Islam and adherents are found across Asia, with some of their spiritual centers being in Iraqi Kurdistan.

The Kurds, in terms of population size at least, are significant, although it is impossible to obtain accurate demographic figures for Kurds from the countries in which they reside for political reasons. They number perhaps as many as 25 million people, spread through Turkey (12 million), Iraq (5 million), Iran (6 million), Syria (1 million), the Former Soviet Union (1 million), and with at least 1 million living overseas in Europe, North America, and Australia as part of the Kurdish diaspora.[11] As such, they constitute the fourth-largest ethnic group in the region (after Arabs, Turks, and Iranians) but do not have a state of their own. In the Middle East, the Arabs have several Arab states, the Turks have a Turkish state (and there are several other "Turkic" states in Central Asia), the Jews have the state of Israel, and the Iranians have one of the longest-running "states" in history. There is no comparable entity named Kurdistan. The gains made by 3 million Palestinians are far greater than those made by nearly 30 million Kurds. Another artificial state, Yugoslavia, has been deconstructed into its component entities, and tiny Kosovo has been deemed a necessary addition to the political map. Yet the Kurds, as the largest stateless people in the world, remain without a national homeland. This injustice is, and will increasingly be, a major destabilizing force in the volatile politics of the Middle East.

## SOCIAL AND POLITICAL CONTEXT

The social and political organization of the Iraqi Kurds reflects the tensions of a traditional (and at times isolated) people who have been exposed to the forces of modernity at a rather late moment in their history. Originally semi-pastoral nomads, the traditional structure of Kurdish social and political organization was inherently tribal. The tribe was a sociopolitical unit with territorial limits based upon kinship and descent.[12] Kinship was effectively the defining feature of tribal membership, but it was apparent that as tribal groups expanded divisions also appeared, so that many Kurdish tribes may trace their origins to separations from other larger tribes. Combined with kinship was the mechanism of patrimonial leadership, whereby the control and authority of the tribal head was predominant. A further feature of Kurdish tribalism was derived from the distinctive topography that shaped Kurdish activities. The fissured nature of Kurdish geography, with its high mountains and deep valleys, meant that interaction between tribes was relatively limited, allowing each to develop with a certain degree of isolation from the others. From this isolationist conditioning, Kurdish tribes (and, arguably, the Kurdish tribal mindset) have remained exclusive entities, which compete among themselves and are historically slow to embrace change. However, the history of Iraq in the twentieth century is one of having change thrust upon it.

The effects of modernity upon what had been a tribal sociopolitical system brought with it associated stresses and strains. The preeminence of the tribes in northern Iraq was countered by the expanding urban centers of Erbil and especially Suleimaniyah. These cities became focal points for the development of class-based political groupings influenced increasingly by left-wing political ideals. It was this division between the tribal sociopolitical groups in the mountains, complete with their unquestioning loyalty to their tribal heads, and the left-wing nontribal urbanites who attempted to promote ideals of socialism (and nationalism) that became the major faultline running through Kurdish politics today.

While the Kurds are the largest ethnically distinct group in the world to remain stateless, their ability to promote a unified identity has historically failed. Confronted by the national interests of the states in which they reside, with inept and fractured political leadership and a lack of a cohesive identity crossing the imposed boundaries of the Middle East, Kurdish nationalism has been too weak to flourish alongside the more organized nationalist agendas of the Turkish, Iranian, or Iraqi states. To break the Kurds, states with dominion over parts of the Kurdish region have often resorted to violence, and nowhere has this been more apparent than in Saddam's Iraq. The West has a long history of selective blindness toward atrocities committed against the Kurds. The Kurds indeed have always been victims of prevailing geopolitical realities, such as the perceived threat posed by Iran to the Persian Gulf region, or the power of the Iraqi economy fueled by its petroleum reserves. The sad fact is that, in this era when Tony Blair speaks of an "ethical foreign policy" and George W. Bush emphasizes the democratic rights of Iraqis, the natural oil formations of Iraqi Kurdistan and the interests of neighboring, reactionary states remain as influential in the foreign policies of major powers today as they were in the formation of Iraq nearly a century ago.

## THE DEVELOPMENT OF THE KURDISH NATIONAL MOVEMENT IN IRAQ, 1918–1991

The recent history of the Kurds in Iraq (since 1991) would strongly suggest that they are a people with a high degree of communal identity who are seeking to become an institutional reality at least within the future Iraqi state, if not beyond.[13] The history of the Iraqi Kurds has been dominated by an existential struggle against the overwhelming power of a Sunni Arab-dominated Iraqi state, intent on consolidating the territorial integrity of the country and the position of the Sunnis within it. Saddam was by no means unique in his attempts to quell the rebellious Kurds. He simply was willing to resort to greater and more brutal levels of violence than were his predecessors. It is therefore useful to chart the uneasy development of Kurdish nationalism in Iraq throughout the history of the Iraqi state, identifying the preeminent figures in its development up to the post-1991 period. The period after 1991 has to be treated separately as, to all intents and purposes, Iraqi Kurdistan became a separate country and the characteristics of its political movements changed as Kurdistan increasingly became an institutionalized region with an indigenous Kurdish government.

Throughout the modern history of Iraq, Kurdish political activity has often been complex and confusing. Parties, tribes, movements, militia, socioeconomic groupings, and religious beliefs have interacted with foreign intervention and personal squabbles—resulting in a volatile and frequently violent brand of political activity. Allies could turn to enemies seemingly at the blink of an eye, and, conversely, the most entrenched opponents became amicable partners when the need arose. However, a constant feature of Kurdish political life has been the lack of ability of Kurdish leaders to translate easily stated notions of Kurdish nationalism into real political and military solidarity on the ground when dealing with Baghdad. Instead, Kurdish parties chose to use their limited forces to fight each other in parochial internal competition for leadership of the Kurdish national movement in Iraq. Such fighting was destructive in an immediate material sense, and in a longer-term political sense as Baghdad took advantage of these natural faultlines in Kurdish politics. Kurdish "successes" in Iraq were often merely the success of one party or group over its competitors, with the actual relationship between the Kurds and Baghdad changing little in terms of securing any form of autonomy. However, with U.S.-led regime change, the Kurds were thrown into the limelight and the different Kurdish leaders and organizations were suddenly regular features on the international news; Jalal Talabani and Massoud Barzani (the leaders of the Patriotic Union of Kurdistan [PUK] and the Kurdistan Democratic Party [KDP] respectively) became convenient examples of progressive political leaders proving that Iraqis could be democratic and peaceloving, given half a chance. Parochial concerns were seemingly suspended as Kurdish leaders, unaccustomed to intense media attention, attempted to appear unified and sincere in their quest to remove Saddam.

How real is this rapprochment is and how successful the Kurdish de facto state in the north of Iraq has been need to be assessed. As the Kurdish parties are now one of the most powerful forces (if not the most powerful) within the post-Saddam environment, it is necessary to understand the political history of conflict and rivalry that still colors the actions of the major parties and politicians, and how the ideology of Kurdish nationalism developed throughout the mid-twentieth century in an Iraq that ruled its Kurdish minority more through violence than by patronage.

## State Formation and the Kurds in the Aftermath of World War One

In the aftermath of World War I, Kurdistan was a pawn on the chessboard of the great powers. Hopes of an independent Kurdistan, which had been hinted at by the British, were dashed as regional geopolitical concerns proved to be more pressing for the victorious British and the reconsolidating Turkey. After early hopes of an independent Kurdistan emerging from the ashes of the Ottoman Empire, the opposition of Ataturk in Turkey, combined with the fragmentary nature of Kurdish political leadership and the machinations of the British, meant that Kurdistan was divided by imposed political borders into its contemporary segments. The necessity of producing a viable political entity from the southern Mesopotamian region (the *vilayets* of Basra and Baghdad) led the British to betray their previous promises of autonomy to the Kurds and effectively saw the Kurdish northern region joined with Baghdad and Basra to form Iraq. Behind this decision was a combination of political, military, and economic considerations. Even at this point, the British were keen that Iraq be dominated by Sunnis rather than by the Shi'a, even if they were forced to identify Kurds as Sunnis; militarily, Mesopotamia could be defended from the mountains far more easily than from the plains; and, most significantly, there were indications of large oil reserves under Kurdish territory at Kirkuk.

This "viable" political entity turned out to be viable only to the extent that the central government was prepared to use coercion to tame the rebellious Kurds. The methods employed by the British to deal with the Kurds in the post–World War I period set the blueprint for successive Iraqi regimes to follow and refine. The British first attempted to co-opt the Kurds into the Iraqi state by seeking the allegiance of powerful tribal leaders through the recognition and enhancement of their localized power structures. Financial aid was given to tribal leaders, and military support was offered in order to ensure the compliance of key tribes. The goal, of course, was to maintain British control over Kurdish territory. But as the local power of various Sheikhs strengthened and the unwillingness of the British to cede further authority became apparent, the central government and their British sponsors turned to the tools of coercion in order to control their headstrong creations. The most famous of these earlier Kurdish figures was Sheikh Mahmoud Barzinji of Suleimaniyah. A prominent tribal chief, Sheikh Mahmoud was cultivated by the British to act as local governor of the region. However, when he began to entertain notions of national leadership and royalty, the British turned to aerial bombing and the gassing of villages to deter him.[14] This pattern characterized the relationship between Baghdad and Iraqi Kurdistan for the remainder of the century. However, as the ability to "buy" Kurdish support was heightened by the increased oil revenue, the same wealth also enabled Baghdad to undertake increasingly grievous military assaults against the Kurds.

The empowerment and reinvigoration of the tribal political structure in Kurdistan, with prominent *Aghas* (chieftains of tribes) placed in positions of authority throughout the region, was not only a source of concern for the British and Iraqi governments. Tribal leadership may have been acceptable to many Kurds, but it occurred at a time of social upheaval in Iraq and Kurdistan and many resented the self-proclaimed position and associated authority of the tribes.[15] Fueled by the success of the communist revolution in Russia, a new class of nontribal, educated professionals was emerging in the rapidly expanding towns and cities of Iraqi Kurdistan. The aftermath of World War I therefore saw two dynamics emerge, both products of British intervention. First, "southern" Kurdistan was incorporated into Iraq for reasons external to the Kurds themselves and placed under Arab government at a time of emerging Kurdish nationalism. Second, the British empowerment of tribal notables created tension within Kurdistan as a new nontribal political class was emerging in the cities. The legacies of both these dynamics are still apparent in today's Iraq.

## The Formation of the Kurdistan Democratic Party

The rise of Kurdish nationalism in Iraq and the inherent division between the tribes and urbanites came together in the formation of the KDP.[16] The KDP is the oldest and most established of the Iraqi Kurdish political entities, with other key parties, including the later PUK, forming from divisions within the KDP itself. The KDP was formed in 1946 and reflected the growing Kurdish nationalist sentiment that emerged in Iraq in the aftermath of World War I. Based on the earlier Iranian KDP (KDP-I), the KDP was from the outset an uneasy alliance between the tribes and the urban intelligentsia. Each side had different leaders, with the tribes under the control of the most influential tribal head of the time, Mulla Mustafa Barzani, and the intelligentsia under the sway of intellectuals, such as the poet Ibrahim Ahmed and later his protégé Jalal Talabani. It was an uneasy relationship, bringing together two groups that had little in common ideologically. For example, the urban left considered the tribes to be reactionary and feudal, benefiting a few important leaders at the expense of the masses. Thus, they favored policies that aimed to redistributing land equitably—a stance that was clearly threatening to the interests of prominent tribal leaders whose political influence was directly related to the quantity of territory under their control.

However, irrespective of the divergent class-based interests, both groups needed each other. Mulla Mustafa had secured a position of importance within the Kurdish national movement in Iraq as an inspirational leader fighting for the interests of his people in the inhospitable mountains of the north. His legendary ability to withstand the military onslaughts of the Iraqi government meant that he occupied a place of respect and admiration in the hearts and minds of the tribal (and some of the urbanite) Kurds. He was, in effect, a natural rallying point—a charismatic figurehead granting moral legitimacy to any Kurdish political movement. However, the popular power base of the Kurds was increasingly urbanized, and the methods and experience of the politicized intelligentsia became increasingly significant as organized political activity developed. The intelligentsia was dominated by Kurds from the Suleimaniyah region, or those resident in the major cities of Iraq, including Baghdad. Chief among these were Ibrahim Ahmed, followed by Jalal Talabani. Ahmed was an educated, urbanized Kurd, devoid of tribal sentiment and with strong social democratic convictions. His experience as the Iraq operations coordinator of the KDP-I in the early 1940s, combined with his skill in organizing political forces, gave him the necessary organizational skills and ideological background to mobilize the left wing of the Iraqi Kurds.

Mulla Mustafa therefore provided the legitimacy and Ahmed provided the organizational skills and knowledge of how to operate in the urban and national setting. For the Kurdish national movement to develop beyond small-scale tribal revolts and limited pamphleteering in the cities, Mulla Mustafa formed an uneasy alliance with the urban intelligentsia of Ibrahim Ahmed. This union was all the more pressing because the tribes and the intelligentsia occupied distinct geographical areas. The tribes loyal to Mulla Mustafa were located in the northwest of Iraqi Kurdistan, in the high mountainous areas, whereas the intelligentsia was mainly centered in the cities of Suleimaniyah, Kirkuk and, to a lesser extent, Erbil. Thus the KDP was formed, with Mulla Mustafa as its President. Initially, he attempted to dominate the Party by appointing a pliant leftist as Secretary General, Hamza Abdullah. However, with the collapse of the Kurdish Mahabad Republic in Iran in 1947 and the subsequent exile of Mulla Mustafa to the USSR, Ibrahim Ahmed was elected Secretary General in 1951 and the Party became dominated by the intelligentsia.[17]

## Toward Division

The Iraqi monarchy was overthrown in 1958 by Abdel Karim Qassim. After utilizing the support of the KDP in the coup d'etat, Qassim quickly pursued policies designed to divide the political strength of the Kurds. Soon after assuming power, he enacted a series of agricultural reforms designed to weaken the interests of the major landowning tribes. As a consequence, the alliance between the tribes and the urbanites was shattered. The landowning tribes, recognizing the military power of the Barzanis, reached an agreement with Mulla Mustafa that pitted the Barzanis against the Iraqi government in return for the support of the major Kurdish tribes. Conversely, the Kurdish unions (farmers, engineers, and so on) pledged their allegiance to the KDP of Ahmed and Talabani as it was in their interests to accept Qassim's policy and weaken the feudal system that characterized Kurdistan at the time.[18] By 1960, Iraqi Kurdistan was in turmoil. The KDP Political Bureau continued to recognize the leadership of Mulla Mustafa out of political necessity, yet the radicalization of the tribes caused by the agricultural reforms fomented a crisis between the Kurds and Baghdad, and the KDP was implicated by association. After Qassim rejected a joint proposal from Mulla Mustafa and the KDP regarding Kurdish rights in March 1961, Mulla Mustafa issued a proclamation to all Kurds to take up arms against the forces of Iraq—effectively signaling the commencement of the Kurdish Revolution in Iraq—on September 11.

After the February 1963 coup d'etat that removed Qassim and briefly gave the Ba'ath Party the reins of power in Baghdad, Mulla Mustafa accepted policies on behalf of the Kurdish people without the prior consent of the KDP Political Bureau. Most contentiously, he accepted a cease-fire without Political Bureau involvement and then further accepted an alliance with the Ba'ath regime, which allowed the unopposed return of government forces to the region and abolished political parties (including the KDP) while allowing the tribes to continue with their activities. This period heralds the appearance of a seemingly irrevocable political split between the tribes and the intelligentsia. The policies of Baghdad and Mulla Mustafa's acceptance of them resulted in the urban nationalists splitting from the tribal leadership, and this tit-for-tat squabbling did little to enhance the strength-in-unity of the Kurdish national movement.

By the time the Ba'ath assumed power for the second time (in 1968), Mulla Mustafa was the preeminent political force in the region, and his unopposed authority over northern Iraq forced the Ba'ath regime to negotiate with him. The Vice President of Iraq and future Kurdish nemesis himself, Saddam Hussein, traveled to Kurdistan and met with Mulla Mustafa. At the time, concerned about the stability of the nascent Ba'ath regime and the destabilizing effect Mulla Mustafa could have on Iraqi politics, the Ba'ath were prepared to grant more or less anything to ensure their own survival. Indeed, Saddam presented Mulla Mustafa with blank sheets of paper on which the Kurdish leader could write his demands. Saddam took back to Baghdad a deal that was the best ever offered to the Iraqi Kurds, known as the March Agreement. It was a lesson in humility Saddam would neither forgive nor forget.

The March Agreement saw the inclusion of five Kurds in the cabinet of Iraq. The Kurdish language was permitted in official discourse, and Kurdish language publications were legalized. Outstanding problems included the status of Kirkuk and the mechanism by which the autonomous area would be identified. While the Ba'ath was effectively playing for time, the Kurds grasped the opportunities presented to them with both hands. One of the Kurdish negotiators of the March Agreement and Minister of Northern Affairs in the reconstituted Iraqi government, and later influential political actor in the *de facto* state of the 1990s, Sami Abdul Rahman described the 1970–1974 period covered by the March Agreement as a "golden era." During these years, the Kurds learnt the skills of local administration and direct governance, skills that were to prove useful in the 1990s.[19] The agreement, however, was short-lived. As the Ba'ath regime steadily solidified its power base, Mulla Mustafa became increasingly antagonistic toward Baghdad. The Ba'ath had little incentive to accede to Kurdish territorial demands, and Mulla Mustafa had no option but to either concede or seek support from outside. Ever the proud leader, he chose the latter option. The Kurds refused to seal their border with Iran, appealed to the U.S. for aid, and accepted support from Israel. Faced with the possible involvement of the Kurds with three rivals of the regime, the Iraqi government again resorted to its proven tools of manipulation. In 1974, the Ba'ath went ahead with the implementation of a watered-down version of the March Agreement (named the Autonomy Law), and negotiated its acceptance not with Mulla Mustafa, but with 600 anti-Barzani Kurds, including those of the Ahmed-Talabani faction. Mulla Mustafa rejected the Autonomy Law and prepared to fight Baghdad once again, expecting the support of Iran to see him through. With the benefit of hindsight, it comes as no surprise that the strategy failed.

In what is perhaps the prime example of the naïveté that characterised the approach of the Kurds toward the subtleties of diplomacy and the speed with which deals could be done and undone, Saddam pulled the rug from under their feet. On March 6, 1975, at the Organization of Petroleum Exporting Countries (OPEC) Conference in Algiers, Saddam and the Shah of Iran settled all outstanding differences, and both agreed to maintain border security. The lifeline of the Kurdish *peshmerga* of Mulla Mustafa was destroyed. Barzani called an end to the Kurdish Revolution on March 23, 1975 and sought refuge in Iran, never to return alive to Iraqi Kurdistan. The KDP was removed as a political force and the Iraqi government moved quickly to secure its hold on Kurdistan. It seemed that the struggle for a Kurdish entity in Iraq had been weakened by the inherent inability of the tribalists and urban intelligentsia to present a unified front, as well as the ability of Baghdad to exploit their divisions.

Determined not to have the ethnic status of Kirkuk questioned in the future, the government embarked upon a comprehensive campaign aimed at altering the demographic characteristics of the whole of Iraqi Kurdistan, including Erbil, Dohuk, and Suleimaniyah, but especially Kirkuk. Rural settlements were erased and the population rehoused in purpose-built settlements close to urban areas. The government even gerrymandered the administrative boundaries of Kirkuk to ensure that Arabs were a majority in the key areas of the city, and Kirkuk province was renamed "*Al-Tame'em*" (which translates as "nationalization") to give it a more Arab nationalist flavor. Human Rights Watch estimates that several hundred thousand non-Arabs were evicted from northern locations and removed to desert locations in southern Iraq or in camps along major roads between 1976 and 1986.[20]

The early 1970s, culminating in 1975, was therefore a watershed period for the Kurdish national movement in Iraq. The period had seen the Kurds enjoy the highest levels of autonomy and political development to date, yet exposed their inexperience when dealing with the external states and their weakness when dealing with the Ba'ath regime. After seemingly having secured autonomous rights in Kurdistan, the grail was lost and Saddam politically outmaneuvered the Kurds with ease, forcing the "immortal" Mulla Mustafa into early retirement.[21]

## The Formation of the Patriotic Union of Kurdistan

Mulla Mustafa's demise left the field wide open for leftwing political leaders, typified by Jalal Talabani and other KDP figures, to stretch their political wings and resurrect the revolution. Mulla Mustafa's sons, Idris and Massoud, continued to head the KDP, though in exile in Iran, but their dominance was now challenged by a new wave of political leaders. Of particular significance was the emergence of new left-wing groups, including the Maoist-inspired *Komala* (brotherhood) dominated by Nawshirwan Mustafa Amin with the support of Talabani, and the Social Democratic *Bezutnawa* (Movement) led by the charismatic Ali Askari. These two formations combined under the leadership of Talabani to form the PUK on June 1, 1975. The PUK was significantly different from the KDP. It did not recognize the preordained right of any tribe to head the Kurdish national movement in Iraq and was openly disdainful of the role played by the Barzanis, blaming them for the failure to secure Kurdish autonomy. The support base of the PUK was in the urban centers of Iraqi Kurdistan—especially in Suleimaniyah, Erbil, and Kirkuk—but the party also had a considerable following amongst the Kurdish population of Baghdad.

The mid-1970s saw Iraqi Kurdistan packed with new political-military organizations vying for power, influence, and territory in what was a veritable pressure cooker of internecine competition. On occasions, the inherent internal divisions erupted into open violence. In a vicious skirmish in 1978, for example, the PUK lost perhaps their most able politician when Ali Askari was captured and executed in Hakkari by KDP forces under the leadership of Sami Abdul Rahman. The loss of what was the moderate wing of the PUK (*Komala* was far more radical) created a political imbalance within the PUK, which Talabani had to manage; its repercussions are still being felt today, as indicated by the fact that the majority of PUK leaders emanate from the far left and all originated from *Komala*.

The KDP also displayed serious internal instability. In a situation reminiscent of the old Mulla Mustafa–Ibrahim Ahmed disagreements, Sami Abdul Rahman espoused his own leftist principles and fell foul of Mulla Mustafa's tribally minded son Idris Barzani. The KDP again split in the late 1970s, with Abdul Rahman leading his intelligentsia away to form the Kurdistan Popular Democratic Party (KPDP) in opposition to the KDP, but in no way friendly toward the PUK. In addition, Islamist groups found new popular support as Kurds became disillusioned with tribalism, the KDP, and the leftist agenda of Talabani. The perceived success of the Islamic Revolution in Iran in 1979 was an impetus for the establishment and development of Iraqi Kurdish Islamist organizations, including the Islamic Movement of Kurdistan (IMK) of Sheikh Othman Abdul Aziz and, succeeding him, his brother Mulla Ali Abdul Aziz. The growing fragmentation of Kurdish politics precluded the emergence of a united front with which to confront the Ba'ath regime in Baghdad. It also allowed the Iraqi Kurds to be manipulated by a succession of neighboring powers, who used the political fragmentation of the Kurds to fund and support different groups against Saddam. Similarly, Saddam supported various Kurdish groups to fight against their fellow Kurds, transforming the north of Iraq into a zone of civil war and proxy intervention rolled up into one nightmarish flashpoint. But, for the Kurds, the nightmare was about to turn a great deal more terrifying.

## Genocide and Reprieve

Following the Islamic Revolution in Iran in 1979, Saddam Hussein seized the opportunity to strike a mortal blow at Iran and regain the territorial concessions given away under the Algiers Agreement of 1975. On September 22, 1980 Saddam launched his offensive against Iran, and the Kurds found themselves located in a war zone and being forced by circumstance to fight as proxies. Both Iraq and Iran supported different formations of Kurdish parties against each other throughout the 1980s, but, more often than not, the Kurds found themselves fighting alongside the forces of Iran. Facing resurgent Iranian/Kurdish activity in the north of Iraq, Saddam adopted draconian measures to remove permanently the threat posed by the persistently rebellious Kurds to his regime.

Saddam authorized the *Anfal* campaign, which planned for the systematic depopulation of rural Iraqi Kurdistan in order to remove the *peshmerga* presence from the region, and to deny to the Kurdish parties the facilities to resurrect and maintain a military presence. The campaign, pursued with enthusiastic brutality by Saddam's cousin Ali Hassan Al-Majid, who became known as

"Chemical Ali" through his infamous activities, saw Iraqi forces laying waste to approximately 4,000 Kurdish villages with conventional and chemical weapons.[22] The rural population was "processed" and rehoused (though a great many were simply executed) in designated collective settlements (*mujama'at*) positioned near major urban centers and military garrisons. In March 1988, Saddam committed what many consider to be his ultimate crime by bombarding the city of Halabja with chemical weapons and nerve agents after PUK and Iranian forces had occupied the area. At least 5,000 civilians died in a matter of hours in what was the most devastating use of unconventional weapons against a civilian population since World War II.

By 1990, the Kurds were at their lowest ebb. The *Anfal* campaign had devastated the *peshmerga* and the rural areas of Iraqi Kurdistan had been depopulated. Politically, the KDP was weakened by its internal divisions and the PUK was recovering from its own ideological headaches of promoting either pure "communism" or following nationally orientated "socialism." The presence of both parties within Iraqi Kurdistan was limited; instead, they had to operate out of Iran. It seemed that the glories of the 1970 autonomy period were totally out of reach—yet autonomy and virtual independence was about to be thrust upon the Kurds when they were at their most devastated and politically fractured.

Saddam's miscalculated advance into Kuwait in 1990 began a sequence of events that would culminate with the formation of a Kurdish de facto state and the first stage of the managed partition of Iraq. Following the expulsion of Iraqi forces from Kuwait by the forces of the Allied coalition in early 1991, popular uprisings occurred in the north and south of Iraq. In Iraqi Kurdistan, the Kurdish uprising commenced in Raniyah on March 4, and soon spread to the major Kurdish population centers. As the scale of the event became clear, forces from the KDP and PUK assumed control of the insurgency. By March 19, southern Kurdistan was under Kurdish control for the first time since 1970 and, arguably, since the inclusion of Kurdistan into Iraq nearly 70 years previously.[23]

Again, however, as in the post–World War I period, the West and neighboring powers were not prepared to see the Kurdish region exist independent from Baghdad. The uprisings of the Kurds and Shi'a in 1991 were perhaps met with more fear in Washington and London than they were in Baghdad. It became painfully clear that the fall of Saddam had not been envisaged and was not an acceptable outcome to the situation. The West preferred a return to the "old days," a pre-Kuwait status quo, and certainly not a new political order that had space to spare for an independent Kurdistan. The triumph of the Kurds and Shi'a was therefore short-lived as the expected Allied support failed to materialize. Saddam moved his Republican Guard into the rebellious areas and, from March 28 onward, the Kurds were forced out of the major cities and into the mountains bordering Iran and Turkey. Kirkuk, once again, was ravaged by government forces keen to erase the non-Arab coloring of the city. As noted by Human Rights Watch, the Kurdish exodus from Kirkuk following the 1991 uprising turned into permanent displacement, which would require nothing less than the removal of Saddam to rectify.[24]

By the beginning of April, news channels were broadcasting scenes of deprivation and human suffering on an immense scale in the Zagros mountains. Men, women, and children were shown huddled together, freezing to death as Turkish (NATO) soldiers looked on, the U.S. military seemingly impotent in its ability to assist. On April 5, the UN Security Council passed Resolution 688 demanding an end to the repression of citizens in Iraq, but, on the ground, the numbers of refugees continued to swell. The Allies attempted to resolve the problem by establishing a small "safe haven" near Dohuk on April 18. However, it was a month too late, as approximately 1 million Kurds had reached the Turkish border by the end of the month, with more on the way.[25] Even though Saddam had been devastated by his defeat in Kuwait and had lost control of 15 out of Iraq's 18 provinces, the Kurdish leadership had no alternative but to seek an accommodation with the regime in order to curtail the humanitarian catastrophe occurring in the mountains.

Both sides were weak. Saddam could not adequately garrison the north, nor continue to fund its civilian operation from the depleted coffers of Baghdad. The Kurds lacked the strength to eliminate the presence of central government forces from the region. The result was a stalemate, with the status of Kirkuk once again proving to be an insurmountable obstacle to securing an acceptable peace between the government and the Kurds. In October, Saddam removed all offices of the government from the north and imposed an economic blockade against Iraqi Kurdistan, leaving a vacuum that paralysed the civil administration of approximately 4 million people.[26] However, Kirkuk remained firmly under the control of Baghdad, and, with the U.S. no-fly zone being located several miles north of Kirkuk, Saddam was free to continue with the tried-and-tested techniques of Arabization.

The de facto state was thus born. To say that its birth had occurred under traumatic circumstances is something of an understatement. Yet this anomalous entity survived and developed institutions of government that served the Kurds in an increasingly efficient manner. The reasons for its birth can be found in the geopolitical peculiarities of Iraq at the time. The weakness of Saddam, combined with the desperation of the Kurdish people and the attention of the international community, facilitated the emergence of a Kurdish-controlled Kurdistan. In effect, the Kurds secured their traditional demands for self-government by precipitous and dangerous accident, rather than by conscious and planned design.

## THE DEVELOPMENT OF THE KURDISH NATIONAL MOVEMENT IN IRAQ, 1991–2003

It is perhaps to be expected that the sudden appearance of "Iraqi Kurdistan" as a de facto state caused considerable consternation in Ankara and Tehran. Western capitals were similarly perplexed as they were faced with diplomatic envoys from the new entity requesting bilateral assistance, seeking the support of the West in removing Saddam from power, and pledging a commitment to establishing a pluralistic democratic government in northern Iraq as the first stage in implementing federalism across the whole of the country. It was, perhaps, too much too soon for Western politicians to accept unreservedly. The appearance and survival of the new de facto state was also something of an embarrassment for Baghdad, where Saddam's regime had expected the leadership of the fractious Kurds to capitulate to its authority rather than confront the burden of administrating an area and people devastated by war and facing an uncertain future. However, survive is what the fledgling entity did, although its early years were made as difficult as possible by the activities of Ankara, Tehran, and Baghdad.

### The Formation of Kurdish Government

The concerns of regional powers were heightened after May 19, 1992 when the Iraqi Kurds held regional elections and formed the Kurdistan National Assembly (KNA). The results of the election directly reflected the divisions endemic within Kurdish society since the mid-twentieth century. There was an almost equal divide between the KDP and PUK, with both parties securing close to 50 percent of the seats in the KNA, while the Assyrians were allocated the remaining 5 of the 105-seat unicameral assembly. With the major parties evenly matched, a "50–50" power-sharing system was adopted in which key executive positions of government were shared. Massoud Barzani (by now undisputed President of the KDP) and Jalal Talabani (Secretary-General of the PUK) remained outside the offices of government, but acted as arbiters of the political system from their respective party political bureaus.[27] The political system displayed dangerous structural instability, and the survival of the

Kurdistan Regional Government (KRG) was directly dependent upon the maintenance of cooperation between the KDP and PUK. However, faced with a potentially operational state system in Iraqi Kurdistan, neighboring powers embarked in earnest on undermining the already tenuous stability by encouraging or coercing the KDP and PUK into political (and, at times, military) acts against each other. By 1993, the de facto state was in danger of being ripped apart by the political machinations of Turkey, Iran, and Iraq.

Of course, neither the KDP nor the PUK were wholly innocent as Iraqi Kurdistan descended into the depths of civil war. Both parties maintained their mutual antipathy and competed for resources, influence, and prestige, with the struggling KRG being the theatre in which their fight was enacted. Massoud Barzani, as the son of the legendary Mulla Mustafa, the head of perhaps the most powerful tribal formation in the region, and the undisputed leader of the most established Kurdish political party, viewed his right to lead the Kurdish national movement in Iraq as irrefutable. Similarly, Jalal Talabani, with his long history of involvement with the Kurdish cause as perhaps the prime political activist of his generation, with extraordinary skills of political manipulation, and with control of a burgeoning, vibrant political party with urban (and, increasingly, mass) roots, believed that he was the rightful heir to the leadership of the Iraqi Kurds. With the 50–50 power sharing system effectively making the Kurdish governmental system moribund, the two parties carved out mutually exclusive cliques within the structures of the new government with the PUK Prime Minister, Kosrat Rasoul—a figure of immense standing within the PUK and almost certainly the leader-in-waiting—promoting figures close to him to positions of authority, and the KDP maintaining its hold on the national assembly with the speaker being Jawher Namiq (from the KDP's political bureau). The KDP also maintained its control over the key revenue-generating point at the Turkish border near Zakho, thereby ensuring that it had direct access to resources that were not available to the PUK. KRG security services became proxies for the two parties, with each spying on the other, and Kurdish government became totally unable to deal with the serious problems afflicting the region because the focus of politicians, bureaucrats, and civil servants was on defeating their power-sharing partners.

Beyond these differences, the animosity that continued to exist between the KDP and PUK had few other causative factors. Ideological differences were minimal; both parties had moved to the center of the political spectrum and attempted to portray themselves as moderate leftists (albeit with a belief in the preeminence of the Barzanis on the KDP side). With undisputed leadership of the Kurdish national movement in Iraq as the prize, the competition between the two political organizations remained inherently personal and focused on basic disagreements such as access to resources and domestic political petty squabbling.

If this personal rivalry was not enough to rip Iraqi Kurdistan apart (which it certainly was), the political economy of Iraq in the 1990s meant that there was now a new dynamic introduced into the competition—control of illegal Iraqi oil shipments and the associated revenue. Saddam had established an oil-smuggling route through territory controlled by the KDP, with the active involvement of senior Barzani family members. The taxation of this trade at the crossing point between Saddam's territory and Kurdish-controlled territory, and then into Turkey, along with associated service revenue, meant that whoever controlled Dohuk and Zakho had the potential to earn several million dollars a week. It was a prize the now wealthy KDP was not going to relinquish, and one that the increasingly impoverished PUK needed to maintain any sort of financial (and therefore military) parity with the strengthened KDP.

## From Unity to Division

The combination of internal and external pressure was simply too much for the Kurdish political system to bear, and the task of destabilizing it proved to be reasonably straightforward. By 1994, four-way meetings were taking place between representatives of Iraq, Iran, Turkey, and Syria. At the top of the agenda was the *de facto* Kurdish entity and how to ensure its demise. The inherent structural competition that existed within the KRG meant that descent into conflict required little more than a push here and a spark there—and within the territory there was certainly no shortage of either. By 1994, a bitter civil war had erupted between the KDP and PUK, which was as much about securing revenue for the parties as it was about leadership of the Kurdish national movement.

Concomitant with this intra-Kurdish melee, new political actors and agendas also appeared. Political Islam had been a powerful variable in Iraqi politics for many decades, and Kurdistan had its fair share of Islamist political parties. Some of these parties, including the Islamic Movement of Kurdistan (IMK), had formed as early as the late 1970s and had fought against Saddam's regime during the 1980s. However, it was the development of the *de facto* state and the subsequent political instability which was an endemic characteristic of Iraqi Kurdistan in the mid-1990s that gave Islamist parties the space and opportunity to become a force in the region. The most popular of the Kurdish Islamist parties was, and remains, the Kurdistan Islamic Union (KIU) led by

Salahadin Baha'adin. Part of the Muslim Brotherhood (a political organization which spans the Middle East), the KIU does not possess a *peshmerga* force and, as a "noncombatant" party, it enjoys a great deal of popular support. However, it is the activities of the more militant Islamist factions that attracted international attention, and particularly the *Al-Qaeda* associated *Ansar al-Islam*. Originally named *Jund al-Islam*, *Ansar* was an offshoot of the more established Islamist parties in the region, including the IMK, and the Islamic Group of Kurdistan (IGK) led by Mulla Ali Bapir, an ex-military commander of the IMK from Raniyah. As an amalgamation of the more militant factions of the military wings of these movements, *Ansar* reportedly received financial support from *Al-Qaeda* and incorporated several dozen Arab-Afghans into its ranks. From 2000 onward, *Ansar* was beginning to be a serious security concern for the PUK and KDP. In March 2000, Barzani's trusted lieutenant, the Christian Franso Hariri, was gunned down by assailants from *Ansar* as his convoy drove through the suburbs of Erbil. Barely a year later, the senior PUK political bureau member Dr. Barham Salih, was lucky to survive an assassination attempt in Suleimaniyah that killed several of his bodyguards. The PUK could never mount a military assault against the *Ansar* strongholds at Biyara and Tawella strong enough to remove the threat because it was suspected that *Ansar* received logistical support from Iran. Instead, Talabani would have to wait until early 2003 for U.S. forces to destroy the organization's infrastructure with an aerial bombardment in the early days of Operation Iraqi Freedom. However, even though the bases are no more, it seems certain that *Ansar* or offshoots of it have maintained a covert presence throughout the north, and are spreading throughout Iraq.

Other non-Kurdish groups also migrated to what became known as "Free Iraq." These included the two major U.S.-sponsored opposition groups—the Iraqi National Accord (INA) of ex-Ba'athist Dr. Iyad Allawi, and the Iraqi National Congress (INC) of Dr. Ahmed Chalabi. Both set up headquarters in Salahadin near Erbil. The KDP and PUK were active participants within Iraqi opposition groups, and were most notably components of the umbrella INC. Yet, even under the umbrella of the INC, conflict between the KDP and PUK persisted. As the relationship between the KDP and PUK deteriorated in the period after the 1992 elections, Chalabi often acted as a negotiator between the two and enjoyed some limited successes. However, he could not prevent the tension developing into a full-scale civil war by 1994, which saw the PUK occupy Erbil and Suleimaniyah, with the KDP retaining control of the valuable revenue-generating areas of Dohuk and the northern parts of Erbil province.

As an indicator of later dynamics within the Iraqi opposition, the PUK maintained strong links with the INC, whereas the KDP took a more cautious approach. The differences in this relationship were highlighted by the INC–PUK operation conducted against Saddam's northern forces in March 1995.[28] The PUK was a full partner in the venture, which ultimately failed after U.S. support (not for the first time) failed to materialize. Conversely, the KDP refused to become embroiled in an escapade that threatened the joint oil-smuggling venture with Saddam and that risked prompting a full-scale conflict with the Republican Guard. The situation between the KDP and PUK remained tense throughout the remainder of 1995 and the first half of 1996. By June, it seemed to be clear that hostilities would again break out. The PUK accused the KDP of maintaining a secret dialogue with Baghdad, while the KDP countered with the charge that the PUK was receiving support from the Iranian Revolutionary Guards. By mid-August, Barzani was becoming increasingly concerned by the alleged PUK–Iran link and lodged a series of appeals with the U.S. administration to ensure the security of the KDP. His appeals fell on deaf ears, particularly as Barzani was not deemed to be a suitable ally in the north after his failure to support previous U.S. initiatives. With nowhere else to turn, Barzani sought the support of Saddam to remove the threat posed to the KDP by the PUK, and to Iraq from Iranian insurgents. Saddam leapt at the chance to lend a hand and stir the pot of Kurdish politics. It also presented him with an ideal opportunity to remove the troublesome Chalabi and the INC from its Iraqi Kurdish operating bases and humiliate its primary sponsor, the U.S.

Iraqi forces invaded the city of Erbil on the morning of August 31, 1996 in coordination with KDP *peshmerga*. The subsequent routing of INC and PUK forces from the city and its environs was completed quickly. The INC lost several hundred of its followers when its camp at Qushtapa, ten kilometers south of Erbil, was overrun by the Republican Guard who captured and executed Chalabi's men. The PUK also would have lost hundreds of *peshmerga* if not for the actions of Kosrat Rasoul, the prime minister and PUK military commander, who staged a fighting retreat that entered the folklore of the PUK. The devastated PUK fled to Suleimaniyah and then into Iran, leaving the entirety of Iraqi Kurdistan under the control of Barzani—if only briefly. With Saddam's forces withdrawn, Talabani launched a counterattack after regrouping in Iran, and forced the KDP out of Suleimaniyah. The subsequent cease-fire line between the two—which runs southwest to northeast from Koysinjaq to Haji Omran—became an established feature on the political map of Iraqi Kurdistan.[29]

## Toward Institutionalization

Since 1996, Kurdish-controlled Iraq has been divided into two areas. The KDP retained the entirety of the governorate (province) of Dohuk, with most of Erbil governorate, including the capital city of Erbil itself. The KDP therefore occupies the northwestern portion of Iraqi Kurdistan, with its government residing in Erbil, and the KDP headquarters located nearby in Salahadin. The PUK retains the entirety of the governorate of Suleimaniyah, with a large portion of Kirkuk governorate (though not including the city of Kirkuk itself) and a small part of Erbil governorate. The PUK's governmental apparatus remains mainly in the city of Suleimaniyah, with its party structure divided between this city and its political bureau complex at Kalarcholan.

Government in each of the *de facto* statelets is by the dominant political party, and the two administrations are effectively one-party systems. After the last inconclusive round of KDP–PUK fighting in 1997, conditions within the autonomous region improved markedly, particularly when compared with the rest of Iraq. The beginning of the oil-for-food deal under the provisions of UN Security Council Resolution 986 allocated 13 percent of Iraqi oil-export revenue to the northern governorates, improving considerably living standards in the north. The improvements in the north did not go unnoticed by the rest of Iraq, with Kurdistan earning the nickname of "Little Kuwait" for its seemingly blossoming economy. These economic developments were matched by a normalization of political relations between the two parties due to the U.S.-brokered Washington Agreement of September 1998, which called for increased cooperation between the KDP and PUK with a future focus on multiparty elections to unify the two statelets and administrations.[30] The Kurdish governments, divided as they were, became increasingly institutionalized, with cabinets sitting in Erbil (under the premiership of Nechervan Barzani, Massoud's nephew) and in Suleimaniyah (under the premiership of Dr. Barham Salih), and by 2001 had presided over the lives of the Iraqi Kurds for a decade.[31]

This is a simple fact, but one which obviously has serious implications for reintegrating Iraqi Kurdistan back into Iraq. People aged 10 in 1991 are, in 2004, 24-year-old adults with little recollection of life under Saddam's regime. Kurdish is now the standard language rather than Arabic; a separate economy and unit of currency (the Kurds kept the "old" Iraqi dinar rather than using the new notes printed by Saddam after the invasion of Kuwait) resulted in an economy that operated independently of Baghdad; and "government" in the north became associated with "Kurdish" rather than "Iraqi." To all intents and purposes, the people of the north are now more Kurdish than Iraqi and their reintegration back into Iraq will be fraught with difficulties. Since the destruction of the World Trade Center in September 2001, and the subsequent removal of Saddam from his seat of power in Baghdad in the spring of 2003, this reintegration of Iraqi Kurdistan back into Iraq proper is now a subject of very real and passionate debate.

## SEPTEMBER 11, 2001 AND THE IRAQI KURDS

September 11 changed the delicate balance that had kept the Kurds safe in their geopolitical anomaly in the north of Iraq. The survival of the *de facto* Kurdish state in its current form was dependent, perversely, upon the continued survival of Saddam himself. With Saddam in power, the Kurds and particularly the KDP enjoyed an almost symbiotic relationship with Baghdad. While the regime was too weak to project its power and authority for any continuous length of time over the north and was made impotent by the debilitating effects of sanctions, the Kurds offered a useful channel for sanctions-busting and generating revenue. With Saddam removed, the situation has been radically altered.

For the leadership of the Iraqi opposition, it was readily apparent that the regime of Saddam Hussein would be implicated in the terrorist attacks of 9/11. For the Kurdish leadership, the hope was also there. However, to a higher degree than any other Iraqi opposition party, the KDP and PUK had a great deal to lose. As the attention of George W. Bush turned toward Iraq, the KDP and PUK were well aware that the political gains made since 1991 were about to be threatened by a possible change in the status quo. This is, therefore, what can be termed the "Kurdish dilemma." It is undeniable that the personal desire of members of the Kurdish leadership and the vast majority of the Iraqi Kurdish population was to see the demise of Saddam and the establishment of multiparty democracy in Iraq. However, the potential losses to the income of the parties (and to the KDP in particular), to political standing in Iraq and in the international community, and to the security and safety of Iraqi Kurdistan if any potential attempt at regime change backfired, was and remains a serious concern.

In the minds of U.S. policy makers, Middle Eastern states, and other interested nations, Iraqi Kurdistan is part of Iraq. U.S. policy makes it abundantly clear that a Kurdish state is not an envisaged acceptable outcome. The Kurdish strategy toward regime change has therefore focused on its age-old concerns of securing autonomy from Baghdad and attempting to gain some form of control over the strategically valuable Kirkuk region.

The Kurds' main problem is that they are highly vulnerable in a post-Saddam Iraq. The likelihood of the no-fly zones continuing is minimal. Sanctions were lifted in April 2003, and no provision was made to maintain any specifically Kurdish share of the Iraqi oil revenue. Furthermore, the illegal oil-smuggling route from Mosul through Dohuk into Turkey has ceased to be a revenue-generating mechanism for the KDP. The ultimate fear, of course, is that once more the Kurds will be sacrificed to broader geopolitical concerns of maintaining the territorial integrity of the Iraqi state by allowing a government in Baghdad leeway to undertake repressive actions against the disloyal, and now confident, north.

There are also key institutional issues to address. Between them, the KDP and PUK may have a militia 80,000 strong. The number would be in excess of 100,000 if other groups were also included. U.S. policy indicated early on that there would be no immediate attempt to disarm the Kurds, whereas virtually every other militia was ordered to stand down their forces. However, the presence of an independent Kurdish militia threatens the continued existence of a unitary Iraq. An independent army represents a capacity to resist central authority and the option to pursue an independent foreign policy. For the Kurds, however, the maintenance of the *peshmerga* is of practical and symbolic importance. No longer willing to be defenseless in case of aggression from any future Iraqi government toward Kurdistan, statements indicating a Kurdish willingness to demobilize the *peshmerga* could be rescinded with alacrity if instability continues to be the norm in the post-Saddam Iraq.

## THE KURDS: KEY ISSUES

### Legacy of Conflict

As the largest nation without a state in the Middle East (and, arguably, the world), the Kurds have been a constant source of instability in the region. Efforts to assimilate the Kurds by force—most notably in Turkey and Iraq—have largely failed both because the Kurds themselves have a deep-rooted sense of their own "uniqueness" and identity, and because they have been prepared to defend themselves rather than capitulate to superior forces. The Kurds are the perennial "rebels" of the Middle East, and the region as a whole will never be truly at peace until a solution is found to the Kurdish problem. The current situation in northern Iraq is, perhaps, the beginnings of such a solution. Finally, the Kurds have something tangible to show for their terrible suffering. The Kurds' fragile experiment in self-governance has survived and prospered despite all the odds, and despite the pernicious attentions of neighboring powers. Recent visitors to Iraqi Kurdistan speak in glowing terms of the emergence of a genuinely pluralistic and tolerant society, in which the Kurdish government has made strenuous efforts to guarantee the political and cultural rights of all groups inhabiting the area. Some even speak on an emerging "Kurdistani" identity, shared by Turkomans and Assyrians as well as Kurds, as a consequence of their shared experience since 1991. The history of Iraq demonstrates clearly that the Kurds are prepared to fight doggedly for self-determination, and that they can never be comprehesively defeated militarily. Not even the most brutal and militarized regime in Iraq's history—that of Saddam in the 1980s—succeeded in quashing the rebellious spirit of the Kurds. Barely three years after the horrors of the *Anfal* campaign, the Kurds were once more rising in open rebellion against central authority.

It has taken nearly a century of armed struggle for the Kurds to achieve the level of autonomy currently enjoyed. There is no reason to suppose that they will sacrifice this without a struggle. The minimum requirement for the successful reintegration of the Kurds into the state of Iraq is, therefore, a post-Saddam political order characterized by pluralism, cultural tolerance, and a high degree of regional autonomy—precisely the sort of government that Iraq has never enjoyed. Even if agreement can be reached on the contours of such a regime, there is no reason for the Kurds to trust that guarantees of autonomy will be respected in the future. Indeed, history suggests that the Kurds would be very foolish to take such guarantees at face value. In times of extreme weakness, Iraqi regimes have been prepared to offer much to the Kurds, only to renege on the deal once power at the center has been consolidated. The crux of the Kurdish problem in Iraq is a fundamental incompatibility between the level of autonomy demanded by the Kurds, and that which central governments have been prepared to tolerate. In an environment of flourishing consensus and trust, this issue could possibly be resolved, but the Kurds have been consistently betrayed by almost everyone.

## Legacy of Betrayal

The traditional Kurdish adage that Kurds have no friends but the mountains is in fact an accurate reflection of the Kurdish experience during the twentieth century. Almost every power in the region has, at one time or another, been a temporary "friend" to the Kurds. The Kurds have been used repeatedly by the U.S., Israel, and Iran to destabilize the state of Iraq, then left to their fate once immediate strategic goals have been achieved. Of course, viewed from the perspective of successive Iraqi governments, the Kurds have enthusiastically embraced every opportunity to betray the state of Iraq—most notably during the Iran–Iraq war. Trust is a commodity in short supply on both sides of the equation. Perhaps the aftermath of the 2003 war will break the established historical pattern. Having once more allied with the U.S. against the central government, perhaps Kurdish interests will be defended regardless of broader strategic calculations. Or, perhaps someone within the Bush Administration will recognize that if the democratization of the Middle East is the long-term strategic goal, then this process should not begin by sacrificing that only part of Iraq (and more or less the only part of the Middle East) that resembles a democracy. If Iraqi Kurdistan's fragile experiment in pluralism and tolerance is not protected, it will almost certainly not survive. When not fighting against the central government, the Kurds have routinely turned their guns on each other. It would take very little for an outside power (Turkey, say) or a newly assertive central government to sabotage the Kurdish experiment by playing off one side against the other. If the U.S. is serious in its democratization mission, this must not be allowed to happen.

## Arabization and the Status of Kirkuk

The status of Kirkuk has long been at the epicenter of friction between the Kurds and Arab Iraqi governments. For the Kurds, Kirkuk is the spiritual capital of Kurdish nationalism; for Arab governments, control of Kirkuk equates to control over the Kirkuk oilfield. In turn, Kurdish control over Kirkuk oil revenues would provide the Kurds with the economic wherewithal to secede from the state of Iraq.

For Saddam, the Arabization of the northern regions under his control served many purposes. He still remembered the passion by which Kurds claimed the city, and the incessant demands the Kurdish leadership made in its attempt to secure dominion over the city. As if the depopulation of the region in the 1970s and 1980s had not been enough, the recalcitrant Kurds summoned the strength to again dispute Baghdad's authority over the city during the uprising of 1991. The Iraqi government therefore first had to secure the Arab future of the city and its oil. Second, the expulsion of non-Arabs from their homes and forcing them to flee to autonomous Kurdistan would place a severe burden upon the new Kurdish authorities, and possibly one which they did not have the capacity to resolve.

Non-Arab families were systematically targeted by the government security services and Ba'ath Party officials and were pressured to undertake the following steps: (1) officially alter their national identity by registering as Arabs; (2) become members of the Ba'ath Party; and (3) if of appropriate age, join one of the pro-regime militias (including the *Al-Quds* Army or the *Fedayeen Saddam*).[32] If these steps were not undertaken (and they often were not) the unfortunate family would be expelled and forced to travel to the Kurdish autonomous region. Once there, the local authorities had little option but to place them in tented cities on the outskirts of the major towns, or to allow them to settle in previously derelict settlements or slums. The standard of living of these displaced "Kirkuki" Kurds was extremely low and they often fell outside the official safety net of the UN oil-for-food program as they had been stripped of ID cards and UN ration documents. To all intents and purposes, the displaced Kirkukis did not officially exist in the eyes of the Iraqi government or UN agencies. The land left behind by the non-Arab evacuees was resettled by the government with Arabs loyal to the regime, with reports indicating that Palestinians had also been granted the right to reside in the area. The feeling of the displaced non-Arabs remained resolutely to return to their places of origin at the earliest opportunity. That time came with the removal of Saddam; Kirkuk, along with other Arabized areas, threatens to be a city of ethnic competition and has the potential to be a bloodbath as returning non-Arabs attempt to evict the settled population.

## CONCLUSION

To say that the Kurds did not enjoy an easy twentieth century is a gross understatement. The problem of being a non-Arab minority in an essentially Arab state, combined with their own intrinsic and enduring internal rivalries, has meant that Iraqi Kurdish history since the formation of Iraq has been characterized by one catastrophe and tragedy after another. Sadly, there is little evidence to indicate that the new century will herald an improvement. Still caught in the parameters of colonial boundary-makers of a century ago, the Kurds in Iraq managed to secure, through adversity, an autonomous region in Iraq; it exists against the wishes of all, yet serves the people of the area in an ever-more efficient manner. Is Iraqi Kurdistan therefore the model that we should really be pursuing for the rest of Iraq? Or could it in fact be the indicator of what may be required to truly resolve the "Iraq issue"—that of the managed partition of a state which should not have been formed in the first place? If the Iraq issue is to be truly resolved, it will require more than replacing a dictatorial regime. The constant strain of holding together the state of Iraq has fostered violence and dictatorship. Perhaps there simply is no other way to ensure the territorial integrity of the state; thus, if Iraq is not to "fail" as a state, it is destined to be ruled by coercion. The alternative is to partition the state of Iraq. Kurdistan has arguably been the festering sore negating the legitimacy of the Iraqi state, yet it could now be the talisman of a peaceful transition through managed partition. Kurds undeniably have their own serious internal problems, yet they have still managed to preside over a viable entity for a decade with the assistance of the UN and the international community. Outside of Israel and Turkey, Kurdistan is the closest there is to a functioning democratic entity in the Middle East. If an independent Kurdish state is what is required to preserve this, then this option needs to be seriously contemplated.

## CHAPTER EIGHT

# THE DEMOCRACY DILEMMA

## INTRODUCTION

AT 8 P.M. ON WEDNESDAY MARCH 19, 2003, the Bush Administration's 48-hour deadline for Saddam to leave Iraq expired. Shortly thereafter, the campaign to remove Saddam's regime by force—code-named "Operation Iraqi Freedom"—began in earnest. More importantly, this date also marked the concrete beginning of a revolutionary foreign policy doctrine on the part of the U.S.—one that pledged to use preemptive war as a means of securing U.S. national security. Less noticed, but of equal significance, the attack on Iraq marked the "first phase in a grand design for the moral reconstruction of the Middle East."[1] The design, forged by a "cabal" of neoconservatives in and around the Administration, had been in place long before the events of 9/11. It was, in part at least, a recognition that the traditional U.S. policy toward the Middle East—propping up reliable but repressive dictatorships—was no longer viable. The events of 9/11 demonstrated in painfully stark detail that the Middle East had become a festering swamp of virulent anti-American sentiment, and that the American mainland was no longer immune to the effects. Rather than address the immediate causes of resentment—U.S. support for Israel, U.S. troops in Saudi Arabia, the sanctions on Iraq—the plan focuses on the perceived root causes of anti-U.S. sentiment in the Middle East—namely, political repression and poverty. Address these, so the argument goes, and you drain the swamp. The broad outlines of the plan are straightforward. Remove the regime in Baghdad and bring democracy to Iraq. Once firmly established, a democratic Iraq becomes a "beacon" of light amid the darkness of repression. One by one, repressive regimes in the Middle East will collapse (either with or without U.S. "assistance") and democracy and prosperity will rise triumphant in their place. In this way, a zone of "democratic peace" will emerge at the heart of the Arab World, rendering the region infinitely safer for both the U.S. and Israel. The plan concedes that the War on Terror will not be won on the battlefield, but in the hearts and minds of potential future terrorists in the Middle East.

To some, the so-called "Democratic Domino" theory appears a work of visionary genius, to others, a monumental folly, but what no one can doubt is the sheer scale of its ambition. One awestruck observer described it as "the most daring experiment in imperial idealism in the whole of human history."[2] In a speech delivered to the American Enterprise Institute in February 2003, President Bush made clear—perhaps for the first time in public—that the democratic domino theory had become official Administration policy.

> The world has a clear interest in the spread of democratic values, because stable and free nations do not breed the ideologies of murder . . . A new regime in Iraq would serve as a dramatic and inspiring example of freedom for other nations in the region.[3]

When the President of the world's only remaining superpower makes a statement like this, people tend to pay attention. From this point onward, the credibility of the Bush Administration hinges on its capacity to deliver on this promise made to the Iraqi people. With the invasion of Iraq, the U.S. embarked on a path that will either end in "nothing less than the moral reconstruction of the Middle East," or it will end in disaster. Either way, the path begins in Baghdad. If the U.S. creates chaos in Iraq, or treats it as a colonial acquisition, rather than constructing a peaceful, democratic order, then the repercussions for U.S. strategic interests in the region as a whole could be devastating. It is in this high-stakes context that one must assess the U.S.'s likelihood of success.

## HISTORICAL CONTEXT

When nation builders begin the process of piecing together the remains of Iraq they will find very little in the way of raw material to work with. Iraq was an artificial British creation, stitched together from the wreckage of the Ottoman Empire. Two key British decisions—to append the Kurdish-dominated province of Mosul to the Arab-dominated provinces of Baghdad and Basra, and to continue the Ottoman tradition of governing through Iraq's minority Sunni Arabs—effectively condemned Iraq to a painful future. Throughout Iraq's history, the Kurds have never willingly participated in the state of Iraq. Sporadically during the 1920s, and again during World War II, the Kurds fought stubbornly to assert their independence against central control. The identity of the power at the center has never mattered greatly to the Kurds. From 1961 to 1991, the Kurds conducted what can only be described as a low-level civil war against central authorities. At times, as in 1975, 1988, and 1991, the war reached full-scale proportions. Subsequent to 1991, the Kurdish region has functioned as a *de facto* independent state, complete with political institutions, armed forces, and a functioning civil society. The "golden age" of Iraqi Kurdistan will not be yielded without a struggle. The minimum requirement for the Kurds in a post-Saddam environment is a continuance of the status quo. Realistically, it is difficult to see how it is possible to reintegrate the Kurds back into the state of Iraq given that the Kurds have *never* been integrated into the state of Iraq. Nor is it difficult to understand why, after the *Anfal* campaign of 1988, and the brutal suppression of the 1991 uprising, harmonious relations between Kurds and an Arab-dominated government in a unified state of Iraq will not be achieved overnight. Viewed from the Arab perspective, the Kurds have always been traitors to the Iraqi state, willing to ally themselves with any foreign power to fight against the Arab population. Few Arabs in Iraq shed tears for the Kurds of Halabja. Many thought the Kurds got what they deserved for betraying the Arab cause.

The sectarian (Sunni/Shi'a) divide has always been more complex. The Shi'a are not a homogenous group, and the degree of geographic integration among Sunnis and Shi'a has always been much greater than between Kurds and Arabs. In the shrine cities of the south, the Shi'a religious leadership has periodically infused the sectarian divide with political meaning. But the target has traditionally been the *secular* nature of all regimes of the Iraqi Republic, and the attempts by successive regimes, especially the Ba'ath regime, to exert central control over religious life in the south. Beyond this, more radical Islamic groups, such as *al-Dawa* and SCIRI, have made clear their intentions to spread, by violent means if necessary, the Islamic revolution. To the extent that the sectarian divide has become politicized, it threatens the unity of the Iraqi state. The return of perhaps 400,000 religious radicals from Iran will serve to fuel the fire. However, the extent to which religion has become politicized within the Shi'a population as a whole is probably limited. Historically, Shi'a discontent has focused on the perpetual Sunni dominance of all positions of power within the Iraqi state.

Resolving the Kurdish problem and sustaining Sunni hegemony have meant that, more often than not, violence has been the key currency of governance in Iraq. The cycle of violence—whether inflicted by the government against dissenting groups or vice versa—has escalated in intensity over time. It is no coincidence that Iraq's most brutal leader (Saddam) was also its most durable. It may be that, in its current geographic configuration, Iraq is ungovernable in the absence of a strong, ruthless leader at the head of a powerful, highly centralized coercive state. Over time, growing oil revenues provided the Iraqi state with the resources to penetrate society and further tighten control. This process reached its zenith under Saddam during the 1970s when the Iraqi state, serving the interests of the Ba'ath Party (and thereby, Saddam), came to dominate the political, social, and economic life of Iraq. The elusive quest to forge an inclusive Iraqi national identity was pursued with energetic vigor under Saddam. Existing ties of loyalty were shattered, to be replaced by ties of loyalty to Saddam himself via the Ba'ath Party. The goal was to atomize the Iraqi people, then reconstruct a glorious new vision of "Iraqi Man"—a being that transcended sectarian and ethnic divisions and that owed primary allegiance to the state of Iraq and its "Great Leader." This was an epic attempt to create a collective identity for the people of Iraq; a combination of social engineering on a massive scale and liberal doses of violence. But it failed, as had all efforts by previous Iraqi regimes, because it proved impossible to create an Iraqi identity that could bind together Sunni and Shi'a while simultaneously accommodating the Kurds in the north. Displays of national unity have been few and far between. The rebellion against the British in 1920, and the dogged defense of the homeland against Iran between 1980 and 1988, solidified Iraq's Arab majority, but did nothing to integrate the Kurds.

Iraq has always been a difficult country to govern. Over time, it has become progressively more difficult, not just because of internal divisions, but also because external powers have found it increasingly difficult to resist interfering in the internal affairs of Iraq. Since the early 1960s, almost every important regional power (including Israel, the Soviet Union, and the U.S.) has, at one time or another, sought to exploit Iraq's internal divisions for strategic gain. Usually this has taken the form of funneling resources to either the Kurds or the Shi'a Islamic parties in order to weaken and destabilize the central regime. Fostering rebellion in the north and south may have served the strategic interests of regional powers, but the Kurds and Shi'a have paid a heavy price for serving as surrogates. The coherence of the state of Iraq has also suffered as a consequence. The immense challenge of creating a shared sense of national unity in Iraq has been rendered virtually impossible by perpetual external interference.

The complex and traumatic legacy of 80 years of Iraqi history will prove difficult to overcome. In the absence of a strong centralized state willing to resort to violence to impose internal stability, it remains to be seen whether Iraq can be held together as a coherent territorial entity. The real problem is, and always has been, that democracy in Iraq will terminate Sunni dominance of state structures. No doubt some form of power-sharing arrangement can be implemented that protects the minority Sunni Arab population and guarantees them at least some say in the direction of the state; but any form of democracy will require the Sunnis to cede a sizable quantity of the power and influence they currently enjoy. Almost overnight, the Sunnis will go from a position of political dominance to one of subservience. This will not be easy to swallow. If history is any guide, the Arab component of Iraq has been most strongly united when the state itself has been faced with an external threat. Initially, the threat was provided by the British (1920), and subsequently by the Iranians (1980–1988). A U.S. occupying force has great potential to achieve the same effect.

## WHAT WILL IT TAKE TO SUCCEED?

The U.S. cannot democratize Iraq, still less the Middle East, at the point of a gun. This is to say nothing more than that to function at all, democracy requires the consent of the governed. Democracy cannot be forced onto an unwilling population. At present, to put it mildly, there is deep mistrust of U.S. intentions in the Middle East. Indeed opinion polls in Western Europe indicate that even the U.S.'s traditional allies consider the war against Iraq to be a war about access to oil. The news is considerably worse from the Arab world. Not only is the Bush Administration deeply unpopular, but the few polls available indicate that the vast majority of Arabs still prefer to believe that 9/11 was a self-inflicted wound designed to justify a "crusade" against the Muslim world. The war against Iraq will have done little to improve President Bush's approval ratings in the Middle East. The dilemma for the U.S. then is how to convince a deeply skeptical and inherently hostile region that the war with Iraq was not just a brutal neoimperialist enterprise to gain control over the world's second-largest reserves of oil. Put bluntly, in the battle for hearts and minds, the U.S. starts with a scorecard of close to zero. To be optimistic, the U.S. will probably get one chance at this. If the economic, political, and social reconstruction of Iraq enjoys widespread popularity among the Iraqi people, then this will go a long way toward convincing the region of the U.S.'s benign intentions. Whether or not the U.S. is even afforded the opportunity to do this depends largely on the reactions of the Iraqi people to U.S. military occupation. Any goodwill will soon fade if the U.S. does not deliver on its promises. At present, with U.S. troops struggling to provide even the most minimal levels of law and order, let alone the efficient delivery of basic utilities, the situation looks grim.

## WHAT DOES IT TAKE TO SUSTAIN DEMOCRACY?

If the answer to this question were truly known, presumably the world would be full of stable, consolidated democracies. Optimism during the 1990s concerning the ease with which states with no previous track record of democracy could be "democratized" has now been forced to confront an uncomfortable empirical reality. Of close to 100 of those countries considered "in transition" to democracy, fewer than one fifth are clearly moving in the right direction. The vast majority have either reverted to former levels of authoritarianism, or appear simply to be stuck in a gray area between democracy and authoritarianism and are going nowhere fast. Overwhelmingly, successful transitions have occurred in geographically/culturally specific concentrations (Central Europe, Latin America) suggesting that political culture matters, and that the "anyone can do it" approach to democratization requires substantial modification.[4] Democracy is apparently more difficult to engineer than previously thought.

Some of the difficulties involved are highlighted by Francis Fukuyama, who advances a (relatively uncontroversial) model of democratic consolidation that envisages "four levels on which the consolidation of democracy must occur."[5] Level one, the most superficial level, involves a normative commitment to the idea of democracy—the point being that democracy cannot long survive unless people believe in it, but also that a widespread belief in the legitimacy of democracy is not sufficient to guarantee a consolidated democracy. Below this level, democracy is consolidated at the level of institutions—constitutions, electoral systems, political parties, and the like. Level three involves the existence of civil society—spontaneously created social structures (interest groups, an independent media, civil rights groups) that exist outside the realm of state control, and serve to mediate the interactions between individuals and the government. Finally, level four, the deepest level, "includes phenomena such as family structure, religion, moral values, ethnic consciousness, 'civic-ness,' and particularistic historical traditions."[6] This is the realm of political culture. Two important insights emerge from this analysis. The first is that as we move from level one through four—from the shallow to the deep—so change becomes progressively slower and more difficult to achieve. It is easier to change institutions than it is to change political culture. There is nothing very controversial about this. The second is that democracy cannot be considered fully consolidated until it is rooted in the political culture of a society. Hence, a society can be convinced of the moral legitimacy of democracy, and the appropriate institutional trappings can be put in place, but the real problems are encountered at levels three and four, because these are beyond the level of social engineering. As Fukuyama puts it,

> I would go so far as to argue that social engineering on the level of institutions has hit a massive brick wall . . . the real difficulties affecting the quality of life in modern democracies have to do with social and cultural pathologies that seem safely beyond the reach of institutional solutions, and hence of public policy.[7]

This assessment, depressingly in accord with the empirical evidence of the last few years, suggests that, at best, the consolidation of democracy is a slow, painful process that is only marginally affected by manipulating institutions. It also offers insights into the magnitude of the task confronting democracy builders in post-Saddam Iraq.

## U.S. OPTIONS

U.S. intentions for the postwar reconstruction of Iraq were never clearly articulated prior to the onset of war. More precisely, a variety of proposals were mooted, almost certainly reflecting divisions within the Bush Administration as to the extent and duration of any postwar U.S. involvement. The configuration of a future Iraqi government and the duration of a U.S. military occupation remain matters of conjecture. However, in essence the options for the U.S. can be distilled down to three: a short-term occupation during which the U.S. makes a serious effort to establish a functioning democratic system, then departs leaving full sovereignty in the hands of a democratically elected Iraqi government; a long-term occupation (ten years or more) during which the U.S. reconfigures Iraqi society in its entirety and makes a concerted effort to establish democratic roots in the country; and, a short-term (two-year) military occupation, followed by the installation of a puppet regime in Iraq and the withdrawal of U.S. troops.[8]

There are, of course, a multitude of possible variations on these basic themes, but taken together, these three options cover most of the potential permutations of answers to the fundamental questions confronting the U.S. at this point in time; first, does the U.S. have any real intention of democratizing Iraq; second, if so, then what level of commitment—in terms of time, treasure, and blood—is the U.S. prepared to devote to this task; and third, how much control does the U.S. intend to exercise over Iraq both during and after the process?

## Option 1: Democracy Lite

This option assumes that the U.S. is prepared to devote considerable time, energy, and resources to the process of democratization in Iraq—but that direct U.S. military involvement in the process will terminate once Iraq's first democratically elected government is up and running. Perhaps a small international "peacekeeping" force is left in place to help a new democratically elected government find its feet, but beyond this, Iraq's democratic experiment is left to its own fate. The template for this "democracy-lite" option would be based broadly on experiences in Bosnia, or Kosovo, and the underlying assumption is that the prospects of democracy emerging in Iraq without significant, direct external involvement are minimal.

While democracy continues to prosper in such unlikely terrain as India, one cannot rule out completely the potential for democracy to take root in Iraq. But by any realistic assessment, the prospects are not good. Fukuyama's idea of layers of democratic consolidation can help to illustrate some of the difficulties involved. During a two-year military occupation, the U.S. can realistically hope to affect developments at the two most superficial levels identified by Fukuyama—the normative and the institutional. The prospects of a vibrant civil society emerging from the political wreckage of Iraq in so brief a period of time are slim to zero; similarly, the likelihood that democratic norms and values will become embedded in the political culture of Iraq in anything short of decades is remote indeed. The best the U.S. can hope to achieve over a two-year period is to implant democracy at the normative and institutional levels. But even here, there are some serious, perhaps insurmountable, obstacles to be overcome.

*Level One: Democratic Norms.* At level one—the normative level—what evidence is there that the Iraqi people will consider democracy to be a "right," legitimate system of government? Certainly, many prominent figures in the exiled Iraqi opposition movement seem convinced of the moral legitimacy of democracy. But most of these figures have lived outside Iraq—many in Western liberal democracies—for decades. For example, Ahmed Chalabi, the urbane leader of the Iraqi National Congress, has lived a life of extreme comfort since he departed Iraq in 1956. It would be unsurprising indeed if Chalabi did not accept the legitimacy of a democratic order. But Chalabi, and many other prominent opposition figures, have existed on a different planet from average Iraqis over the last few decades. Other opposition groups—SCIRI and *al-Dawa*, for example—are known to be much more ambivalent, even hostile to the idea of a Western-style democracy; and these two groups are going to constitute a much more significant presence in Iraq than are the likes of Chalabi. Indeed, the whole question of the future political role of Shi'a religious leaders (which is likely to be significant) raises important concerns about the compatibility of Western democratic norms and those of politicized Islam. At the procedural level, the idea of resolving disputes peacefully via the institutional mechanisms of democracy need not create problems, but at the substantive level, democracy is associated with a raft of values—such as gender equality, universal suffrage, and freedom of speech—that may prove more difficult for the Shi'a religious establishment to tolerate. For Sunni Arabs, the advent of democracy, even at the procedural level, spells the death knell of Sunni dominance over the Iraqi state. Moreover, the hardcore of anti-Western, anti-Zionist, pan-Arab sentiment has always emanated from the Sunni triangle. It is optimistic to expect Sunni Arabs to accept normatively a democratic system "imposed" on Iraq by a Western, "imperialist" power (and, not inconsequentially, a power that is Israel's staunchest ally) and that guarantees their future political subservience in the state of Iraq.

Among ordinary Iraqis, the little information available makes for depressing reading. According to a recent survey, Iraqis are almost completely apathetic about the nature of the political system that emerges after the war. Disturbingly, many seem to long nostalgically for a return to the "golden age" of the 1970s, a period not noted for its political liberalism. Said one Iraqi, "Before the war and the sanctions, our dinar was strong and our purchasing power was the envy of the Arab world. We want to return to the period of prosperity our parents lived through in the 1970s."[9] Given the immense suffering endured by the Iraqi population over the last 20 years, it is not surprising that stability and survival are the primary concerns of most Iraqis. Esoteric debate about the moral legitimacy of political systems is not a priority. This does not bode well for the introduction of a political system that demands and relies on popular participation.

*Level Two: Political Institutions.* Ordinarily, decisions concerning the type of electoral system, whether to have a presidential or parliamentary system, and the degree of power assigned to the central government relative to the regions, are important, but not matters of life and death. In the case of Iraq, no doubt most interested parties will agree in the abstract that power needs to be shared among the Kurds, Shi'a, and Sunnis (and perhaps, the Turcomen and Assyrians). Such a division of power could be accomplished in a variety of ways. A collegial executive comprising one Shi'a, one Kurd, and one Sunni is an obvious solution (though clearly one that does not accurately represent these groups in proportion to population). Beyond this, the problems occur. Does each group get a veto over policy decisions, in which case this arrangement is prone to perpetual gridlock; or are decisions made on the basis of majority rule, in which case the Kurds can be permanently outvoted by the Arabs? The template for the former is the arrangement dreamed up for the governance of Bosnia in 1995. Bosnia is an instructive example because it provides a reasonable approximation of the nature of the situation that confronts Iraq, that is, serious ethnic and (potentially) religious unrest with a veneer of stability provided by a Western occupation force. In the case of Bosnia, each of the three major groups (Croats, Bosniacs, and Serbs) is represented in a collegial presidency. While the exact process is inordinately complex, each group has an effective veto over all presidential decisions. Combined with a barrage of classic checks and balances, the provisions of the Bosnian constitution provide precisely the sort of strong guarantees that were deemed necessary to protect any minority group. Such a system will need to be adopted in Iraq to safeguard the Kurds. The problem (which will almost inevitably occur in Iraq as well) is that in the absence of a basic foundation of trust among groups, the system of checks and balances has almost completely paralyzed the central government. By all accounts, the Bosnian constitution has been a disaster for all concerned, and has served to heighten rather than reduce ethnic tensions. Bosnia's most recent elections in 2002 saw dramatic gains for virulently ethnic/nationalistic political parties, which now dominate the political process in the failed state of Bosnia. A continued NATO presence is probably all that prevents the resumption of serious ethnic violence in Bosnia. The parallels with a post-Saddam Iraq are ominous. The deeper problem with power-sharing arrangements such as collegial executives is that they have a tendency (as in the case of Bosnia) to codify and solidify existing ethnic or religious divisions. Affording constitutional and institutional recognition to the existence of distinct groupings may serve merely to encourage such groups to think and act as distinct entities.[10]

Yet decisions about power-sharing will be straightforward relative to decisions regarding the division of power between central and regional governments. The issue of federalism (the power division between central and local/regional governments) is a political disaster in the making. Once again, there is little disagreement in the abstract about the need for some sort of arrangement for devolving power away from the center. It is clear, however, that each of Iraq's groups has a very different conception of what this will look like in practice. Symptomatic of this difference in perception is the proposal by the INC. The INC website advances a none-too-helpful formula for a democratic Iraq with a federal system and a strong central government. But herein lies the problem. This is probably exactly what a future democratic Iraqi government requires, but to the extent that power is devolved to regional governments, it is taken away from the center; so there is an inherent contradiction between federalism and a strong central government. The INC's formulation is basically a meaningless, lowest-common-denominator "soundbite," which attempts to obscure the fundamental conflicts that exist among Iraq's various groups on the issue of federalism. To simplify somewhat: the Kurds are unlikely to settle for anything less than the degree of autonomy enjoyed since 1992; the Sunni and secular Shi'a opposition want to retain a strongly centralized state; and the religious Shi'a opposition wants to establish local autonomy in certain spheres (religion, education), but otherwise favors a strong central state. As it stands, the degree of autonomy demanded by the Kurds is far in excess of what the other groups are prepared to tolerate.

Once we get into details, the plot thickens further. The Kurds favor "ethnic federalism," whereby regional boundaries are drawn to coincide with the distribution of ethnicities; other groups (including the Turks) have explicitly rejected this in favor of "territorial federalism," in which regional boundaries may or may not coincide with ethnic/sectarian population distributions. The future battle lines are drawn. The Kurds want clearly demarcated zones of autonomy in which Kurds are the dominant majority and they will fight to include Kirkuk within this autonomous region. Somewhat ambitiously, the Turcomen population—numbering perhaps one million, and concentrated in Kirkuk and Mosul—have called for the establishment of a Turcomen "federal unit" to include the cities of Mosul and Kirkuk. This formula is supported by Turkey, and the Turks have declared themselves willing to intervene militarily in the event that Kirkuk is incorporated into a Kurdish autonomous region. Thus far, all those involved in discussions of a post-Saddam Iraq have simply avoided addressing these explosive issues.

Beyond issues of territorial delimitation, the more basic concern of how to divide power between levels of government has yet to be seriously engaged. Critical issues to be resolved (just to mention two) include the status of religion and the future role of militia forces. In the first case, the problem is not one of religious tolerance—Iraq actually has a relatively good record here—but of the degree of autonomy afforded to the religious establishment in the Shi'a south. The likely demands of the Shi'a, as reflected in the 2002 "Declaration of the Shi'a of Iraq," include guaranteed autonomy for "teaching circles" (the *hawzas*), and "the right to establish independent schools, universities and other teaching establishments and academies."[11] Historically, organized religious opposition to the central government has emerged from educational institutions, and has been championed by prominent religious scholars. Hostility has traditionally erupted in response to the efforts of avowedly secular regimes at the center (notably the ICP-supported Qassim regime and the Ba'ath regime) to advance the cause of individual rights and liberties—particularly changes to the status of women—and to control the religious establishment's sources of revenue and educational infrastructure. It seems likely that after the fall of the Ba'ath regime, Shi'a Islam in Iraq will become radicalized by the return of nearly half a million Shi'a exiles from Iran. The presence in Iraq of some of Shi'a Islam's holiest sites (especially the shrine cities of Karbala and Najaf) could turn southern Iraq into a magnet for Islamic fundamentalism. The evolving relationship between a hardcore of Islamic fundamentalism in the south and a secular, liberal democracy in Baghdad should be interesting to observe. The key question remains whether Western liberal democracy or organized religion will have greater appeal to the majority Shi'a population.

The question of what to do about the proliferation of private armies in Iraq is critical, but deeply problematic. For obvious reasons, in most federal systems, the armed forces are placed under the control of the central government. Even in Switzerland, one of the most highly decentralized political systems in existence, Article 58 of the constitution states clearly, "the use of the army is a federal matter." A post-Saddam Iraq will resemble Afghanistan to the extent that there will be numerous well-armed militia forces, each defending particular tracts of territory, and none overly inclined to lay down arms. To give some idea of the likely scale of this problem, it is worth noting that during the war, there were (at least) five separate armies operating in northern Iraq—not counting Turkish or coalition forces. Add to this the numerous tribal militias dispersed throughout the country, and the magnitude of the internal security problem becomes apparent. But the real problem here will be the two (PUK and KDP) Kurdish forces. In light of the recent historical record of Kurdish/Arab relations, it is inconceivable that the Kurds will simply demobilize their *peshmerga* fighters. Historically, their tenacious military resistance against central rule is the only thing that has afforded any form of autonomy to the Kurds. But if the *peshmerga* remain, what will be their legal status in a new Iraqi federation? The time will come when the central government will need to enforce the rule of law in Iraqi Kurdistan. How will this be done? To take just one possible example, for most of the 1990s, the Turks have enjoyed an informal right of "hot pursuit" (the right to cross the Turkish/Iraqi border) in their brutal struggle against the Kurdistan Workers Party (PKK). In fact, for most of the period, Turkish armed forces have occupied parts of Iraqi territory under the guise of fighting a counterinsurgency war. It is very easy to envisage a scenario under which one of the major Kurdish groups would clash with the central government over whether this should continue or be curtailed. Under this scenario, how is the central government's decision to be enforced? The reality is that the existence of independent, well-armed, battle-hardened armies in the north means that central government edicts will be unenforceable. The Kurds may choose to obey, or they may not, but in the latter case, any attempt by the center to enforce the law will result in bloodshed. The broader problem is that the Kurds will need to compromise—especially over the emotional issue of the future status of oil-rich Kirkuk—yet there will be no incentive to do so while the Kurds retain their capacity to resist enforcement, either politically, through the exercise of veto power, or militarily, through their *peshmerga*. Additionally, if, as some experts have suggested, the Kurds are legally permitted to retain their armies as militias of a federal unit, why should other units of a future federation not be extended the same privilege? Should SCIRI's militia army—the 10,000-15,000–strong Iranian backed *Badr* Brigade—be afforded the same privilege? Where does this end? The only realistic parallel to this sort of arrangement is the situation in Bosnia, where the constituent "entities" retain their own armed forces—and thus, their capacity to resist rule from the center. In practice, this has produced a paralyzed central government that is unable to enforce its will. Today, Bosnia is two separate states in all but name. A similar situation in Iraq would please the Kurds, but it would mean the end of Iraq as a coherent territorial entity.

A counterargument could be made, and is made by those optimistic about the future of a democratic federal Iraq, that these are details that can be ironed out at some point through a process of compromise and consensus. Perhaps; but these have not been prominent sentiments historically in relations between the Kurds and the center. It is also worth noting that when moving beyond the level of detail, the bigger picture provides few grounds for optimism. Federalism is a highly sophisticated form of democracy. Successful federal arrangements presuppose the existence of a stable democratic order. It is unsurprising that almost all real-world examples of successful federal arrangements are located in Western Europe (Switzerland, Austria, and Germany, for example), or in the Anglo-Saxon world (the U.S., Canada, Australia). Beyond this, there are isolated instances of functioning federalism (Brazil, India) but the record is not good. The obvious conclusion (one supported by almost all the research), is that the requirements for successful federalism greatly exceed those for successful democracy.[12] The basic requirements are much the same (consensus among decision-makers, willingness to compromise, acceptance of the rule of law, a strong independent judiciary to arbitrate political disputes, and so on), but these are required not just among branches of government at the center, but also at different levels of government. Federalism necessarily involves "relatively complex systems of division and sharing of powers and authority," which in turn requires "populations with a supportive, or at least congenial, political culture."[13] Summarizing what he considers the "accepted body of knowledge in the field," one of the leading experts on federalism states, "the existence of civil society is vital to the idea of federalism"; furthermore, "ethnic nationalism is probably the strongest force against federalism," and hence "ethnic federations are the most difficult of all to sustain."[14] The problem, then, is that the simplest part of reconstructing Iraq politically will be to get some sort of democracy working. But above and beyond this, mutually acceptable federal arrangements will need to be established that can encompass bitter ethnic divisions and a tense sectarian divide.

But what may prove to be the deepest problem confronting nation-builders in Iraq is that Iraq has always been governed by a strong authoritarian center. It may be indeed that dictatorial rule from the center is the logical product of governing an inherently artificial state, riddled with all manner of factional strife. If this is the case, then the elimination of the regime's governing institutions (the Ba'ath Party, various militia groups, security services, and so on)—essentially, the institutional "glue" that holds together the state of Iraq—coupled with a massive decentralization of power from the center to the regions will likely precipitate the beginning of the end for the state of Iraq.

*Advantages of Option 1.*    From a U.S. perspective, the obvious advantage of option 1 is that it removes U.S. troops out of harm's way in relatively short order. Iraq is likely to be a very dangerous place for U.S. troops for the foreseeable future, and waning domestic support for a continued and costly (in terms of money and casualties) operation may play a critical role in determining the length of the occupation. The runup to the November 2004 presidential election may prove decisive here. If U.S. troops are still locked in bloody combat operations against a significant resistance force, the temptation to campaign on a "bring the boys home" platform may prove irresistible. Moreover, if the U.S. can at least begin the process of reconstructing Iraq's infrastructure, and leave behind a new Iraqi constitution and an elected democratic government, this would be a victory of sorts. The U.S. would have liberated the Iraqi people from the tyranny of Saddam, established the institutions of democratic governance, and then left the people of Iraq to govern themselves. The departure of occupying U.S. troops would also be popular among many if not most Iraqis; the obvious exception would be the Kurds, who may fear, with some justification, that they are being "thrown to the wolves."

*Problems with Option 1.*  The most obvious problem with option 1 is that the chances of democracy prospering in Iraq in the aftermath of a U.S. troop withdrawal are minimal. Over two years, some meaningful progress can be made on the reconstruction of Iraq's physical infrastructure; U.S. forces may even be able to impose some semblance of law and order, but there are clear limitations on what can be achieved in so short a period of time. The Iraqi social structure has been decimated by years of war and sanctions, Iraq's economy is a disaster area, the bureaucracy is barely functioning, and Iraq currently has no armed forces or means to preserve internal security. In short, the Iraqi state needs to be entirely rebuilt from the ground up. This will not be achieved in two years. Grafting democratic institutions onto a hollow state structure is not a recipe for success.

Reaching agreement among Iraq's various groups on the design of democratic institutions is, in itself, a major challenge, and the U.S. cannot avoid playing an important but intrusive role in the process. The importance of the role is that only the U.S. can provide the framework of coercion to force groups to compromise when, as appears inevitable, there are fundamental disagreements over the design of the new government. Only the U.S. can provide a guarantee that deals struck between groups will be adhered to. But this guarantee will endure only as long as a significant U.S. military presence remains in Iraq. It will also be an intrusive role in that it will inevitably involve the U.S. "taking sides" in support of one group over another. U.S. preferences will, therefore, become embedded in the Iraqi constitution. This is unavoidable, but it means that not only will the U.S. be imposing a *system* of government on Iraq (the Iraqis are free to choose any system they want—so long as it is democratic), they will also be dictating the *mechanics* of such a system. Once U.S. troops have departed and there is no overarching power to enforce deals, the system will survive only to the extent that the system itself is perceived as legitimate by all the parties. Few can reasonably expect that a system imposed by an external power that refuses to stay and police the system it created will enjoy widespread legitimacy in the eyes of the Iraqi population. More plausibly, the system will be perceived for what it is—an imposed expression of U.S. values and preferences rather than those of the Iraqi people.

Over a two-year period, the U.S. can, perhaps, convince the people of Iraq of the normative legitimacy of democratic governance (though different groups may have widely differing interpretations as to what democracy should look like in practice); it may also be possible to cobble together a constitution that parcels out power in a broadly representative way while protecting minority rights. Thus, the U.S. can realistically hope to make inroads into the first two levels of democratic consolidation identified by Fukuyama (the normative and the institutional). What cannot be achieved in so short a period is consolidation on the deeper levels of civil society and political culture. A vibrant civil society and a supportive political culture cannot simply be "engineered" into existence in the same way as institutions, and certainly not in two years. But it is precisely at these levels that the success of the democratic experiment in Iraq will be determined.

*Prospects for Democracy in Iraq Under Option 1.* The chances of democracy in Iraq surviving much beyond a U.S. withdrawal cannot be good. Almost none of the conditions conducive to democratic consolidation will be present. The reconstruction of the Iraqi infrastructure—social, political, and economic, as well as physical—will barely have begun; the political system itself will probably be perceived by many Iraqis as an "illegitimate," alien imposition; the Kurds will be cast adrift once more, dependent for their protection on paper guarantees outlined in a constitution that may or may not be adhered to by an Arab-dominated central government; certain groups of Sunni Arabs will undoubtedly resent their precipitous loss of power and status; and a host of potential "spoiler" groups will be poised to sabotage the democratic experiment. Democracy is far easier to destroy than create, and an unconsolidated democracy, covered in U.S. fingerprints at the heart of the Middle East, will be an easy target.

Under these circumstances, the most plausible result of option 1 is a prolonged struggle to gain control over the levers of power. Under democratic rules, this struggle is resolved via popular election, but power struggles in Iraq have never been resolved in this way. Regime changes in Iraq have traditionally involved struggles among rival groups of Sunni elites, with the outcome determined by which group can effectively control the coercive instruments of the state. Several of these coups have involved serious bloodletting, but none has led to prolonged military confrontations between rivals for power. Power in the Iraqi state has always been heavily concentrated at the center, and the state has always possessed well-developed coercive institutions (the army and internal security apparatus), meaning that new leaders coming to power on the back of a coup have inherited the existing institutions of an authoritarian state largely intact. Transfers of power have, therefore, been accompanied by minimal levels of social upheaval; establishing control over a small number of key, strategically placed coercive institutions has normally been sufficient.

The Iraq of two years hence will bear no resemblance to the Iraq of old. If all goes according to plan, Iraq will be a democratic state in which power is highly decentralized, and in which coercive institutions will play a much less prominent role. Saddam's collection of internal security organizations, the Republican Guard, the Special Republican Guard, and even the Iraqi regular army have already been dismantled. The Iraqi armed forces may well have been reconstituted by this point, but not on the scale of previous years. Any struggle for power that ensues in the aftermath of a U.S. departure will be infinitely more complex than previously because power will be heavily dispersed throughout the system. It will no longer be possible to capture the Iraqi state by controlling a few key power nodes. Moreover, the struggle for power will no longer be restricted to competition among rival Sunni groups. This is a recipe for major civil upheaval. If this occurs, it will not necessarily be a war driven by ethnic or sectarian hatred, though these may well be exploited; it will be about establishing control over a greatly weakened state structure. This may prove to be an unduly pessimistic scenario, but it is surely more plausible than the alternative, which is that democracy consolidates and thrives in such inhospitable terrain. If the U.S.'s goal is to democratize Iraq, and from there, the whole of the Middle East, option 1 is highly unlikely to achieve that end. It may be possible for an external power to impose a successful democracy in Iraq, but it will take a lot longer than two years.

## Option 2: Prolonged Occupation

Option 2 assumes a significantly greater (10–15 year) commitment on the part of the U.S. during which Iraq is treated as an imperial possession. All important decisions are made by American administrators, the U.S. military remains a significant presence to guarantee internal stability, and the economic, social, and political structure of Iraq is totally reconstructed from the bottom up. During this period, there is no pretense that Iraq is in control of its own fortunes; all significant decisions are taken by an American occupation force, then imposed on the Iraqi people (whether they like it or not). But the goal is to establish the firm foundations for a future democracy. The obvious blueprints for option 2 are the U.S. occupations of Germany and Japan in the aftermath of World War II.

Essentially, the U.S. needs to replicate its performance in Japan and Germany. In some respects, the parallels between creating democracy in Iraq and what it required in Germany and Japan are apt. The education system in Iraq will need to be entirely revamped, unknowable numbers of people will need to be "deprogrammed" after 30 years of Ba'athist rule, the economy will need to be reconstructed from the bottom up, corruption that has reached epidemic proportions will need to be rooted out, generations of Iraqis schooled in the idea that America and Israel are the bitter enemies of the Iraqi people will need to be persuaded otherwise—and so the list could continue. The Iraqi state needs to be reconstructed before any attempt can be made to implant democracy. Unlike the cases of Germany and Japan, this will need to be done in the midst of a deeply hostile region, and it will need to be done while holding a fragmented country together. Japan and Germany were, at the time, two of the most ethnically homogenous countries on the face of the earth. Iraq is not.

If the U.S. wants to give democracy any chance of survival in Iraq, it will need a level of commitment at least on a par with that devoted to Japan. This will mean long-term military occupation. It is worth remembering that democracy was forced on the Japanese—the U.S. imposed democratization from above. The U.S. even wrote Japan's constitution, then railroaded it through the Japanese Parliament. It was an occupation in which "General MacArthur and his command ruled their new domain as neocolonial overlords, beyond challenge or criticism, as inviolate as the emperor and his officials had ever been."[15] It was, in the words of one observer, "the last immodest exercise in the colonial conceit known as 'the white man's burden.'"[16] Vital to the success of this neocolonial enterprise was the figure of the emperor. It was through the emperor that MacArthur ensured the compliance of the Japanese people. No comparable figure exists in Iraq.

Nonetheless, a long-term U.S. military occupation will at least offer some prospect of a survivable democracy emerging in Iraq by the end of the period. The critical function U.S. troops can serve is to provide a framework of stability, backed up by the threat (or use) of coercive force. The deals made and compromises reached during the process of haggling over the constitution can be enforced because the U.S. can ensure compliance. For example, a hypothetical deal between Kurds and Arabs could involve the city of Kirkuk remaining outside a Kurdish autonomous region, in return for which the Kurds receive a guaranteed annual income from the Kirkuk oil field. Based on historical experience, the Kurds would be extremely naïve to take on trust that an Arab-dominated central government would ultimately respect such a deal. The long-term presence of U.S. troops can provide a guarantee that all parties comply with deals struck. The advantage of this is that Iraqi democracy can function even in the absence of mutual trust among Iraq's groups. Hopefully, over time, as the political representatives of Iraq's groups interact on a daily basis and in an atmosphere of stability, so the bonds of trust will begin to emerge.

In addition to resolving many of the problems over political institutions, a long-term U.S. presence will facilitate the evolution of civil society and, perhaps, the genesis of a democratic political culture in Iraq. At the end of 10 to 15 years of military occupation, the U.S. will leave in place a set of political institutions embedded in something deeper. Ideally, Iraqi democracy will be consolidated at the level of civil society and will therefore have some chance of becoming a self-sustaining phenomenon. But it is important to recognize the magnitude of the challenge involved here. Consolidating democracy at the two deepest levels identified by Fukuyama will not be easy because, in simple terms, there is little in the way of raw material to work with.

*Level Three: Civil Society.* Civil society can be defined as "the realm of spontaneously created social structures separate from the state that underlie democratic political institutions."[17] These social structures—comprising, among other things, active interest groups, watchdog groups, community associations, and a free press—are, according to many, "a necessary precondition of stable democratic institutions."[18] Others have used the term "social capital" to refer to the reservoirs of "trust, norms and networks" that bind the social fabric of a country and in turn, affect significantly the prospects for an effective democratic order.[19] To use an analogy, civil society is the topsoil onto which the seeds of democratic institutions are sown. The quality of the soil determines the likelihood of the seeds germinating.

In Iraq, the process begins from a position of sowing seeds onto concrete. The golden age of Iraqi civil society occurred under the latter years of the monarchy. Even then, this was a civil society comprised of elites, which never penetrated the vast majority of the population. Since 1968, when the Ba'ath assumed power for the second time, civil society in Iraq has simply ceased to exist. The nature of totalitarian regimes is such that the elimination of civil society is consciously pursued by the regime, because the existence of autonomous social structures beyond the direct control of the state is perceived as a threat. No one should underestimate the effectiveness with which the Ba'ath regime succeeded in shattering any vestige of civil society that may have lingered on beyond the overthrow of the monarchy in 1958. In terms of social structures beyond the control of the regime, almost all have been dismantled. This atomization of the Iraqi people—which included a concerted effort to inculcate in the young a sense of loyalty to the regime more fundamental even than family ties—cannot but have had a devastating effect on future prospects for the emergence of civil society. At the same time, after 1991, the regime fortified certain structures. In particular, the 1990s witnessed the birth of "neo-tribalism" in Iraq—a strange perversion of traditional tribal values coupled with the channeling of favors and material benefits to certain tribal groups at the expense of others. Viewed (extremely) optimistically, the tribes could provide some form of stability in post-Saddam Iraq. Many tribes, for instance, span the sectarian divide and thus serve to integrate rather than divide the Arab population of Iraq. More realistically, the existence of multiple, heavily armed tribal groups used to operating relatively free from direct central control could degenerate into a large-scale version of Afghan warlordism.

Nurturing the seeds of civil society in Iraq will be a long and painful process. It will involve providing a social, economic, and political context conducive to the emergence of moderate groups, such as trade unions, professional associations, and political parties committed to the democratic process; at the same time, it will also require the U.S. to make difficult decisions about how to deal with "immoderate" groups, such as Islamic fundamentalists, anti-Zionist groups, or, more pertinently, anti-American groups.

*Level 4: Political Culture.*   At the deepest level, political culture encompasses factors such as religion, moral values, ethnic consciousness, and the like. This is the deeper soil within which the germinated seeds of democratic institutions establish strong, durable roots. This is the deepest level at which a democracy must become embedded in order to be considered fully consolidated, and it is a level that is beyond social or political engineering. In Fukuyama's words, "Culture can be defined as a-rational, ethical habit passed on through tradition."[20] Culture does not change rapidly, but over the course of generations. At this level, of course, uncomfortable questions arise about whether the norms and values associated with the Western liberal democratic tradition are even compatible with the norms and values of an Arab Islamic society. This is a complex debate (to say the least), and one that cannot be proven either way. But empirically, the record of stable democracies in the Arab world is not good. In 2001, the highpoint of democracy in the world, 121 (63 percent) of the world's 192 countries had democratically elected governments. Of the 16 Arab states, none was democratic. Nor has an Arab state ever been governed democratically for very long.[21] The closest to an exception here is actually Iraq which, under the monarchy, at least maintained a reasonable pretense at being democratic. But in no sense did democracy penetrate into the culture of society. At best, one might describe it as an elected oligarchy. The record of Islamic countries is slightly better. In 2001, of the 45 countries with Muslim majorities, 11 had democratically elected governments. Note, however, that this figure comprises countries like Nigeria, the democratic credentials of which are marginally convincing at best. In terms of countries that could be classified as "free" by western standards, there is only one example—Mali.

None of this is to argue that an Arab or Islamic democracy is inherently oxymoronic, but rather to highlight the magnitude of what needs to be done in Iraq. The creation of a successful, consolidated democracy in Iraq would dwarf America's achievements in Germany or Japan. It would be history's first fully functioning, consolidated Arab democracy. For democracy to survive and prosper in Iraq will require a massive commitment on the part of the United States. Iraq (with the exception of Iraqi Kurdistan) has enjoyed nothing resembling a functioning civil society since the early 1950s, and has never had a democratic political culture. More often than not in Iraq's history, political disputes have been resolved through the use of violence rather than at the ballot box. Iraq is not a latent democracy, waiting to explode into life the moment the shackles of oppression have been cast aside. Civil society and a supportive political culture will need to be created from scratch and this will take time— generations perhaps. A 10–15 year U.S. military occupation is the minimum that will be required to give democracy in Iraq a chance of succeeding.

*Advantages of Option 2.*   Option 2 is different in kind from option 1. It recognizes that bringing democracy to Iraq is in the vital strategic interests of the U.S., and that this will require a massive commitment of resources and manpower to achieve. A commitment of this order of magnitude will go some way toward convincing skeptics that the U.S. is serious about democratizing the Middle East. Over a 10–15–year period, Iraq can be completely reconstructed from the ground up; the oil infrastructure can be brought back online, vital utilities can be restored, Iraq's once-proud social support network can be reconstituted, and the U.S. can leave in place a democratic system of government that stands some chance of surviving a U.S. departure. During this period, law and order, protection against external interference, and social stability will be guaranteed by U.S. military forces, and "spoiler" groups can be rooted out and eliminated. Ideally, at the end of this period, the cycle of violence that has haunted relations between Kurds and Arabs will have been broken and a stable, prosperous, democratic Iraq will have a real chance of succeeding as a nation.

*Disadvantages of Option 2.*   There are two very obvious drawbacks to option 2. First, it is unclear how long the American public will be prepared to tolerate an occupation that consumes sizeable economic resources and results in significant U.S. casualties. The assumption that the costs of occupation and the reconstruction of Iraq can be met using Iraq's own resources is (at least in the short term) plainly false. Most analyses estimate that it will take up to six years before Iraq's oil infrastructure is capable of producing oil at pre-1991 levels. In the meantime, Iraq's physical and social infrastructure will need to be reconstructed, and the cost of this, if done properly, will run into the hundreds of billions of dollars. The cost of occupation alone is running at over $1 billion a month and the news that Iraq's own resources are to be used to pay for the military occupation of the country is unlikely to be well received by the Iraqi people. But the most politically inflammatory issue is likely to be U.S. casualties. Pacifying a country the size of Iraq will not be accomplished without significant losses, and as the death toll mounts, public pressure for the withdrawal of U.S. troops will intensify. The U.S. public has simply not been well prepared for a commitment of this magnitude. In fact the Bush Administration's estimate prior to the start of the war was that U.S. troops would be out of Iraq within 60 days of the declared end of the war. Clearly, this estimate is proving to be woefully inaccurate.

But the most significant problem with option 2 is that it essentially requires the Iraqi people to yield sovereignty over their own country for a 10–15–year period. During this period, the U.S. would control Iraq's resources, decide what is, and is not, an "acceptable" political party, exercise a monopoly over the use of violence, and impose a political system of its own devising on the Iraqi people. It is simply unrealistic to expect the majority of Iraqis to tolerate an occupation of this type and duration. Indeed, one of the few things that currently unites Iraqis is a shared desire to see the occupation terminated as soon as possible and control over Iraq returned to Iraqis. Even erstwhile allies of the U.S., such as the INC, have made it clear that long-term military occupation is not an option. Only the Kurds seem likely to support an extended period of military occupation. As long as U.S. troops remain on the ground in Iraq, the Kurds have a good chance of retaining their autonomous existence in northern Iraq. But the reaction of Iraq's Arab population to a prolonged occupation is likely to be less hospitable. The British have traveled this road before, and it is a road drenched in blood. As the British learned to their cost, the only sure way to unite Iraq's Arab population is to forcibly occupy Iraq and to impose an alien system of government that lacks popular legitimacy. The British-imposed Hashemite monarchy proved to be fairly durable, but it could never command widespread respect or affection because it was fatally tainted by its association with the British. During the period of direct rule

(1920–1932), the British faced a major rebellion that united Iraq's Arab population (1920), and continual unrest from the Kurds in the north. The British administered heavy doses of violence to maintain order, and the U.S. must be prepared to do the same. But the goal of the British was only to pacify Iraq and maintain some form of internal order; the U.S. has the much more ambitious task of turning Iraq into a functioning democracy. This will require the widespread and *active* participation of the Iraqi people. It is somewhat optimistic to expect Iraqis to be wildly enthusiastic about being ruled by a country that is responsible for the devastation of Iraq and the deaths of hundreds of thousands of Iraqis through sanctions and war.

Option 2 embodies precisely the scale of commitment that will be required if democracy in Iraq is to survive in the long term, but it is not feasible politically. The future is never certain, but the most plausible outcome of option 2 is that over time, domestic resentment at the continuing drain on the U.S. economy and the interminable stream of body bags returning from Iraq will intensify, and resistance in Iraq to a "neo-colonial" occupation will harden. The U.S. may well end up with its own version of the West Bank, but on a scale that dwarfs anything the Israelis have to deal with.

## Who Wants a Democratic Iraq?

Viewed on a regional level, the broader issue becomes who will and will not support a strong, stable, prosperous, democratic Iraq? If the U.S. succeeds beyond all expectations in Iraq, who will favor this outcome? History indicates the importance of this issue. Throughout Iraq's history, but especially after 1958, one of the key factors affecting the internal stability of Iraq has been the willingness of outside parties to intervene to destabilize the fragile ethnic/sectarian balance. Iraq is an easy target—far easier than other states in the region. At various times, this has resulted in major external interference, using the Kurds as a surrogate to target the central regime. At other times, Iran has used the Shi'a in the south as its fifth column. The list of countries that have found themselves unable to resist the temptation to intervene is long; it includes the U.S., Iraq, Syria, Israel, the Soviet Union, Jordan, Kuwait, Turkey, and Saudi Arabia (pretty much every country in the region, in fact). Presumably, for the state of Iraq to enjoy the stability necessary to nurture democratic roots, this will need to stop. Among states in the region, few will welcome a strong, democratic Iraq. For most of the states in the region, the ideal form of government for Iraq was, and is, a weakened, contained Saddam-like regime. It is certainly not a strong, prosperous democracy allied with the West. Iraq is surrounded by states (with the possible exception of Kuwait) that have a vested interest in seeing the democratic experiment fail. It is implausible to think that they will not seek to influence the course of events in Iraq.

Certainly, Iran, Syria, and Saudi Arabia will not rejoice if the U.S. triumphs. If nothing else, the first two cannot help but think that they are in line to become the next dominos. A stable, democratic Iraq will leave the U.S. free to turn its attentions elsewhere. Iran is an original member of the "axis of evil," and Syria must fear impending membership. These two states have every incentive not to let the U.S. succeed. No doubt the U.S. will issue stern warnings against interference in Iraq—so this interference will take the form, as it always has, of using surrogates in Kurdistan and the south. Beyond this, it is difficult to see how the Gulf monarchies will embrace the democratization of the Middle East with open arms. In particular, the Saudi ruling family survives in power because it has bought off the Islamic threat—both through financial inducements, and by maintaining a strictly Islamic political and social system. But this is a very delicate high-wire act, which would come tumbling down rapidly if Western liberal values were introduced into the Saudi system. In light of this, Saudi Arabia has every incentive not to let the U.S. succeed in Iraq. Perhaps the most pertinent question is whether the U.S. itself even wants democracy to succeed. This will depend on what emerges as a consequence. Historically, the ideologies that have successfully traversed the sectarian and/or ethnic divides are anti-imperialism, anti-Zionism, pan-Arabism, Islam, and Communism. None of these can look particularly attractive to the U.S.

Evidence from elsewhere (Russia, Bosnia, and Kosovo for example) suggests that when peoples are released from a sustained period of totalitarian rule, they are inordinately susceptible to extremist political forces. The atomization of Iraq's population has broken down traditional ties of loyalty to the extent that the people are likely to grasp at the first ideology that makes them feel part of something larger. Whether this expresses itself as a revitalization of Islamism, or an extremist Arab-based ideology, the political parties that emerge to reflect these forces will not be sympathetic to the West, still less to a continued occupation by U.S. forces. If democracy produces parties that embrace these ideologies—and it is extremely difficult to envisage where more moderate ideologies are going to spring from—then the U.S. will have to decide whether or not to abide by the products of this process. Will the U.S. accept a pan-Arabist, anti-Zionist elected government in Iraq? This would rather defeat the purpose of the whole exercise. The most likely outcome would be that the U.S. interferes behind the scenes to ensure the "right" election results. But the more the U.S. is drawn into this sort of activity, the less indigenously "Iraqi" the government looks, and the more likely it is to be seen as a colonial imposition. The British have been here before.[22]

## Option 3: The Puppet Regime

This leaves option 3. This is, in many ways, the default option. In its broad outlines, this option would involve the selection of an Iraqi puppet to put an Iraqi "face" on an American military occupation. The role of the puppet would be to convince the Iraqi people that they should cooperate with U.S. forces, that the U.S. is a friend to Iraq's people, not an enemy, and generally to soften the edges of complete American dominance. After perhaps two years of direct American rule, during which some of Iraq's infrastructure is rebuilt, the armed forces and police de-Ba'athized and reconstituted, and Iraq's oil is brought back online, direct American rule ends, to be replaced by the chosen "face." Some form of democratic exercise (probably carefully controlled) is staged, and the puppet is elected overwhelmingly to executive office, promising to abide by democratic norms and to work with Iraq's diverse populations to forge a new constitution for the democratic governance of Iraq. Behind the scenes, the puppet's regime is heavily dependent on the U.S., and the U.S. retains a decisive say over the direction of policy. The U.S. retains military basing rights in Iraq both to police the region, and to ensure the "stability" of the new regime during its difficult, formative stages. Such a scenario could evolve either by design, or by accident. By design, it would indicate that the "democratic tsunami" the U.S. promised would engulf Iraq, and from there, the Middle East, was an elaborate bluff/lie; by couching the war as the first phase in a crusade to liberate the oppressed people of the Middle East, the Bush Administration's goal was to win support for the war from diverse populations (the Iraqi people, the American public, and world opinion), but the intention was never to democratize Iraq. The intention all along was to implant a pliable leader into the heart of the Arab World. The ideal leader would not look very different from Saddam Hussein (i.e., authoritarian, able to preserve Iraq's unity, and *secular*)—but would have to be significantly more user-friendly. Western oil supplies would be guaranteed, U.S. troops could leave Saudi Arabia to its own fate, and the U.S. would have a new, strategically vital operating base from which to police (or invade) problematic regimes in the region (Iran and Syria).

It is also plausible that this scenario unfolds even if democratizing Iraq was the original intention. Perhaps after a brief honeymoon period during which the euphoria of liberation ensures cooperation, reality sets in with a jolt.

Iraq—pride of the Arab World, and location of Shi'a Islam's holiest shrines—is now under complete foreign domination. Worse, it is domination by the hated American–Zionist axis. Prominent religious leaders in the southern shrine cities, fortified by the return of nearly half a million exiles from Iran, speak out against the occupation of holy ground by an infidel invader. The newly established and U.S.-administered "Ministry of Religious Affairs" attempts to silence dissent.[23] Resentment grows—fueled by organized Shi'a groups such as al-Da'wa and SCIRI—and is discretely funded by Tehran. Resentment gives way to terrorist activity. Occupying troops are targeted in a suicide bombing campaign. The steady stream of body bags returning to Washington turns U.S. public against the occupation. The U.S. desperately needs a way to get troops out of Iraq without losing face. A puppet government offers the least-worst option. In truth, this is only one among numerous possible scenarios that could lead the U.S. to withdraw in short order without leaving a democratic Iraq in its wake. Indeed, considerably more pessimistic scenarios are depressingly plausible. Even if a U.S. occupation is broadly popular among average Iraqis, there are a host of potential groups that could spearhead resistance, ranging from Islamic extremists to renegade units of Saddam's *Fedayeen*. The potential for violent interethnic (or intertribal) conflict in post-Saddam Iraq is also high. In particular, the city of Kirkuk is a tinder box waiting to ignite. Perhaps 300,000 Kurds wait in refugee slums in northern Iraq, ready to return to their homes in Kirkuk. These homes are now occupied by ethnic Arabs as a consequence of Saddam's sustained policy of "Arabization." The Turks wait in the wings, ready to intervene with military force if Kirkuk's large Turcomen population is threatened. The endless possibilities for internal violence that the removal of Saddam's repressive regime could unleash will need to be policed by U.S. forces. The question is not whether U.S. forces are capable of performing this function (they clearly are) but rather how long the American public is prepared to tolerate the loss of American lives to win the peace in Iraq. Of course, under a best-case scenario, regime change ushers in a period of relative calm and stability that enables a functioning democratic order to be established. Perhaps this will occur. If it does not, we can expect the Bush Administration rhetoric to change subtly. The word "democracy" will be exorcised from official discourse; the word "stability" will increasingly take its place. The U.S. role in the liberation of Iraq will be stressed—its role in *constructing* democracy afterward will be downplayed. The Iraqi people, we will be informed, must build democracy for themselves. But the regime left in place will be, at best, marginally democratic, and the prospects for the emergence of a stable democratic order in Iraq will be essentially zero.

*The Advantages of Option 3.* Option 3 is not without its appeal. Not only does it remove U.S. troops from a very dangerous place in short order, it would also allow the U.S. to avoid the accusation that it is imposing its own vision of government on the Iraqi people. The responsibility for creating democracy will be placed on the people of Iraq. Meanwhile (presumably) the U.S. will ensure that it retains some influence over a new regime, even once U.S. troops have departed the scene. A puppet regime will also absolve the U.S. of responsibility for dealing with some very prickly, potentially explosive issues—such as how to create a mutually acceptable balance of power within a new government among Sunnis, Shi'a, and Kurds, and how to reconcile conflicting demands for strong central government with those for a decentralized political order. In short, the U.S. will simply sidestep all the most intractable problems involved in creating democracy in Iraq. Responsibility for resolving these will pass to an Iraqi regime. Additionally, such a regime will lend itself to strong, centralized governance. This will ensure stability (at least temporarily) and safeguard the territorial integrity of Iraq. While certainly not democratic, the replacement regime will be a significant improvement for the Iraqi people. Any puppet regime will, by definition, be morally preferable to Saddam's regime. It could scarcely be otherwise.

*Drawbacks of Option 3.* Tempting as it may appear, option 3 would be seriously detrimental to U.S. interests. It would also, in all likelihood, spell disaster for Iraq. Despite inevitable claims to the contrary, option 3 would be widely perceived as a violation of a basic U.S. commitment to bring democracy to the people of Iraq. A deeply skeptical international community will have its worst suspicions confirmed. The U.S.-British war will be judged retrospectively as an unprovoked, aggressive war against a Third World country in pursuit of narrow self-interest. Claims by President Bush that "Iraqi lives and freedom matter greatly to us," and pledges to bring "hope and progress into the lives of millions"[24] will be dismissed as cynical deceptions. America's reputation, already badly damaged by the diplomatic trainwreck at the United Nations, is on trial in Iraq. If America does not deliver on its promise to bring democracy to Iraq, then it is difficult to see anything but a significant increase in worldwide anti-American sentiment. At this point, the idea that America could actually win the hearts and minds of the Arab world evaporates entirely. Prior to the onset of war, most experts were already predicting that the use of force against an Arab Muslim country at the heart of the Middle East would radicalize an entire generation of Arab youth. In the short term, this can only harm the U.S. in its war against global terror.

There is always the remote possibility, of course, that the Iraqi equivalent of Nelson Mandela will emerge like a phoenix from the ashes to help heal the historical wounds of a badly mutilated society and to champion Iraq's triumphant march toward democracy. Chances are slim, however. Even if the U.S. evades responsibility for democratizing Iraq, some form of leadership structure must be left in place and it is not at all clear where this will come from. The Iraqi Governing Council (IGC) has the structure, it is broadly representative of Iraq's diverse factional groupings, and, at least rhetorically, is united around the need for a federal democratic Iraq. But the IGC has demonstrated itself to be bitterly divided. Rhetorical consensus around the use of words such as "democracy" and "federalism" mask the basic truth that the various groups represented within the IGC interpret these terms in radically different ways. If the IGC cannot come close to meaningful agreement on the future of Iraq from the safety of five-star London hotels, it is unlikely to find consensus any easier in the turbulent environment of Baghdad.

In terms of individuals who could serve as the acceptable "face" of American occupation, there simply are no obvious contenders. Such an individual would have to be acceptable to Sunnis, the Shi'a, and the Kurds. INC leader Ahmed Chalabi fits the bill demographically, but is virtually unknown inside Iraq. A prominent former army officer offers certain advantages. Until its dissolution the Iraqi army remained one of the institutions most respected by ordinary Iraqis, and one of the few institutions that has historically served to integrate rather than divide Iraqi society. Such a leader would almost certainly be a Sunni Arab, both because the available selection of high-ranking Shi'a officers is limited, but also because it is unlikely that the overwhelmingly Sunni Arab officer corps would accept Shi'a leadership. It is also unclear how those army officers who chose to surrender to coalition forces rather than fight (assuming those who chose to fight will be terminally out of contention for a leadership position) will be judged by Iraqis. They may be viewed as cowards and traitors to the state of Iraq, or as heroes who chose not to defend a brutal repressive regime. Either way, if the U.S. leaves Iraq in the hands of a military leader, it will be difficult indeed to sell this as a victory for democracy.

Beyond the specifics of who would front a puppet regime, a more significant issue concerns the likely fate of such a regime once a U.S. military occupation ended. With all of the most difficult questions regarding power-sharing arrangements and the division of power remaining to be resolved, and no real foundation for democracy in place, there are really only two possible outcomes. First, a struggle for power among Iraq's various groups ensues, leading to a wholesale breakdown in law and order and possible civil war. Second, the regime, like all previous Iraqi regimes, realizes very quickly that authoritarian rule and the use of force are the necessary components of stable governance in Iraq. The U.S. helps prop up the regime from afar, in return for which Iraq becomes a pliable client state for the U.S. Back to the future for the state of Iraq. A third possible outcome—that the regime embarks on a dedicated, long-term effort to implant democracy, and is ultimately successful—is as credible an outcome as it has ever been for Iraq. The idea that Iraq can find its own way to democracy flies in the face of 80 years of history. It assumes that the basic building blocks of a stable democratic order are already in place in Iraq, and that once liberated from the yoke of an oppressive regime, democracy will emerge as the natural state of being for the people of Iraq. This is a fantasy. Democracy does not occur spontaneously, and certainly not overnight.

## CONCLUSION: PONDERING ALTERNATIVES

The U.S. is currently in a very dangerous position. Having promised to bring democracy to Iraq, and from there, to the whole of the Middle East, the U.S. now finds itself occupying a country that seems less than enthusiastic about tolerating the long-term military occupation that will surely be necessary if the U.S. is to deliver on its promise. Of the three options outlined above, option 1 seems closest to what the Administration had in mind before the outbreak of the war; option 2 is what it will take in order to give democracy some chance of survival in Iraq, but this option is unlikely to be acceptable to either the U.S. or Iraqi people; option 3 is probably the most likely to occur. The dilemma then is that the one option that could plausibly result in a stable, democratic Iraq is politically unacceptable, while the other two options may well precipitate the violent fragmentation of the state of Iraq. The U.S. is in the process of dismantling the remaining institutions of the Iraqi state, and as it does so, it risks dissolving the "glue" that has held the state together for over 80 years. At this point, it may be wise to ponder an alternative option.

### Option 4: The Managed Partition of Iraq

One option, that of allowing the state of Iraq to split up, has barely entered the debate as a possibility. To the extent that it has, it has been in the form of promises on the part of the U.S. to preserve the territorial integrity of the Iraqi state. The promise was made primarily to reassure the Turks that an independent Kurdistan would not result from the conflict. In return, the Turks were supposed to permit the U.S. to launch a northern front from their territory. In the end, the Turks reneged on their side of the deal. As an option, the managed partition of Iraq is far from ideal; it is just better than any other option currently under consideration.

*How would this occur?*    The most obvious objection to the partitioning of Iraq is that it would be an imposed solution. Once again, a western imperialist power redraws the map of the Middle East to safeguard its own strategic/economic interests. This is an important objection, because if indeed a partition of Iraq were to be imposed unilaterally by the U.S. it is difficult to see how these borders would be considered legitimate by anyone in the region. This would be a fragile solution. The trick is not to *impose* this as a solution, but to provide the Iraqi people themselves with the opportunity to decide the issue. The outlines for this are already in place. The Pentagon's plan to divide Iraq into three segments, a north, center, and south, is how the process begins. This creates three autonomous units governed under the loose auspices of a single state. These units should be governed through existing structures on the ground. In the case of the south, this means governing though tribal leaders, the religious leadership, and organized Islamic groups such as SCIRI and *al-Da'wa*. The likelihood of this resulting in any form of democracy is slim, but that is not important. The goal would not be to impose democratic institutions on any unit, but to allow each unit to govern itself according to its own preferences.

Clearly, in the case of Iraqi Kurdistan, governance would be through the two major Kurdish factions (the PUK and KDP) along with representatives of the Turcoman and Assyrian communities. In practice, the administration of Iraqi Kurdistan would continue much as it has for the last decade or so. In other words, what is the closest thing to a functioning (though imperfect) democracy in the region would not be disturbed. The goal of administering three separate units instead of one single unit is to avoid precisely the MacArthur syndrome. In so far as the U.S. inevitably will be the power behind the throne, it is vital to minimize the impression of overweening American power. The administration of postwar Iraq should devolve power away from the center as much as possible. Iraq can be governed as three parts much more easily, and less oppressively than it can as a single unit. As the situation evolves, each unit makes its own choices about the priorities for reconstruction and begins to forge its own economic relations with surrounding nations. Natural trading partners for the north are Iran and Turkey, for the center, Syria and Jordan, and for the south, the Gulf monarchies. Assuming that some form of equitable distribution of oil revenue can be negotiated (similar to the oil-for-food program administered by the UN), the Iraqi oil industry's export routes are naturally divided into three. From the oil fields of the north, the pipeline stretches to Turkey; from the Kirkuk field to the southwest, a pipeline (currently closed) exports to Syria; and from the oil fields of the south, the obvious route is out through the Gulf. The goal would be to establish autonomous economic relations between the three units and other countries, and to avoid channeling the decision-making process through a centralized administration. But this will be a temporary arrangement that allows reconstruction to proceed without having to encounter the problems associated with defining the final features of a central government.

The governing of Iraq does not need to be enshrined immediately in a set of inviolate constitutional principles; government can be regionally organized, flexible, and sensitive to the diverse social structures on the ground. Some form of loosely organized, largely powerless central government can be established to provide an umbrella over the whole. This can be made deliberately powerless and given to the Iraqi exile community to run, or can be constitutionally engineered to produce paralysis. A replication of the constitution of Bosnia perhaps.

In terms of security forces, the Kurds will not disband the *peshmerga*, so each unit must be allowed to organize its own security forces. Again, this will resemble the situation in Bosnia. But the division of Iraq into three units is not the end goal. It is a temporary means of proceeding with the reconstruction that enables each unit to evolve in the most natural direction, and the populations of each unit to determine how this is organized. After a certain period (perhaps two to three years), the time will come for the Iraqis themselves to determine a political future for Iraq. The first question on the agenda does not concern the type of political system to be put in place, but the most fundamental decision of all. Do the Iraqis want to stay together as a state, and if so, what are they prepared to compromise in order to achieve this? This suggests the need for a referendum, preceded by an honest and open dialogue among Iraqis themselves as to whether there is any future for the state of Iraq. The referendum would be held in each of the three units, and if the majority on any unit votes to secede from Iraq, this decision must be accepted. The advantage of this approach lies in the incentives it provides to the major political players involved. For those who favor preserving the territorial integrity of Iraq, the goal will be to win over those who are more ambivalent. This will require a willingness to compromise on important principles. To retain the Kurds as part of the Iraqi state for example, it may be necessary for Arab Iraqis to allow them the autonomy to govern themselves as they have been doing for the last

12 years. This will become a struggle for the hearts and minds of the Iraqi people, which is as it should be.

There are three possible outcomes of such a process. First, all three units stay together as a coherent state; second, the Kurds secede while the remaining Arab-populated units stay together; and third, there is a three-way division resulting in a northern Kurdish state, central Sunni/Shi'a state, and a southern Shi'a state. Based on past history, the first outcome is possible, but the Kurds will need a lot of persuading that it is in their best interests to remain part of the Iraqi state. The third outcome is probably the least likely. The most likely outcome is the second of these, in which case the Arab state of Iraq (or, perhaps, Mesopotamia) coexists with an independent Kurdish state. Given that all three outcomes are possible, the advantages and disadvantages of each need to be considered in turn.

*A United Iraq.*    If all three units of the Iraqi state hold together, then on the surface, nothing has changed. Iraq will occupy the same territory it has always occupied. But something very significant will have changed. For the first time in Iraq's history, this will be a *voluntary* union. The Kurds will have freely chosen to enter into a union with the Arab Iraqi state. The vote that produces this outcome can be considered the first expression of true national identity in Iraq's modern history. If nothing else, this outcome would be the first stage in a long process of healing the deep wounds of history. At this point, Iraq has a chance of being ruled by something better than the Ba'ath Party, because the strains of forcing the parts to remain whole will have been removed. Whether a democratic Iraq results from this is an open question, but some of the compromises likely to precede such a vote are basically the compromises that will need to be made at some point anyway. For example, if, as seems reasonable to assume, the Sunnis favor maintaining the state of Iraq in its current configuration, then they will have to accept that their days of dominating the decision-making process in Iraq are over. Power will have to be shared with the Shi'a.

There are no obvious downsides to an outcome that maintains the territorial integrity of the state of Iraq. Turkey may complain about the degree of autonomy enjoyed by the Kurds, but the time has come for Turkey to stop interfering in the politics of Iraq. If this takes an ultimatum from the U.S., then so be it. What comes out of this may or may not be democratic, but it will be a system chosen by the Iraqis themselves, rather than imposed on them by the U.S. At least in Kurdistan, there is a strong possibility that if allowed to enjoy the same degree of autonomy as previously, over time, a viable democracy can emerge. The potential is already there.

*The Two-State Outcome.*    If the Kurds are genuinely afforded the opportunity to determine their own future, then the probable result will be an independent Kurdish state in the north of Iraq coexisting with an Arab entity to the south. To avoid this outcome, the Arab population must be prepared to tolerate a degree of Kurdish autonomy that they have never previously been willing to accept, and the Kurds must take it on trust that an Arab-dominated central government will not renege on promises made when (subsequently) in a position to do so. Neither seems likely. Rather, it seems plausible that the Kurds would elect to fulfill their long-cherished dream of independence. The possibility of an independent Kurdish state raises a number of important concerns, but on balance, an independent Kurdistan resolves more problems than it creates.

Where would the borders fall? Given that there has been no reliable census in Iraq since 1957, the exact distribution of the Kurdish population relative to the Arab population in northern Iraq is unknown. Nonetheless, certain cities, Erbil and Suleimaniyah, for example, are indisputably Kurdish, while Mosul is clearly Arab-dominated. An independent Kurdish state would not, therefore, include Mosul within its borders. The status of Kirkuk is the obvious sticking point. As a result of decades of ethnic cleansing, Arabs almost certainly form a plurality, if not an absolute majority in Kirkuk. However, Arab and Kurdish perspectives on the significance of Kirkuk differ. For the Kurds, Kirkuk is their Jerusalem; for successive Arab regimes, the core issue has always been control over the large Kirkuk oil field. These two issues are separable in that the inclusion of Kirkuk in an independent Kurdistan does not necessarily entail Kurdish control over the oil reserves. Kirkuk the city should be part of a Kurdish state; Kirkuk the oil field (at least in its entirety) need not be. Other than the inclusion of Kirkuk, the boundaries of an independent Kurdish state would not differ significantly from the already established boundaries of the autonomous Kurdish region.

⊰⊱    ⊰⊱    ⊰⊱

Would a Kurdish state survive? A Kurdish state in northern Iraq would be small in terms of population; somewhere between 4 and 5 million. It would also be land-locked and surrounded by much larger, more powerful, and probably hostile states (Turkey, Syria, Iran, and an Arab state to the south). An unprotected Kurdistan would not last five minutes in such an environment. The only way an independent Kurdistan can be sustained as a viable entity is to establish a permanent U.S. or international military presence there. The establishment of military bases in Kurdistan would be tantamount to a guarantee of protection. As such, Kurdistan is perhaps the only part of Iraq in which the population would welcome U.S. troops enthusiastically. From a U.S. perspective, Kurdistan would actually be an ideal location from which to police neighboring "rogues" (Iran and Syria), without requiring troops to set foot on holy ground or Arab territory. Rather than constituting an onerous long-term burden on the U.S. then, the prospect of policing the region out of Kurdistan could more accurately be perceived as an opportunity.

Economically, Kurdistan's prospects would be better than they first appear. Optimally, some form of agreement could be negotiated with the Arab state to the south whereby Kurdistan would receive a proportion of the revenues from the Kirkuk oil field. Over the longer term, Kurdistan is in fact very well placed to become a regional trading hub. Located at the crossroads of three great civilizations (Turkish, Arab, and Persian), it is not difficult to envisage Kurdistan emerging as an important commercial center for the region. Initially, there is likely to be considerable hostility toward a nascent Kurdish state—especially from Turkey. Over time, however, once Kurdistan becomes an internationally recognized reality, Turkey would have little option but to open up trade routes through the newly established entity. Simply put, if Turkey wants to have any trade relations with Iraq, then goods cannot avoid traversing Kurdish territory. The presence of U.S. military bases and, perhaps, 30,000 to 50,000 foreign troops would also provide a significant contribution to the Kurdish economy.

Politically, the potential danger is one of implosion. Relations between the two main Kurdish factions—the PUK and the KDP—have not always been amiable, to say the least. In the mid-1990s indeed, this tense relationship erupted into open military conflict and came close to ripping apart the Kurds' fragile experiment with democracy. Since 1997, the animosity between the two organizations has diminished considerably and the *de facto* Kurdish state has been governed as essentially two separate entities. Clearly, if the likely consequence of creating a Kurdish state were a resumption of civil war, then this would rather seriously undermine the argument in favor of independence. Yet there are several reasons why this is unlikely. First, strong international support will impart a stability sufficient to prevent this from occurring; second, the collapse of the unified Kurdish government, though partly self-inflicted, was precipitated primarily by external interference on the part of neighboring powers. Again, the U.S. can flex its military muscles if necessary to prevent a repetition of this. Third, the leaders of both factions, Barzani

(KDP) and Talabani (PUK) have extremely powerful incentives not to destroy what may prove to be the Kurds' one chance at independent statehood. History will judge neither man kindly if personal rivalry is permitted to sabotage Kurdish independence. Finally, since 1997, both parties have demonstrated a capacity for peaceful coexistence—not just with each other but also with other ethnic and religious minorities located within Iraqi Kurdistan. Kurdistan may not be procedurally democratic (both entities are essentially governed as one-party statelets), but it is liberal and tolerant.

⚛    ⚛    ⚛

How would Turkey respond? Not very well, obviously. Turkey's concerns would focus on the status of approximately one million ethnic Turcomen residing in northern Iraq (mainly in Kirkuk and Mosul) and the possible impact of an independent Iraqi Kurdistan on Turkey's own sizable Kurdish population. Turkey's Kurds—geographically concentrated in the southeastern portion of the country—number anything up to fifteen million. Sporadically since the 1920s, then continuously since 1984, Turkish Kurds have struggled violently with a central government that has simply refused to recognize their existence as a distinct ethnic group. The government's "solution" to the Kurdish problem has been to rely on brute military force, an approach that has resulted in up to 30,000 Kurdish deaths, wholesale ethnic cleansing, and the destruction of 3,000 to 4,000 Kurdish villages since 1984. The capture of Abdullah Ocalan—leader of the main Kurdish resistance force, the Kurdistan Workers' Party (PKK)—in 1999 ushered in a period of relative calm. Ocalan announced a cease-fire from his prison cell and declared himself willing to pursue a political solution to the problem of Kurdish rights in Turkey. The fear in Ankara, presumably, is that an independent Kurdistan in Iraq would reignite the armed struggle in Turkey, potentially threatening the territorial integrity of the Turkish state. If valid, this fear would constitute a powerful argument against the creation of a Kurdish state in Iraq. As a NATO member Turkey has long been the key strategic ally of the U.S. in the region; it is also secular, somewhat democratic, and a vital geographical and psychological bridging point between the Western and Muslim worlds. The implosion of Turkey would be an unmitigated catastrophe for Western (and, obviously, Turkish) interests in the Middle East. Yet the prospects of a Kurdish state in northern Iraq precipitating massive instability in Turkey is extremely remote. In fact, a strong case can be made that a Kurdish state would impart stability to the strategic environment. For most of the 1990s, for example, the KDP has collaborated actively with Turkish military forces to crush PKK activities in northern Iraq. It is highly unlikely that either Kurdish faction would jeopardize newly won independence in order to support the PKK. In fact it is more plausible to assume that once Iraqi Kurds have something tangible to lose (statehood), they will have a vested interest in cooperating fully with Turkey to resolve the PKK problem. The elimination of the PKK as a viable force may even allow Turkey to fundamentally reappraise its approach to the Kurdish question. Certainly the chosen approach to this point—violence and brutality—has done little but inflict pain on the Turkish state. It has enabled Turkey's generals to maintain an unhealthy influence over a supposedly democratic civilian government, it has been a steady drain on the Turkish treasury (to the tune of $8 billion a year), and it has resulted in Turkey compiling one of the worst human rights records on the planet. If, as most in Turkey seem to favor, the future of Turkey lies with Europe and membership of the European Union (EU), then this is simply inconceivable until these issues are addressed. This will require a peaceful and *civilized* resolution to the Kurdish issue. Turkish preferences on the Kurdish question are not irrelevant—Turkey is, after all, an important Western ally—but this cannot mean that Turkey retains a *de facto* veto over the future of Iraq.

While the disadvantages associated with creating an independent Kurdistan in northern Iraq should not be underestimated, these must be balanced against a number of powerful arguments in favor of such a development. First, there is a compelling moral case for Kurdish statehood. No other ethnic group in the Middle East, perhaps in the world, suffered to the same extent as the Kurds during the course of the twentieth century. The strategic calculations of the great powers of the 1920s carved up the Kurdish nation and condemned its people to live as perpetual minorities in someone else's state. Nowhere have Kurds been treated as anything other than second-class citizens, and in Turkey and Iraq, their treatment has been close to subhuman. The attitude of the West in general, and the U.S. in particular, has been cynical in the extreme. When strategically convenient, the Kurds in Iraq have been encouraged to challenge central authority and provided with the material wherewithal to sustain rebellion; when no longer convenient, they have been deserted and left to their fate. Naturally, this did not prevent the suffering of the Kurds from being exploited to the maximum degree by the Bush Administration in the lead up to the war in 2003. Apparently, the use of chemical weapons against the Kurds in 1988 provided sufficient justification for a war to remove Saddam but is insufficient to justify what the Iraqi Kurds really deserve, which is their own state.

Second, despite concerns in some quarters that a Kurdish state would destabilize the region, based on the evidence of the twentieth century, it would be difficult to imagine how anything could make the Kurds more of a destabilizing influence than they already have been. Especially in Turkey and Iraq (and to a lesser extent in Iran) the Kurds have been a perpetual source of internal instability. In Iraq they have provided external powers with a ready-made surrogate army with which to destabilize a succession of central governments. With little to lose and their autonomy to preserve, the Kurds have proven to be more than willing accomplices. A Kurdish state would give the Iraqi Kurds something to lose and an incentive to promote rather than undermine stability in the region. It is precisely the *absence* of a Kurdish state that has made the Kurds such a dangerous influence at the heart of the Middle East.

Third, as the U.S. becomes embroiled in what is starting to look like a full-scale guerilla war in Iraq, and the presence of U.S. troops generates an increasingly hostile reaction from ordinary Iraqis, the idea that a unified Iraq will be the first democratic domino to fall in the Middle East begins to look a little optimistic. The only part of Iraq that looks capable of sustaining democracy at present is Iraqi Kurdistan. By insisting that Kurdistan remain part of a unified Iraq, the U.S. runs the risk of destroying the very political force that it seeks to unleash in the Middle East. A less ambitious, but much more realistic goal would be to use an independent Kurdish state as the first domino to fall in the region. Kurdistan would be a less significant domino than Iraq, but in a region not noted for its democratic traditions, anything is better than nothing.

Finally, it is worth noting that an independent Kurdish state is already in existence in all but name. The Kurds have their own governing institutions, control over territory, defined borders, and capable armed forces. Kurdish governments sit in Erbil and Suleimaniyah, KDP *peshmerga* patrol the streets of Mosul, and Kirkuk is governed by a Kurdish mayor. International recognition of this reality on the ground is really the only missing piece of the jigsaw. At this point it is difficult, if not impossible, to envisage how Iraqi Kurdistan can be peacefully reintegrated into the state of Iraq.

☗☗    ☗☗    ☗☗

What happens to the rest of Iraq? The remainder of Iraq would be largely ethnically homogenous. Geographically, it would look something like ancient Mesopotamia with the majority of the population located in the "land between two rivers." Ethnically and historically, this new state of Mesopotamia would be much more coherent than the old state of Iraq. Critically, the removal of Kurdistan from the equation would make Mesopotamia significantly easier to govern. The constant strain of using military force to maintain the territorial integrity of the Iraqi state would be removed, as would the capacity for external powers to use the Kurds as surrogates to destabilize the central government. That Iraq has been governed by a succession of militaristic, violent regimes is due, in no small measure, to the intractability of the Kurdish problem. Remove the problem and there is the possibility that Mesopotamia could be governed by something more appealing than the Ba'ath Party. This may, or may not look much like a democracy, but it would be a significant move in the right direction.

The removal of four to five million Sunni Kurds from Iraq would, of course, leave the remainder even more numerically dominated by Shi'a. Would Mesopotamia become vulnerable to a Shi'a fundamentalist takeover? This is possible but unlikely. Regardless, if Iraq is destined for fundamentalism, the retention of Kurdistan in the state of Iraq will not prevent this. It will, however, spell the end for the Kurds' brave democratic experiment in the north. However, it is unlikely that the majority of the Shi'a—particularly those living in the central part of Iraq—would embrace a fundamentalist state with open arms, and such a development would provoke strong resistance from the Sunni population. If the process of Iraq's political reconstruction begins with a regionally based vote on the future viability of the state itself, then those groups intent on pushing for an Islamic state (SCIRI and *al-Da'wa*, for example) will need to recognize that the fulfillment of this goal may well result in the disintegration of the Arab part of the Iraqi state into two separate entities. The three-state outcome would be potentially problematic in some respects but is not without its advantages.

*The Three-State Outcome.*    The details of this eventuality would be messy. Unlike the Kurdish region in the north, there is no natural dividing line that neatly separates Iraq's Sunni and Shi'a populations. A boundary line based around the 33rd parallel (adjusted to account for natural features) would create two states with roughly equal populations (about 10 million); an overwhelmingly Shi'a state of Basra in the south, and a mixed Sunni/Shi'a state of Baghdad in the center. The former would include the shrine cities of Karbala and Najaf, the latter, the Sunni triangle stretching northwest from Baghdad to Mosul, and from there, south to the Syrian border. Basra would inherit Iraq's southern oil fields including the massive Rumaila field (Iraq's second largest in terms of reserves); Baghdad would gain the lion's share of the Kirkuk oil field (shared with Kurdistan), smaller fields around Mosul, and any untapped oil riches in the western desert. Both Arab states would have sufficiently large populations and enough economic resources to ensure survival, yet neither would be powerful enough to threaten neighbors or pursue schemes for regional hegemony.

There are three potential concerns with the three-state outcome. First, the prospect of some form of Islamic state emerging in the south becomes distinctly plausible; second, if this occurs, it may provide an opportunity for Iran to expand its influence into, or even assimilate the southern, oil-rich part of Iraq; and third, the partition of a major power in the region would leave Iran as the unchallenged hegemon of the Gulf. From the perspective of the U.S., none of these prospects is particularly appealing. At the same time, it is easy to exaggerate the dangers involved here. There is probably a very good chance that some form of Islamic state would take hold in the southern part of Iraq. Such a state would (obviously) not be democratic, nor would it be favorably disposed toward the U.S. On the positive side of the ledger, an "Islamic state of Basra" would be a small state in terms of population and would lack the power to create problems for other states in the region. More importantly, separating off the source of Shi'a fundamentalism from the rest of Iraq would eliminate any prospect of an Islamic state taking root in a unified Iraq. Sometimes the leg must be amputated to save the body. Neighboring Iran would certainly seek to influence the course of events in Basra (as it has persistently in Iraq as a whole), but this does not mean that Basra would become a mere puppet of Iran. Historically, the relationship between indigenous Iraqi clerics and clerics of Persian origin has been one of rivalry rather than collaboration. As the Iran–Iraq war illustrated, sectarian identity does not trump ethnicity in the complex relationship between Iraqi and Iranian Shi'a. The 1991 *intifada* provided further evidence that Iranian-sponsored religious organizations such as SCIRI command limited support within Iraq; thus there is every reason to believe that an Islamic state of Basra would be an indigenously Iraqi affair.

The argument that the partition of Iraq would leave Iranian power unchecked in the Gulf region is superficially plausible but basically flawed. U.S. power—whether operating out of bases in Kurdistan or Gulf monarchies such as Qatar and Bahrain—would check Iranian power. This argument also assumes that the balance of power logic employed by the U.S. to date has been successful. In fact it has been a disaster. In supporting the brutal dictatorship of the Shah of Iran until 1979, the U.S. helped precipitate the Iranian Revolution. After 1979, U.S. military and economic support for the equally brutal regime of Saddam enabled Iraq to emerge as the largest military force in the region. Since the 1970s, the Gulf region has been host to an Islamic fundamentalist revolution, a vicious eight-year war between the region's two major powers, an invasion of Kuwait, and two coalition wars against Iraq. This is not an impressive record of stability. It is also precisely this "enemy of my enemy" logic that has fostered such deep resentment toward the U.S. in the region. The broad strategic vision underlying the invasion of Iraq in 2003 represents a tacit acknowledgment that the policy of supporting one murderous dictator to balance the power of another has failed disastrously.

The managed partition of Iraq is far from an ideal solution to the dilemma that currently confronts the U.S. as it seeks to bring some semblance of order to the country. But there are no good options left, only less bad options. The U.S. is committed to democratizing Iraq while preserving its territorial integrity as a state. If the U.S. insists on adhering to both of these commitments it is heading down a road that ends in disaster. It is time to consider alternative options.

# EPILOGUE

ON MAY 1, 2003, PRESIDENT BUSH STOOD on the flight deck of the USS *Abraham Lincoln*, suitably bedecked in naval aviation gear, and with a "Mission Accomplished" banner conveniently visible in the background, to declare an official end to major combat operations in Iraq. One hundred days later, the President offered his analysis of the prevailing situation in occupied Iraq: "We've made a lot of progress in a hundred days, and I am pleased with the progress we've made."[1] Simultaneously, the White House issued a 24-page report entitled "Results in Iraq: 100 Days Toward Security and Freedom" to trumpet the successes of the U.S.-led occupation. The report detailed such notable achievements as the restoration of water supplies to preconflict levels, the establishment of over 150 newspapers, universal access to health care, and, somewhat optimistically, the institutionalization of democracy as among the "highlights of the successes" in Iraq. The problem for the Bush Administration is that the successes in Iraq (of which there are many) are inevitably overshadowed by the obvious fact that the war is not yet over. If anything, it has morphed into a form of conflict that is much more dangerous now than it was in March 2003. From the perspective of November 2003, seven months after Bush's speech (and eight months after the main body of this book was completed), the outlook for U.S. forces in Iraq and the future stability of Iraq itself does not look good.

There must now be serious doubts about whether the U.S. can prevail militarily over the forces of resistance, still less establish a shining beacon of democracy at the heart of the Middle East. However, the absence of an obvious exit strategy has done nothing to dampen the optimism of Defence Secretary Donald Rumsfeld. Cutting though the complexities of the occupation with surgical precision, Rumsfeld stated, "Our exit strategy in Iraq is success; it's that simple."[2] Absent a clear definition of what would constitute "success," this is an unhelpful formulation. At a minimum (one would presume), success must include U.S. forces defeating a growing and increasingly violent insurgency movement. But if the Bush Administration's statements (both pre- and postwar) are taken at face value, success must also include the establishment of a functioning democracy in Iraq that stands some chance of surviving the departure of U.S. troops. To achieve either task will be anything but "simple," as the first seven months of the occupation illustrated all too clearly.

## GOVERNING IRAQ: THE U.S. EXPERIENCE SO FAR

Iraq is currently governed by the Coalition Provisional Authority (CPA) under the stewardship of former Ambassador L. Paul Bremer and will be until at least June 30, 2004. At this point, according to the current plan, sovereignty is to be turned over to a selected/elected Transitional National Assembly, and the CPA will dissolve. This is the plan, at least. In the meantime, Bremer will continue to exercise complete control over the process of reconstruction. A highly experienced diplomat, Bremer is rapidly discovering what the history of Iraq has always shown—namely, that Iraq is among the most difficult places on earth to govern. Despite this, progress in the reconstruction has been made.

The CPA's website lists some of the most important achievements. By October 2003, for example, the CPA had overseen the reopening of all of Iraq's 240 hospitals, increased public health spending "to over 26 times what it was under Saddam," and administered over 22 million vaccinations to Iraqi children.[3] In the field of education, Iraq's 22 universities and 43 technical institutes have reopened, as have virtually all primary and secondary schools. The CPA has pledged to distribute 72 million new (Saddam-free) textbooks by the end of the school year. According to the *Economist*, these texts will exclude "controversial" content including "all references to Jews and Israel, Sh'ia, Sunnis, and Kurds, and anything critical of America."[4] Also deleted from history is the Iran-Iraq War, the 1991 Gulf War, and any mention of Ba'athist rule. Exactly how much of Iraq's modern history remains after these deletions/rewrites is unclear, but the "de-Saddamization" of Iraqi youths is well under way. Alongside these successes Bremer can point to the restoration of basic utilities to at least the prewar level and an increase in Iraq's oil production to over 2 million barrels per day.

Sadly, these positive achievements have been overshadowed by the political mismanagement of the occupation. Many have blamed this on the Bush Administration's failure to formulate a coherent plan for postwar Iraq prior to the invasion.[5] A more charitable interpretation would be that Iraq is a desperately difficult place to govern and that both administrators of Iraq (initially, retired general Jay Garner, then from May 2003 onward, Paul Bremer) faced a series of intractable problems with no easy solutions. There have been at least three, mutually inconsistent, plans implemented in postwar Iraq. Plan A, supervised by Garner, involved a deliberately modest program of de-Ba'athification (just the top two tiers of the Ba'ath hierarchy were to be purged), leaving key state institutions, structures, and associated personnel largely intact. This was intended to provide the stable foundation on which the reconstruction of Iraq's physical and social infrastructure could proceed. The obvious drawback was that this moderate purge left a large number of high-ranking Ba'athists (mainly Sunni Arabs) entrenched in positions of power. The Iraqi "face" on the occupation was to have been provided by a leadership council (appointed by Garner) that was intended to pave the way for a national convention in June 2003 to choose a transitional government. Garner's tenure was brief, however. As the scapegoat for the waves of anarchy and looting that gripped Iraq in the first few weeks following the collapse of Saddam's regime, and, more generally, the Bush Administration's initial failure to plan adequately for the immediate postwar environment, Garner was unceremoniously evicted from his position in May 2003. The demise of Plan A was confirmed by Garner's replacement, career diplomat Paul Bremer, whose Plan B involved a much more rigorous and far-reaching program of de-Ba'athification. This time the top four layers of the Ba'ath Party hierarchy (comprising in excess of 100,000 people) were purged from state institutions, and the Iraqi army was dismantled in its entirety. At one stroke, Bremer had effectively crippled Iraq's state structure by removing almost all experienced and qualified personnel and added some 350,000 disgruntled soldiers to the growing ranks of Iraq's unemployed. To the tasks of reconstructing Iraq's social, economic, and physical infrastructure, and combating an increasingly well-organized and violent resistance, Bremer now added the task of state-building from the ground up. While it is easy to criticize this approach, realistically, there were no good options open to Bremer. Most Iraqis (understandably) would have deeply resented the retention of prominent ex-Ba'athists in positions of power. Nonetheless, Bremer's actions contributed greatly to the complexities of the reconstruction process.

In place of Garner's leadership council, Bremer opted for a carefully balanced (Iraqi) Governing Council (IGC), selected to faithfully reflect Iraq's religious and ethnic diversity. As a textbook example of power-sharing arrangements, the IGC, and its performance to date, provides an ominous insight into what may lay ahead for the state of Iraq once full sovereignty is restored.

## THE IGC: A TASTE OF THINGS TO COME?

The composition of the IGC reflects an entirely laudable concern on the part of the CPA to give all groups a seat at the table in rough proportion to their presence in society. Efforts were also made to co-opt the most prominent Shi'a parties. Thus *al-Da'wa* was gifted two seats on the Council. SCIRI also secured a prominent position on the IGC, with Ayatollah Mohammad Baqir al-Hakim representing the organization until his assassination at the Shrine of Ali in Najaf by as-yet-unknown (but probably Sunni) perpetrators, to be replaced by his younger brother Ayatollah Abdul Aziz al-Hakim. The Kurds are heavily represented, with Barzani and Talabani taking their places next to the staunchly independent Mahmoud Othman and the rising star of Kurdish politics, Salahadin Baha'adin, of the Kurdistan Islamic Union (an organization associated with the Muslim Brotherhood). Shi'a representatives (mixed between those who may be classed as "religious" and those who are more secular) number 13, Sunni Arab representatives stand at 6, Kurds have 4, and there is 1 Turcoman and 1 Assyrian representative (although the Turcoman representative is not recognized by the main Turcoman parties).[6]

On paper at least, the IGC is, in most respects, a perfect microcosm of Iraqi society. Yet from its inception, the Council has been plagued by problems. First, and most obviously, the IGC was appointed by the CPA rather than elected by the Iraqi people. In practical terms, there was no way to avoid this; the CPA desperately needed something in place as soon as possible to give the impression that Iraqis were participants in their own occupation. The process of elections (preceded by a census and an agreed-upon set of rules for their conduct) would have taken months, if not years, to organize. An appointed body was the only realistic option, but the obvious drawback is that the IGC clearly lacks legitimacy in the eyes of the Iraqi people. It is perceived for what it is—namely, the creation of the CPA. Second, for a governing council, the IGC has done remarkably little governing. In part this reflects the inability of Council members to agree on anything of importance, but it also reflects the harsh reality of where governing power really lies. While the CPA (under Bremer's leadership) retains a de facto veto over Council decisions, the IGC will remain devoid of meaningful power.[7]

Third, while scrupulously demographically representative of Iraqi society, the IGC is unrepresentative in at least one critical respect: the IGC does not just include returning exiles, it is dominated by them. Although all 25 members are meant to be equal, some are more equal than others, with a ruling elite of nine carved out of the Council to act, on a rotating basis, as President of Iraq.[8] Of this core group, only one member (Mohsen Abdul Hamid) can claim to be a true "Iraqi's Iraqi." This preference on the part of the CPA for exiles is understandable. After all, the exiles do have some strong points: they are known quantities for the CPA and understand better than most how to deal with Americans. At least some of the exiles can also be considered reliably pro-democratic, having spent years in the West and having campaigned actively for the overthrow of Saddam.[9] But while exiles such as Ahmed Chalabi may possess all the right attributes on paper (from a U.S. perspective) to play a leadership role in the governance of Iraq (he is a thoroughly westernized, secular Shi'a who is also a very shrewd and intelligent political operator), he is virtually unknown inside Iraq and is laden with political baggage from his dealings in the ex-Iraqi opposition. By stacking the Council with exiles, therefore, the CPA further undercut any claim the IGC might have made to represent the authentic voice of the Iraqi people.

Although it is easy to criticize Bremer and the CPA for the failings of the IGC, the reality is that he is merely experiencing firsthand the acute dilemmas that accompany one country's military occupation of another. Unless the military occupation itself enjoys widespread legitimacy in the eyes of those being occupied, any governing body appointed by the occupying force inevitably will be perceived as illegitimate. But, of course, any military occupation that already enjoys popular legitimacy has no need of an indigenous puppet government to put an acceptable face on the occupation.

The failure of the IGC to function as a credible "voice of Iraq" highlights a deeper problem. Internally, this microcosm of Iraqi society was hopelessly divided. With most of the members coming from the ex-Iraqi opposition—itself riddled with vicious personal squabbles—and with the IGC constructed explicitly along lines of sectarian and ethnic identity, it was a natural progression for the IGC members to act according to sectarian and ethnic interests. The inherent danger with power-sharing arrangements that seek to reflect a society's cleavages at the level of political institutions is that they serve to reinforce rather than reconcile existing societal divisions. This is precisely what happened in Bosnia and, arguably, what is occurring within the IGC. There is no obvious way around this problem; indeed, probably the only way in which the interim government of Iraq could have been structured was by attempting to create some form of collegial authority according to ethnic and sectarian divisions. But the apparent "unworkability" of the IGC—even in its current, powerless form—provides few grounds for optimism that the same system will be any more workable when replicated on a national level. The problems played out within the Council are likely to be the same problems that will be played out in Iraq in general. The unwillingness of the

Shi'a religious representatives to accept any solution other than one that would reflect their own numerical dominance and the entrenchment of the Kurdish position on ethnic federalism are but two of the obvious disagreements that have marred the existence of the IGC.

## PLAN C: AN EXIT STRATEGY?

The untimely demise of Plan B in early November 2003 was precipitated by two major considerations on the part of the Bush Administration. First, the month of October and the first two weeks of November witnessed a significant upsurge in the levels of violence inflicted on occupying forces, with over 40 U.S. troops dying in the first ten days of November alone. The search was on for an exit strategy that could turn over sovereignty to the Iraqis sooner rather than later. Second, Plan B envisaged a time line for the restitution of Iraq's sovereignty that required the IGC to agree on something, just to get past the first stage. The IGC had been given a deadline of December 15 to determine a mechanism for selecting delegates to a constitutional convention. Subsequently, the new constitution was to have been put to a referendum, elections held, and sovereignty restored to the democratically elected government of Iraq. Predictably, Plan B never got past the first stage. Recognizing that whoever controls the writing of the constitution ultimately controls the political system, the influential Najaf cleric Grand Ayatollah Ali Sistani issued a *fatwa* demanding that delegates to any constitutional convention be elected directly by the people. Potentially, this would have allowed the Shi'a religious establishment to dominate the process of constitutional design.[10] The popular election of delegates would, of course, require a time-consuming census that would have to be undertaken in the midst of a guerrilla war. The IGC was deadlocked on the issue. To break the deadlock and accelerate the time line, the Bush Administration hurriedly scrapped Plan B and launched Plan C.

The sudden change of plan was an understandable reaction to a rapidly deteriorating security environment, but it was also an embarrassing about-face for Bremer to justify. As late as September, Bremer had described Plan B as "straightforward and realistic," and had outlined in some detail the ordering of the process by which sovereignty was to be handed back to the Iraqis. "The seventh step, dissolving the coalition authority, will follow naturally on the heels of elections. Once Iraq has a freely elected government, the coalition authority will happily yield the remainder of its authority to that sovereign Iraqi government."[11] In short, the CPA would turn power over only to a popularly elected Iraqi government.

Plan C envisages a rather different sequence of events. By February 28, 2004, the IGC "in close consultation with the CPA" is supposed to have drafted and approved a Fundamental Law (FL) that will function as a temporary constitution for Iraq. The FL is to include (among other items) a bill of rights composed of the usual freedoms and protections, a "federal arrangement for Iraq, to include governorates and the separation and specification of powers to be exercised by central and local entities," and a date for its own expiration. The IGC itself is to be dissolved once "elections" to a Transitional National Assembly (TNA) have been held.[12] The process by which members of the TNA are to be elected is somewhat complex. Each of Iraq's 18 governorates is to form an Organizing Committee of 15 members (a mix of IGC and local appointees) that will then convene a Governorate Selection Caucus (GSC) comprising "notables from around the governorate." Each GSC will then elect representatives to the TNA, with the number of representatives in proportion to the governorate's share of Iraq's total population. The TNA is to be elected by May 31, 2004, and will assume "full sovereign powers for governing Iraq" by June 30, 2004. A permanent constitution is due some time in the latter half of 2005 (drawn up by directly elected delegates), with elections for a new Iraqi government to follow before December 31, 2005.

The outlines of Plan C have now been agreed upon by both the CPA and the IGC, so it seems reasonable to assume that there will be at least some effort on both sides to make the plan work. In theory, this is a sensible compromise. The Fundamental Law will obviously be covered in U.S. fingerprints (the CPA has a veto over its provisions), but there is a built-in guarantee that it will govern Iraq only temporarily. Under the plan, Iraq's permanent constitution will be authored by Iraqis and, as such, would stand some chance of being accepted as legitimate. The plan also avoids the problems associated with holding direct elections immediately. The "election" of the TNA takes place as a three-stage process with no direct popular involvement, but because seats in the TNA are to be allocated in proportion to population, the Shi'a will still be the dominant force. Most important from a U.S. perspective, the plan envisages a restoration of sovereignty at a much earlier stage than previously. Full sovereignty will be restored to a transitional government (rather than to a popularly elected government), and the drafting of the permanent constitution will follow rather than precede the hand-over of power. If all goes according to plan, the U.S. will end its role as an occupying force in June 2004. Thus the possibility of an early exit from Iraq is built into the plan.

There are simply no good options left in Iraq, and Plan C is as plausible an option as any at this stage in proceedings. The most obvious drawback with Plan

C is its fiendish complexity. Just to arrive at the stage of a *transitional* government requires a three-stage process involving the selection of delegates (to Organizing Committees) who then select the delegates (to Governorate Selection Caucuses) who then select the representatives to the transitional administration. Presumably, the hope is that by spreading the process out across three distinct stages, no single stage will be significant enough to provoke a life-or-death political struggle. But the downside here is that a drawn-out, multistage process increases the number of points at which political conflict could occur, while the ever-present problem of the initial nondemocratic appointment of first-stage groups will continue to haunt proceedings. To make this plan work will require, at every stage in the process, compromise, consensus, and a willingness to put the welfare of the collective above narrow sectarian/ethnic interests. These are scarcely defining features of Iraq's political history. Moreover, the potential for political conflict is heightened by the compressed time frame envisaged for completion of the process. Implausibly, this three-stage process will have to be completed within a three-month period (from the end of February to the end of May 2004)—an impossibly ambitious timetable under current conditions. Unless the increasingly violent and sophisticated insurgency movement can be defeated, or at least contained, plans for three-stage political processes are largely academic.

## THE SUNNI INSURGENCY

By November 2003, coalition forces in Iraq were facing a conservative estimate of 30 attacks per day with a U.S. fatality occurring on average every 36 hours. Indeed, the first half of November proved to be particularly bloody for the United States, with 40 soldiers being killed in the first ten days alone. The Bush Administration's standard line—that the insurgency comprised a relatively small number of "diehard" Saddam loyalists supplemented by a motley collection of foreign terrorist elements—was embarrassingly undercut by the release of a leaked CIA report in mid-November. The report, authored by the station chief of the Agency's Baghdad office, estimated the number of insurgents at 50,000 (as compared to the prevailing Administration estimate of 5,000) and raised serious doubts about the capacity of coalition forces to defeat the insurgency. Although the source of the insurgency was geographically localized (the Sunni Triangle, encompassing the area between Baghdad, Tikrit, and Fallujah), by November 2003, the insurgents were demonstrating an alarming capacity to conduct sophisticated and highly destructive out–of-area operations.

The identity of the various groups involved remains something of a mystery, but it is clear that the insurgency comprises more than just Saddam loyalists. The website Iraq Democracy Watch provides a running list of resistance groups that now number 29. While loyalist Ba'athist groups, such as the Return Party and Saddam's *Fedayeen* figure prominently, the list also includes Arab nationalist groups (such as the Nasserites), radical Islamic entities (such as Ansar al-Islam and the Army of Mohammed), and Iraqi nationalist groups (such as the Iraqi Resistance Brigades). In reality, then, the insurgency is a complex amalgam of groups that, under normal circumstances, would probably be enemies rather than allies, but are temporarily united in a common desire to drive occupation forces out of Iraq. Beyond this, the common thread that connects these groups is that most, but not all, are Sunni Arab groups. This is a mixed blessing for coalition forces. On the positive side, it indicates that the insurgency has yet to spread much beyond Iraq's minority Sunni Arab population. On the negative side, it means that one segment of the Iraqi population is bearing the brunt of an increasingly violent U.S. counterinsurgency campaign.

With the initiation of operations Iron Hammer and Ivy Cyclone I and II in November 2003, the United States signalled a massive escalation in the level of firepower it was prepared to bring to bear in the Sunni Triangle. One problem with this approach (as identified by the author of the leaked CIA report) is that, historically, the application of brute force to defeat an insurgency has proven ineffective, even counterproductive. The more indiscriminate the violence inflicted, the more alienated the indigenous population becomes, and the greater the level of support enjoyed by the insurgents. The more fundamental problem is that Sunni Arabs already have little to lose by supporting the insurgents. Plan C (or, for that matter, any plan for democracy in Iraq) is a recipe for the political marginalization of the Sunni Arab population. Hence, the Sunnis have no incentive to cooperate in the successful execution of Plan C and every incentive to continue to resist its implementation.

Another problem is that the message conveyed by massive demonstrations of military power (i.e., the United States will prevail) runs counter to the logic of Plan C. Plan C has been widely perceived (whether accurately or not) as providing the option of an early escape route for U.S. forces. Administration officials have strenuously denied this. According to Donald Rumsfeld, "there is no decision to pull out early," a sentiment echoed by President Bush, who pledged simply, "We're staying."[13] But it is far from clear on what basis these statements were made. In the unlikely event that Plan C stays on track, the United States is due to hand over full sovereign powers to the TNA by June 30, 2004. Presumably, *full* sovereign powers will include the power to order U.S. forces out of Iraq, so U.S. forces will remain only if they are invited to by the TNA. It simply does not seem very plausible that the first act of a sovereign Iraqi government will be to endorse the continued presence of U.S. troops in the country. But, of course, this is the beauty of Plan C as an exit strategy. If U.S. troops leave, it is not because they have been driven out by the insurgency, but because they have been "uninvited" out of Iraq by the legitimate sovereign government. In practice, it matters less what the *real* intentions of the Bush Administration are and much more how these intentions are perceived. If the perception is that the Administration is looking for a fast exit, then the message that U.S. forces will prevail over the insurgents, at whatever cost and however long it takes, rings hollow.

## THE SHI'A: POISED FOR POWER

In contrast to the Sunni population, the majority Shi'a population has every incentive to cooperate, at least for the time being, with U.S. plans for the future of Iraq. The implementation of democracy would overturn centuries of Sunni rule and almost certainly produce a Shi'a-dominated government. Whether this results in an Iranian-style theocracy or some moderate form of nominally Islamic state is an open question. The Shi'a population of Iraq is clearly not a homogenous entity that speaks with one coherent voice. It is already clear, however, that the most influential voices from within the Shi'a community belong to religious leaders and that the most organized (and best-armed) Shi'a groups are religious parties such as SCIRI and *al-Da'wa*. Groups like these moved rapidly to fill the power vacuum left in the wake of Saddam's removal. They are now firmly entrenched in most of the major towns and cities of the center and the south.

The voice of revered Najaf cleric Ayatollah Sistani has emerged as among the most influential in post-Saddam Iraq. But other, less moderate voices have also made themselves heard. Of these, Muqtada Sadr is the best-known, and potentially most influential, figure on the radical Shi'a scene. His power base is in Sadr City in Baghdad, but the Sadr Movement has succeeded in spreading its message across the center and the south of Iraq. Sadrists were likely participants in riots against U.S. Marines in Karbala in July and were involved with subsequent riots in Basra in the middle of August. Sadr's authority has not died away, as many observers predicted. Instead, it has increased. The whole of East Baghdad, Kufa, and Samarra is now a Sadr-dominated zone, and his influence is growing in Karbala, Najaf, and Basra. In addition, by the fall of 2003, Muqtada had announced the formation of his own militia (the Mahdi Army), standing at an estimated 10,000 men.

The fact that there is a strong line of political Shi'ism emerging in Iraq should not necessarily be viewed with trepidation. However, Muqtada's variety of Shi'ism is extremely worrying for anyone wishing to maintain the integrity of the Iraqi state, as he is promoting an inherently *exclusive* version of Shi'ism. Far from the more conciliatory gestures of Ayatollah Sistani, the Sadr Movement seeks to impose religious authority over Iraq, to exclude foreign influence, and to subordinate the Sunnis to Shi'a religious leadership.[14] Furthermore, the movement is not particularly dependent upon the figure of Sadr himself. If he did not lead it, another firebrand would take up the cause, and perhaps even more vociferously by relying more heavily on the real hardline Ayatollahs in Iran, including Grand Ayatollah Kadhim al-Haeri, a Khomeini-style radical demanding a strict Islamic government for Iraq. During an interview with the San Francisco *Chronicle's* Robert Collier in mid-November 2003, Haeri referred to the IGC as "puppets of the Americans" and described Plan C as "unacceptable." Quoting a Western diplomat's thoughts on Haeri, Collier noted that "if he returns to Iraq . . . it will be like throwing a match onto gasoline."[15] Asked when he intended to return to Iraq (he has been in Qom, Iran, since 1974), Haeri replied ominously, "in the right time."

## THE KURDS: THE END OF AUTONOMY?

Throughout the period since Saddam's fall, the Kurds have maintained their autonomy in the north of the country, watching the chaotic events in the south unfold with an increasing degree of concern. The north is now economically booming even more than it was during the 1990s. Property developers are moving into the region, encouraged by both the Kurdish authorities and the CPA alike. Unemployment in major urban centers is almost zero due to the huge explosion of construction, and professionals from Baghdad are reportedly moving north to work rather than remaining at home. The journalist Maggy Zanger emphasizes clearly the difference that remains between Kurds and the rest of Iraq when she says "the bloodshed in the Sunni Triangle is watched on Arab satellite channels from afar [in Kurdistan]. It is as distant from the Kurds as it is to viewers in Jordan or London."[16] To all intents and purposes, Kurdistan is, in all but name, another country.

Neither Barzani nor Talabani has ever received any guarantees whatsoever from any American with authority that the United States would support the preservation of Kurdish autonomy and protect the proto-democratic structures that are obviously emerging. Indeed, Paul Bremer now seems to be going in exactly the opposite direction and appears to be pursuing a strategy that, if successful, would create a political structure in Iraq that offers no place for a Kurdish autonomous zone within it. Plan C clearly envisages a form of federalism based on governorates rather than ethnicity. Plan C is, therefore, destined to create political conflict between the Kurds on the one side and pretty much everyone else on the other. The only question is whether this conflict is played out at the stage of drafting the FL (which is required to contain a description of "federal arrangements" for Iraq) or whether the real battle will await the drafting of the permanent constitution. Either way, while the Kurds retain their *peshmerga* forces—by some distance the most capable indigenous military forces in Iraq at present—it is difficult to see how an Arab-dominated central government will be able to force the Kurds to accept an unfavorable settlement without resorting to violent means. Like it or not, there is no easy way to deny the Kurds at least what they already have, and they know it.

## PROSPECTS FOR DEMOCRACY

If the insurgency cannot be defeated, or at least contained at manageable levels, then there is obviously no chance of democracy taking root in Iraq any time soon. The more relevant question is whether Iraq can avoid coming apart at the seams. Civil war remains a very real possibility, perhaps more of a probability at this point. In fact, if U.S. troops are "uninvited" out of Iraq in June 2004, and the (mainly Sunni) insurgency turns its guns on a Shi'a-dominated TNA, with the Kurds mobilizing in the north to protect their entity and consolidate their hold on Kirkuk by removing the Turkic and Arab presence, then Iraq's worst nightmare of civil conflict along sectarian and ethnic lines becomes a reality. The magnitude of the challenge that dilemmas such as these present to the Bush Administration is, therefore, immense. In a November 2003 speech to the National Endowment for Democracy, President Bush reiterated his commitment to democratizing Iraq. While recognizing that it would be a "massive and difficult undertaking," he argued, "it is worth our effort, it is worth our sacrifice, because we know the stakes. The failure of Iraqi democracy would embolden terrorists around the world, increase dangers to the American people, and extinguish the hopes of millions in the region. Iraqi democracy will succeed."[17] If Iraqi democracy does succeed, it will be a stunning achievement for the Bush Administration; if it does not, the negative repercussions will be felt in Iraq and the Middle East as a whole for decades to come.

# NOTES

## INTRODUCTION

1. Ray Wallace, "Is Iraq Even in the World?" (www.mirror.co.uk/printable_version.cfm?objectid=12391630&siteid=50143)
2. The Project for a New American Century (PNAC), *Rebuilding America's Defenses. Strategy, Forces and Resources for a New Century*, Washington D.C.: PNAC, September 2000, p. 14.
3. Mark Danner, "The Struggles of Democracy and Empire," *New York Times*, October 9, 2002, p. 27.
4. John Lewis Gaddis, "A Grand Strategy of Transformation," *Foreign Policy*, November/December 2002, p. 55.
5. *Ibid.*, p. 54.
6. "The National Security Strategy of the United States of America." Washington D.C.: The White House, September 17, 2002, introduction.
7. Gaddis, p. 55.
8. "Polls Apart." *The Guardian*, November 11, 2002. (www.guardian.co.uk/Print/0,3858,4367628,00.html)
9. *Ibid.*
10. Baghdad, Basra, and Mosul were all former provinces of the Ottoman Empire. The Ottoman Empire was largely dismantled as a consequence of military defeats during the course of World War I. What remained became the modern day state of Turkey; the rest was divided up by France and Britain into protectorates (see chapter 1).
11. See chapter 7 for further details on the strategic considerations underlying the decision to incorporate Mosul into Iraq.
12. In very simplistic terms, pan-Arabism is the belief that the various countries of the Arab world will one day be united to form a single, coherent Arab nation.
13. Mark Steel, "Saddam Seems to Have Won Over his Floating Voters," *The Independent*, October 17, 2002, p. 14.
14. Many Iraqi tribes (including Saddam's own) have Sunni and Shi'a branches.
15. This, of course, would depend on where the boundary lines fell, but it is not difficult to envisage a Kurdish-dominated northern state, a Shi'a-dominated southern state, and a central state focused on Baghdad, but embracing the Sunni triangle.
16. An exception here is an article by Daniel Byman in which he proposed that Iraq should be allowed to disintegrate into its constituent elements (Daniel Byman, "Let Iraq Collapse," *The National Interest*, Fall 1996, pp. 48–60).

**CHAPTER 1**

1. The Ottoman Empire, centered on modern day Turkey, encompassed most of the Middle East, the Balkans, and parts of Eastern Europe at the height of its power.
2. The Arab Revolt was a British-orchestrated rebellion against the Ottoman Empire during World War I led by "Lawrence of Arabia," but fought by the Arabs. Implicit throughout was a British promise to allow Arab independence on the cessation of hostilities. This promise was not kept.
3. Faisal ruled in Syria from the end of World War I in 1918 until 1920. At that point, the French, in fulfillment of their mandate, evicted Faisal from the country, preferring to rule Syria directly.
4. Geoff Simmons, *Iraq: From Sumer to Saddam.* New York: St. Martins, 1994, p. 172.
5. Aside from oil concerns, the decision to attach Mosul to the rest of Iraq also afforded the British a buffer zone against a newly resurgent Turkey. The territorial addition was supported by Faisal because it diluted the power of the Shi'a by incorporating (predominantly) Sunni Kurds into the state of Iraq.
6. Iraq's small Assyrian community had been granted a homeland by the British after being driven out of Ottoman territory during World War I. The community subsequently formed the backbone of the Iraqi Levies, a force the British used to guard their air bases in Iraq.
7. Quoted in Samir al-Khalil (pseudonym for Kanan Makiya), *Republic of Fear: The Politics of Modern Iraq.* Berkeley: University of California Press, 1989, p. 160.
8. Phebe Marr, *The Modern History of Iraq.* Boulder: Westview Press, 1985, p. 38
9. In simple terms, pan-Arabism embodies a vision of Arab greatness that will one day be realized through the political union of all Arab countries into one Arab state. The arch villains of pan-Arabism are colonial powers (who have conspired to keep the Arabs in a position of perpetual subservience) and the state of Israel (viewed as an instrument of Western imperial dominance).
10. Said K. Aburish, *Saddam Hussein: The Politics of Revenge.* New York: Bloomsbury, 2000, p. 29
11. See for example, Aburish, pp. 30–31.
12. Aburish, p. 31.
13. Simmons, p. 195. The "power ministries" Simmons refers to are premier, finance, interior, defense, and foreign affairs.
14. *Ibid.*, p. 195.
15. Marr, p. 144.
16. *Ibid.*
17. Yitzhak Nakash, *The Shi'is of Iraq.* Princeton, New Jersey: Princeton University Press, 1994.
18. The two major sources of Shi'a leadership in the south had traditionally been religious and tribal. A unified Shi'a leadership (as occurred during the Iraqi revolt against the British in 1920) was threatening to British rule, and to Sunni dominance over the institutions of state. The goal of the British, then, was to ensure that the Shi'a leadership was kept internally divided.
19. Marr, p. 145.
20. Charles Tripp, *A History of Iraq.* Cambridge: Cambridge University Press, 2000.
21. One exception was the election of 1954, judged by many to be the freest in Iraq's history. However, when the election yielded the "wrong" result (i.e., one that afforded opposition parties too much power in parliament), parliament was

dissolved within less than two months, and a new, better orchestrated election was held to produce the right result.

22. Simmons, p. 179.
23. Tripp, p. 6.
24. Quoted in Simmons, p. 147.
25. The introduction of military conscription in 1934 was a particular bone of contention for the Shi'a. The burden of conscription was to fall heavily on the numerically dominant Shi'a, yet the command structure of the armed forces was to remain dominated by Sunnis.
26. al-Khalil, p. 168.
27. *Ibid.*, p.169.
28. *Ibid.*, p. 170.
29. The catalyst for the *wathbah* was the Iraqi government's conclusion of a new treaty with Britain (the Portsmouth Treaty of 1947). The terms of the treaty were negotiated in secret, and while they actually detailed a significant reduction in British influence (British air bases in Iraq were to come under Iraqi sovereignty, all British troops to be withdrawn) by this point there was widespread hostility to the idea of maintaining *any* military link between Iraq and Britain (Marr, pp. 102–103).
30. The Sunni–Shi'a sectarian split might best be viewed as a "latent" divide in the sense that it could potentially be exploited by Shi'a religious leaders to challenge the legitimacy of the Sunni-dominated center. Fortunately for the regime, religious leadership in the south was internally divided for much of the period between ethnically Persian leaders and those of Arab extraction (Nakash, p. 118).
31. Nakash, p. 112.

## CHAPTER 2

1. See chapter 3 for details of Ba'ath Party organization and doctrine.
2. See, for example, Said K. Aburish, *Saddam Hussein: The Politics of Revenge.* New York: Bloomsbury, 2000, pp. 38–39; Geoff Simmons, *Iraq: From Sumer to Saddam.* New York: St. Martins Press, 1994, p. 219.
3. Phebe Marr, *The Modern History of Iraq.* Boulder: Westview Press, 1985, p. 158.
4. On the cult of personality surrounding Qassim, see, Charles Tripp, *A History of Iraq.* Cambridge: Cambridge University Press, 2000, p. 168.
5. *Ibid.*, p.156.
6. Marr (p. 167) argues that the ICP's continued support for the regime, despite these measures, was due to specific instructions from the mother party in the Soviet Union.
7. Samir al-Khalil, *Republic of Fear: The Politics of Modern Iraq.* Berkeley: University of California Press, 1989, p. 227.
8. Aburish, p. 51.
9. Simmons, p. 226.
10. The Ba'ath's seizure of power in 1963 relied on an uneasy alliance between certain segments of the army's officer corps and the civilian leadership of the Party. The Party needed the armed forces to unseat Qassim and obtain power, while the armed forces needed the Party to control the "street" in defense of the coup.
11. In March 1963, the Syrian Ba'ath had seized power in a military coup, opening up the possibility of a immediate union between Iraq and Syria under the auspices of the Ba'ath Party.

12. Aburish, p. 75.
13. Marr, for example, describes Arif as a "relatively conservative Muslim and a staunch Sunni" (p. 191).
14. Marr, p. 282.
15. Migration from rural to urban areas accelerated during the 1950s, making the streets of major urban areas an increasingly significant political arena.
16. Marr, p. 176.
17. Simmons, p. 218.
18. Aburish, p. 39.
19. Targets included the Iraqi Women's League, the General Union of Students, and the trades unions. The goal (obviously) was to terrorize, but also to eliminate the ICP's capacity to mobilize large numbers of supporters to resist Ba'athist rule.
20. Simmons, p. 227.
21. Quoted in Aburish, p. 54.
22. Marr, p. 179.
23. The ICP's appeal to the downtrodden of Iraq, and its suspicion of Arab nationalism enabled the Party to attract both Shi'a and Kurds.
24. Marr, p. 173.
25. Simmons, p. 243.
26. Marr, p. 172.
27. Robert Soeterik, *The Islamic Movement of Iraq (1958–1980)*. Amsterdam: Stichting MERA, 1991, p. 15.
28. Aburish, pp. 45–46.
29. *Ibid.*, p. 45.

## CHAPTER 3

1. Efraim Karsh and Inari Rautsi, *Saddam Hussein: A Political Biography*. New York: The Free Press, 1991, p. 30.
2. Con Coughlin, *Saddam: King of Terror*. New York: HarperCollins, 2002, p. 76.
3. Quoted in Said K. Aburish, *Saddam Hussein: The Politics of Revenge*. New York: Bloomsbury, 2000, p. 86.
4. Events in neighboring Iran—where a similar move had resulted in the overthrow of the Mossadeq regime in a 1951 CIA-sponsored coup—illustrated the potential dangers.
5. Quoted in Karsh and Rautsi, p. 79.
6. The longstanding dispute over the Shatt Al-Arab—the confluence of the Tigris and Euphrates Rivers which forms part of the southern border between the two countries—had originally been addressed by a 1937 treaty. However, in 1969, from a position of considerable strength, the Shah of Iran unilaterally abrogated the treaty. At the time, the nascent Ba'ath regime was powerless to respond.
7. While the economic development of Iraq under the Ba'ath was heavily state-driven, it was far from rigidly socialist. Indeed, after the start of the Iran–Iraq War, the private sector came to play an increasingly important role in sustaining the war effort.
8. Coughlin, p. 150.
9. *Ibid.*, p. 161.
10. Dilip Hiro, *Iraq in the Eye of the Storm*. New York: Thunder's Mouth Press, 2002, p. 39.

11. After it became clear that the Islamic regime in Tehran would not collapse overnight, Iraq made repeated efforts to end the conflict. Ultimately, the conflict lasted for eight long years because the Iranians refused to accept any outcome other than regime change in Baghdad.

12. Hiro, p. 32.

13. *Ibid.*, p. 32.

14. *Ibid.*, p. 31.

15. Amatzia Baram, *Culture, History and Ideology in the Formation of Ba'athist Iraq, 1968–89.* New York: St. Martin's, 1991, p. 15.

16. *Ibid.*, p. 19. Much like the in Soviet Union, the political institutions of the state (RCC, Parliament, etc.) coexisted with Party institutions in Ba'athist Iraq. Constitutional power was vested in the state institutions, but real decision-making power resided with the institutions of the Party.

17. Amatzia Baram, "The Ruling Political Elite in Bathi Iraq, 1968–1986: The Changing Features of a Collective Profile." *International Journal of Middle East Studies*, vol. 21, no. 4, November 1989, p. 462.

18. Baram (1991), p. 19.

19. The city of Tikrit, located on the Tigris 50 miles North of Baghdad, is close to the birthplace of Saddam and was the major recruiting ground for key positions of power within Saddam's regime.

20. Quoted in Andrew and Patrick Cockburn, *Out of the Ashes: The Resurrection of Saddam Hussein.* New York: HarperCollins, 1999, p. 76.

21. Aburish, p. 162.

22. *Ibid.*, p. 190.

23. At the bottom of the Ba'ath hierarchy was the basic unit of party organization—the party cell (*halaqah*). Comprising between three and seven members, these cells operated at the small village or neighborhood level. A minimum of two and a maximum of seven such cells comprised a party division (*firqah*). Divisions operated in larger villages, factories, schools, and throughout the military and the bureaucracy. Higher up the ladder, party sections (*shabah*), composed of two to five divisions, functioned at the level of a town, large city area, or rural district. Above the *shabah* was the branch (*fira*), which was the Party's provincial-level unit. There were 21 branches of the Iraqi Ba'ath, 1 in each of the 18 provinces, and 3 in Baghdad. Collectively, these 21 branches elected the Regional Command (RC) at party meetings (regional congresses). The RC was the Party's highest policy-making body in Iraq, and its Secretary General (until 1979, Bakr, thereafter, Saddam) was the Party leader.

24. Samir al-Khalil, *The Republic of Fear: The Politics of Modern Iraq.* Berkeley: University of California Press, 1989, p. 251.

25. *Ibid.*, p. 198.

26. Richard H. Pfaff, "The Function of Arab Nationalism," *Comparative Politics*, vol. 2, no. 2, January, 1970, p. 164.

27. *Ibid.*, p. 165.

28. The idea was that power over decision-making was highly concentrated in the hands of a central committee, or a single individual (the centralism element), and that lower levels of the Party had the opportunity to elect the levels immediately above (the democratic element). This structure was supposed to provide efficient decision-making without sacrificing democratic principles.

29. Quoted in al-Khalil, p. 77.

30. *Ibid.*, p. 77.
31. *Ibid.*, p. 85.
32. Coughlin, p. 167.
33. No doubt to the great dismay of Saddam's security services, Amnesty International's 1976 award for worst human rights violator on the planet went to the CIA-trained security services of neighboring Iran—the infamous SAVAK.
34. Aburish, p. 208.
35. Isam al-Khafaji, "State Terror and the Degradation of Politics in Iraq," *Middle East Report* 176, May-June, 1992, p. 16.
36. Aburish, p. 82.
37. al-Khalil, p. 52.
38. *Ibid.*
39. *Ibid.*, p. 56
40. Sandra Mackey, *The Reckoning: Iraq and the Legacy of Saddam Hussein.* New York: W.W. Norton & Company, 2002, pp. 260–61.
41. Quoted in Mackey, p. 263.
42. In addition to a shared ethnicity, Iraq's Shi'a and Sunni populations have also become much more geographically integrated as a consequence of significant Shi'a migration from the south to the center. While accurate census data is not available, by the end of the 1970s Shi'a almost certainly constituted a majority of the population of Baghdad.
43. The Sumerians, the "founders" of Mesopotamian civilization, had, before the onset of the second millennium B.C., already perfected irrigation techniques, learned to write and begun to accumulate libraries of knowledge on astronomy, philosophy, and agriculture. The mighty King Hammurabi, who transformed the city state of Babylon into an empire through military conquest, governed through the rule of law—establishing in the process the concepts that now underpin the entire Western legal system. The brutal Assyrians, who swept down from the north to ransack Babylon, then ruled Mesopotamia with a mixture of brutality and grandeur (not unlike Saddam Hussein), after which King Nebuchadnezzar, a personal favorite of Saddam's, returned Babylon to its former exalted status and achieved immortality in the eyes of Saddam by storming Jerusalem and carting off the Jewish population into captivity.
44. Paul W. Roberts, *The Demonic Comedy: Some Detours in the Baghdad of Saddam Hussein.* New York: Farrar, Straus and Giroux, 1998, p. 206.
45. Baram (1991), p. 33.
46. Quoted in Baram (1991), p. 35.
47. Aburish, p. 114.
48. *Ibid.*, p. 115.
49. al-Khalil, p. 88.
50. Quoted in al-Khalil, pp. 77–78.
51. *Ibid.*, p. 92
52. Phebe Marr, *The Modern History of Iraq.* Boulder, C.O.: Longman, 1985, p. 284.
53. The popularity of Saddam—particularly during the 1970s—is recognized by almost all observers of the period, regardless of how critical their assessment of the Ba'ath regime in other respects.

## CHAPTER 4

1.  Larry Everest, "Fueling the Iran–Iraq slaughter: U.S. 'Weapons of Mass Destruction,' Hypocrisy, and So Much More." *Z Mag* online, September 05, 2002. www.zmag.org/content/showarticle.cfm?SectionID=158ItemID=2292

2.  The best known of these was the huge "victory arch" constructed in Baghdad out two metal forearms (molded in Britain from casts of Saddam's actual arms), each clutching swords that crossed at the apex of the arch.

3.  Hussein Sumaida and Carole Jerome, *Circle of Fear—A Renegade's Journey From the Mossad to the Iraqi Secret Service.* Toronto: Stoddart & Co., 1991.

4.  Iraqi Deputy Prime Minister Tariq Aziz to Arab League Secretary General Chadli al-Klibi, "Iraqi Memorandum to the Arab League," July 15, 1990.

5.  Quoted in Dilip Hiro, *Neighbors Not Friends: Iraq and Iran After the Gulf Wars.* London: Routledge, 2001, p. 28.

6.  Quoted in Geoff Simmons, *Iraq from Sumer to Saddam.* New York: St. Martin's Press, 1994, p. 315.

7.  In all probability, U.S. officials were anticipating a small-scale Iraqi attack to grab the disputed islands of Bubiyan and Warba, rather than an all-out assault to conquer Kuwait.

8.  Mohammed-Mahmoud Mohamedou, *Iraq and the Second Gulf War: State Building and Regime Security.* London: Austin and Winfield, 1998, p. 145.

9.  Andrew Cockburn and Patrick Cockburn, *Out of the Ashes: The Resurrection of Saddam Hussein.* New York: HarperPerennial, 1999, p. 3.

10. PBS Frontline interview with Wafic al-Samarrai, 2001. http://www.pbs.org/wgbh/pages/frontline/gulf/oral/iraqis.html

11. Cockburn and Cockburn, p. 33

12. The sense of betrayal on the part of regular Iraqi troops was certainly justified. Realizing the likely outcome of the war, Saddam withdrew five Republican Guard units back into Iraq, to be replaced by "cannon fodder" units of the regular army. Approximately 70 percent of the Republican Guard thus survived the second Gulf War intact, at great cost to regular army troops.

13. Cockburn & Cockburn, p. 20.

14. SCIRI was formed in 1982 as an umbrella organization for various Islamic groups resisting the Ba'athist regime. The close association of the organization with the Iranian government (Iran supplies money and equipment, and essentially controls the organization's armed wing) has rendered it suspect in the eyes of many Iraqis as an instrument of Iran. See chapter 5 for further details regarding SCIRI.

15. Ofra Bengio, *Baghdad Between Shi'a and Kurds.* Washington Institute for Near East Policy, Policy Focus No. 18, February 1992, p. 10.

16. Cockburn and Cockburn, p. 25.

17. *Ibid.*, p. 43.

18. *Ibid.*, p. 43.

19. For the U.S., the INA's coup option offered a number of advantages. It would require no U.S. military support, it could conceivably be achieved with minimal bloodshed, and it promised to remove Saddam without fundamentally affecting the status quo in Iraq—one Sunni-dominated regime would simply be replaced with another.

20. The very same night as Hussein Kamel's defection, the inimitable Uday Hussein livened up a party outside Baghdad by opening fire with a semi-automatic weapon, hitting and severely wounding his Uncle Watban in the process. Apparently the two had fallen out—a further indication, if any were needed, that all was not well at the court of Saddam.

21. The reason for the defection seems to have been that Hussein Kamel had fallen out with Uday over various military-related business contracts and feared that his various positions in the regime (and maybe even his life) were in jeopardy.

22. In essence, Kamel was calling upon those still in Baghdad to rise up against the regime at great risk, while he himself remained safe in Amman. Moreover, Hussein Kamel was by this point so deeply implicated in the crimes of the regime that it is difficult to understand where he thought his support was going to come from.

23. Cockburn and Cockburn, p. 189.

24. Chlorine is a commonly used precursor in the production of chemical weapons. The import of pencils was prohibited because they contain graphite, a material used in nuclear power reactors.

25. There were two positive achievements Clinton could point to. First, UNSCOM, despite all the odds and in the face of all manner of imaginative deceptions on the part of the Iraqis, had actually rounded up and destroyed a large part of Iraq's capacity to produce WMD. Former chief weapons inspector Scott Ritter estimated that by the end of 1998, 95 percent of Iraq's WMD capability had been successfully eliminated. Second, and again, despite all the odds, the situation in northern Iraq had evolved into a veritable oasis of stability, prosperity, and pluralism. Safe from the immediate reach of Saddam, the two Kurdish parties had finally stopped trying to tear each other apart, and were devoting their energies instead to creating something better for the long-suffering Kurdish people. The status quo in the north—two mini-statelets, one governed by the KDP, the other by the PUK—was far from perfect, but it was a major improvement on anything the Kurds of Iraq had enjoyed in the past, and it was closer to a functioning liberal democracy than almost anything else in the Middle East. The Kurds, finally, were enjoying their "golden age."

26. See, Bob Woodward, *Bush at War.* New York: Simon and Schuster, 2002, p. 49.

27. *Ibid.*, p. 11.

28. Judith Miller and Laurie Mylroie, *Saddam Hussein and the Crisis in the Gulf.* New York: Times Books, 1990, p. 130.

29. Another, less charitable, explanation is that by the 1990s, Saddam had begun to lose his grip on reality, and believed quite literally that he was God's chosen representative on earth. Perhaps the colossal cult of personality, assiduously propagated since the late-1970s, had simply transcended earthly limitations.

30. The two-tiered economy actually kicked in during the end period of the Iran–Iraq war, as did corruption on an epic scale on the part of the ruling regime.

31. Toby Dodge, "Cake Walk, Coup or Urban Warfare: The Battle for Iraq," in Toby Dodge and Steven Simon, eds., *Iraq at the Crossroads: State and Society in the Shadow of Regime Change.* International Institute of Strategic Studies Adelphi Paper, vol. 354, issue 1, pp. 60–76. London: I.I.S.S./Oxford University Press, 2003, p. 65.

32. *Ibid.*, p. 69.

33. For an analysis of what constitutes an Iraqi tribe, see Hosham Dawood, "The 'State-ization' of the Tribe and the Tribalization of the State: The Case of Iraq," in Faleh A. Jabar and Hosham Dawood, eds., *Tribes and Power: Nationalism and Ethnicity in the Middle East.* London: Saqi, 2003, pp. 110–35.

34. See Faleh A. Jabar, "Clerics, Tribes Ideologues and Urban Dwellers in the South of Iraq: The Potential for Rebellion," in Dodge and Simon, *Iraq at the Crossroads*, pp. 162–78, quote p. 171.

35. *Ibid.*, pp. 172–73.

36. Amatzia Baram, "Neo-Tribalism in Iraq: Saddam Hussein's Tribal Policies 1991–96," *International Journal of Middle East Studies*, vol. 29, issue 1, Feb. 1997, p. 14.

37. This is not to suggest that Iraq was otherwise governed according to the "rule of law," but only to make the point that tribal revenge (or honor) killings were legally prohibited; hence, there was a clear contradiction between tribal norms of justice and the state's own legal code.

38. Cockburn and Cockburn, pp. 23–26.

39. Human Rights Watch, *World Report*, 1995.

40. Dieter Bednarz and Volkhard Windfuhr, "Saddam's Survival in the Ruins," reprinted in *World Press Review*, August 1999, p. 16.

41. This explanation suggests that Saddam had indeed succeeded in transforming the population into a massive "cult" of followers.

42. Quoted in Baram, p. 40.

43. Jabar, p. 171.

## CHAPTER 5

1. See Ofra Bengio, *Baghdad Between Shi'a and Kurds.* Washington Institute for Near East Policy, Policy Focus No. 18, February 1992, pp. 2–3, quoting H. al-Alawi, *al-Shi'a wal-Dawla al-Qawmiyya fi al-'Iraq, 1914–1990*, 2nd edition, 1990.

2. Liora Lukitz, *Iraq: The Search for National Identity.* London: Frank Cass, 1995, pp. 3–4.

3. Faleh Abd al-Jabar, "Clerics, Tribes, Ideologues and Urban Dwellers in the South of Iraq: The Potential for Rebellion" in Toby Dodge and Steven Simon, *Iraq at the Crossroads: State and Society in the Shadow of Regime Change.* International Institute of Strategic Studies Adelphi Paper no. 354. Oxford: Oxford University Press/ International Institute of Strategic Studies, 2003, pp. 161–78, quote at p. 162.

4. Graham Fuller and Rend Rahim Francke, *The Arab Shi'a: The Forgotten Muslims.* New York: St Martin's Press, 1999, p. 9.

5. *Ibid.*

6. David Pinault, *The Shiites: Ritual and Popular Piety in a Muslim Community.* New York: St Martin's Press, 1992, p. 4.

7. In Shi'ism, the term "Imam" denotes a member of the *Ahl al-Bayt* who is leader of the Muslim community, regardless of whether they are recognized as such by the Muslim world at large. The recognition of Hassan as the second Imam clearly shows the lack of recognition the Shi'a gave to Muhammad's earlier successors. See Pinault, p. 5.

8. Just as Saddam reached into history to identify himself with figures of honor from Islam's past, including the Saracen leader Salah al-Din al-Ayubi, Ayatollah

Khomeini would similarly refer to Saddam as "Saddam Yazid" in order to try and mobilize Shi'a sentiment against Saddam by associating him with the actions of the Caliph Yazid.

9. Yitzhak Nakash, *The Shi'i of Iraq*. Princeton, N.J.: Princeton University Press, 1994, p. 13.

10. Pinault, p. 6.

11. The *ulama* are recognized by a series of ranks, including *Hujjat al-Islam*, "argument in defense of Islam," *Ayat Allah* (Ayatollah), "the sign of God," and *Ayat Allah al-Uzma*, "the mightiest sign of God." See Pinault, p. 7.

12. See Moojan Momen, *An Introduction to Shi'i Islam: The History and Doctrines of Twelver Shi'ism*. London: Yale University Press, 1985, pp. 297–98.

13. Fuller and Francke, p. 88.

14. Gareth Stansfield, "Politics and Governance in the New Iraq: Reconstruction of the New Versus Resurrection of the Old," in J. Eyal, ed., *War in Iraq: Combat and Consequence*. Whitehall Paper 59. London: Royal United Services Institute for Defence Studies, 2003.

15. Amatzia Baram, "The Radical Shi'ite Opposition Movements in Iraq," in Emmanuel Sivan and Menachem Friedman, eds., *Religious Radicalism & Politics in the Middle East*. Albany, N.Y.: SUNY Press, 1990, pp. 95–126, p. 95.

16. Abd al-Jabar, "Clerics, Tribes, Ideologues," p. 164.

17. T. M. Aziz, "The Rise of Muhammad Baqir al-Sadr in Shii Political Activism in Iraq from 1958–1980." *International Journal of Middle East Studies*, vol. 25, issue 2 (May 1993), pp. 207–22, quote at p. 208.

18. See Joyce Wiley, *The Islamic Movement of Iraqi Shi'as*. Boulder, C.O.: Westview Press, 1992, p. 34.

19. Aziz, p. 209.

20. *Ibid.*, p. 211.

21. Wiley, p. 46.

22. *Ibid.*, p. 47.

23. Aziz, pp. 212–13; Wiley, pp. 47–48.

24. Wiley, p. 49.

25. *Ibid.*, p. 54, quoting Muhammad Baqir al-Sadr, *"Nida' al-Qa'id al-Shahid Ayatollah al-Sadr ila al-Sha'b al-'Iraqi al-Muslim"* (Message of the Martyr Leader Ayatollah al-Sadr to the Muslim Iraqi People), 1980.

26. Wiley, p. 54.

27. Abd al-Jabar, p. 165.

28. *Ibid.*, pp. 165–66.

29. *Ibid.*, p. 166; Amatzia Baram, "From Radicalism to Radical Pragmatism: The Shi'ite Fundamentalist Opposition Movements of Iraq," in James Piscatori, ed., *Islamic Fundamentalism and the Gulf Crisis*. Chicago: University of Chicago Press, 1991.

30. Wiley, p. 60.

31. Kanan Makiya, *Republic of Fear: The Politics of Modern Iraq*. Berkeley: UCLA Press, 1998, p. 107.

32. Abd al-Jabar, p. 166.

33. Wiley, p. 64.

34. *Ibid.*, pp. 62–63, quoting Chibli Mallat, 'Iraq,' in Shireen Hunter, ed., *The Politics of Islamic Revivalism*. Bloomington: Indiana University Press, 1988, pp. 71–87.

35. *Ibid.*, p. 4.

36. See Human Rights Watch, *The Iraqi Government Assault on the Marsh Arabs.* HRW Briefing Paper, January 2003, p. 5.
37. *Ibid.*
38. Human Rights Watch, p. 8.
39. United Nations, *Report on the Situation of Human Rights in Iraq.* February 1995, p. 15.
40. Abd al-Jabar, p. 170.
41. It was also apparent that the Shi'a masses were supportive of the Iraqi nationalist agenda during the Iran–Iraq War, choosing to fight against their coreligionists in Iran for the Iraqi state. This is often, and correctly, viewed as evidence of the "Iraqi" identity of the Iraqi Shi'a. It is also representative of the division that exists between the Shi'a in Iran and those of Iraq.
42. Abd al-Jabar, p. 171.
43. *Ibid.*
44. See Stansfield, p. 75.
45. See Glenn Kessler and Dana Priest, "U.S. Planners Surprised by Strength of Iraqi Shiites," *The Washington Post*, April 23, 2003, p. A01.
46. Juan Cole, "Shiite Religious Parties Fill Vacuum in Southern Iraq," in *Middle East Report Online*, April 22, 2003.
47. *Ibid.*
48. Hooman Peimani, "The ever-threatening Shi'ite Factor," *Asia Times*, April 18, 2003.
49. Stansfield, p. 77.
50. Trofimov, "Shiite Power Struggle Threatens Stability," *The Wall Street Journal*, April 17, 2003, p. 10.
51. "The Declaration of the Shi'a of Iraq," June 2002.

## CHAPTER 6

1. Peter Sluglett and Marion Farouk-Sluglett, "Some Reflections on the Sunni/Shi'i Question in Iraq," in *The Bulletin of the British Society for Middle Eastern Studies*, vol. 5, issue 2 (1978), pp. 79–87, quote at p. 79. The authors Sluglett and Farouk-Sluglett quote as describing Iraq according to its three-way division are: Uriel Dann, *Iraq Under Qassim: A Political History, 1958–1963.* London: Pall Mall, 1969; Majid Khadduri, *Republican Iraq: A Study in Iraqi Politics Since the Revolution of 1958.* London: Oxford University Press, 1969; and Abbas Kelidar, *Iraq: The Search for Stability.* London: Institute for the Study of Conflict, 1975.
2. For example, Ofra Bengio, *Baghdad Between Shi'a and Kurds.* Policy Focus. Washington Institute for Near East Policy, Research Memorandum No. 18, February 1992.
3. Amatzia Baram, "Neo-Tribalism in Iraq: Saddam Hussein's Tribal Policies 1991–1996," in *International Journal of Middle East Studies*, vol. 29, issue 1, February 1997, pp. 1–31, quote at p. 5.
4. Malik Mufti, *Sovereign Creations: Pan-Arabism and Political Order in Syria and Iraq.* London: Cornell University Press, 1996, p. 23.
5. *Ibid.*, p. 24.
6. The Sharifians consisted of several hundred Sunni Arabs who had been serving Ottoman army officers, and many of them were involved in the Arab Revolt of

Sharif Hussein in World War I. David Pool, "From Elite to Class: The Transformation of Iraqi Political Leadership," in Abbas Kelidar, ed., *The Integration of Modern Iraq*. London: Croom Helm, 1979, pp. 63–87, quote at pp. 64–65.

7.  *Ibid.*, p. 65.
8.  Mufti, p. 25.
9.  Hanna Batatu, *The Old Social Classes and the Revolutionary Movements of Iraq: A Study of Iraq's Old Landed and Commercial Classes and of its Communists, Ba'thists and Free Officers*. Princeton, N.J.: Princeton University Press, 1978, p. 26.
10. Ahmed Shikara, "Faisal's Ambitions of Leadership in the Fertile Crescent: Aspirations and Constraints," in Kelidar, *Integration of Modern Iraq*, pp. 32–45, quote at p. 35; Phebe Marr, *The Modern History of Iraq*. Boulder C.O.: Westview Press, 1985, pp. 36–37; Uriel Dann, *The Role of the Military in Politics: A Case Study of Iraq to 1941*. London: Kegan Paul, 1982, pp. 44–50.
11. Mufti, p. 108.
12. Marr, p. 154.
13. Amatzia Baram, "Saddam's Power Structure: The Tikritis Before, During and After the War," in Toby Dodge and Steven Simon, eds., *Iraq at the Crossroads*, pp. 93–114, quote at p. 94.
14. Baram, p. 95.
15. *Ibid.*, p. 96.
16. Phebe Marr, "Iraq: The Revolutionary Experience," in P. J. Chelkowski and R. J. Pranger, eds., *Ideology and Power in the Middle East: Studies in Honor of George Lenczowski*. Durham N.C.: Duke University Press, 1988, pp. 185–209, use of material at p. 191.
17. Amatzia Baram, "The Ruling Political Elite in Ba'thi Iraq, 1968–1986: The Changing Features of a Collective Profile," in *International Journal of Middle Eastern Studies*, vol. 21, 1989, pp. 447–93, quote at p. 448.
18. *Ibid.*, p. 451.
19. Ofra Bengio, "A Republican Turning Royalist? Saddam Husayn and the Dilemmas of Succession," in *Journal of Contemporary History*, vol. 35, no. 4, 2000, pp. 641–53, quote at p. 646
20. Baram, pp. 100–101.
21. *Ibid.*, p. 102.
22. *Ibid.*, p. 104.
23. *Ibid.*, p. 105.
24. Bengio, p. 643.
25. Amatzia Baram, *Building Toward Crisis: Saddam Hussein's Strategy for Survival*. Policy Paper no. 47, Washington Institute for Near East Policy (WINEP). Washington D.C.: WINEP, 1998, p. 27.
26. Baram, "Saddam's Power Structure," p. 97.
27. Baram, *Building Toward Crisis*, p. 27.
28. *Ibid.*; Ken Pollack, *The Threatening Storm: The Case for Invading Iraq*. New York: Random House, 2002, p. 27.
29. Baram, *Building Toward Crisis*, p. 27.

**CHAPTER 7**

1.  For a detailed account of recent Kurdish history, often portraying the Kurds as victim, see Jonathan Randall, *After Such Knowledge, What Forgiveness? My Encoun-*

*ters with Kurdistan*. Boulder, C.O.: Westview Press, 1999. For an analysis that focuses on the more destabilizing aspects of Kurds, see Stephen Pelletiere, *The Kurds and their Aghas: An Assessment of the Situation in Northern Iraq*. Philadelphia: U.S. Army War College, Strategic Studies Institute, September 1991.

2. Identifying "where" Kurdistan is in Iraq has proved to be a historical cause of conflict between the central Iraqi government and the dominant Kurdish political parties. It resulted, for example, in the collapse of autonomy negotiations in the 1970s between Mulla Mustafa Barzani and the Iraqi government, and the removal of Saddam in the spring of 2003 was followed by tension arising over the historical identity of Kirkuk and other northern Iraqi towns. Academics, similarly, have failed to produce a cogent definition of the limits of Kurdistan in general and Iraqi Kurdistan in particular. For this reason, the phrase "the land of the Kurds" is often used, and the delimitation of its area has often been decided upon by population distribution. The Arabization of sensitive areas such as Kirkuk can be seen in its true geopolitical context as forcibly altering the demographic composition and identity of contested zones. For an account of the challenges involved in identifying the extent of Iraqi Kurdistan, see Gareth Stansfield, *Iraqi Kurdistan: Political Development and Emergent Democracy*. London: RoutledgeCurzon, 2003, pp. 27–28.

3. See Human Rights Watch, *Iraq: Forcible Expulsion of Ethnic Minorities*, vol. 15, no. 3 (E). Washington D.C., March 2003, p. 8.

4. Interview with Dr. Latif Rashid, PUK Representative to London, London, June 25, 2003.

5. For an account of the *Anfal* campaign and the destruction of Halabja, see Middle East Watch, *Human Rights in Iraq*. New Haven & London: Yale University Press, 1990, pp. 69–96.

6. Professor Christine Gosden, a geneticist based at Liverpool University who conducted field research in Halabja in the late 1990s, noted that "the occurrences of genetic mutations and cancer in Halabja appear comparable with those who were one to two kilometres from ground zero in Hiroshima and Nagasaki." Quoted in *The Financial Times*, "The Weapons Threat: The Enduring Pain of Halabja." Report by Guy Dinmore, July 10, 2002.

7. See Gareth Stansfield, "Politics and Governance in the New Iraq: Reconstruction of the New Versus Resurrection of the Old," in *War on Iraq: Combat and Consequence*. Whitehall Paper 59. London: Royal United Services Institute for Defence Studies, June 2003, pp. 67–83, reference at p. 79.

8. See Pam O'Toole, "Iraqi Kurds Face Uncertain Future," *BBC News*, April 18, 2003.

9. The 1933 Montevideo Convention on Rights and Duties of States identified "the state" as possessing (a) a permanent population; (b) a defined territory; (c) government, and; (d) a capacity to enter into relations with other states. A monopoly of authoritative binding rule-making is also considered a primary characteristic by political science theorists. See Hurst Hannum, *Autonomy, Sovereignty and Self-Determination: The Accommodation of Conflicting Rights*. Philadelphia: University of Pennsylvania Press, 1990; Sohail Hashmi, ed., *State Sovereignty: Change and Persistence in International Relations*. Pennsylvania: Pennsylvania State University Press, 1997.

10. For a concise account of Kurdish characteristics, see Merhdad Izady, *The Kurds: A Concise Handbook*. Washington D.C.: Crane Russak, 1992.

11. David McDowall, writing in 1992 and extrapolating his figures from the 1978 research of Martin Van Bruinessen, puts Kurdish population figures at: Turkey, 10.8 million; Iraq, 4.1 million; Iran, 5.5 million; Syria, 1 million; other, 1.2 million. David McDowall, *The Kurds: A Nation Denied*, London: Minority Rights Group, 1992, p. 12; Martin Van Bruinessen, *Agha, Shaikh and State: The Social and Political Organization of Kurdistan*. London: Zed Books, 1992, pp. 14–15. Figures collated in Stansfield, *Iraqi Kurdistan*, p. 33.

12. See Van Bruinessen, pp. 50–56.

13. Stansfield, "Politics and Governance in the New Iraq," p. 82.

14. For an account of the rebellion of Sheikh Mahmoud Barzinji see David McDowall, *A Modern History of the Kurds*. London: I.B. Taurus, 1996, pp. 159–63; Stansfield, *Iraqi Kurdistan*, p. 62.

15. See McDowall, pp. 151–59.

16. The party was originally called the Kurdish Democratic Party, but changed its name in 1953 to the Kurdistan Democratic Party to make it more accessible to non-Kurds (Stansfield, *Iraqi Kurdistan*, p. 66).

17. *Ibid.*

18. *Ibid.*, p. 126.

19. Interview with Sami Abdul Rahman, Salahadin, Erbil, April 3, 1998.

20. Human Rights Watch, pp. 9–10.

21. Mulla Mustafa Barzani died in exile on March 1, 1979 in Washington D.C.

22. Ali Hassan Al-Majid became known as "Chemical Ali" after his leadership of the attack.

23. It would appear that, if any party had been involved with the prior organization of the Kurdish uprising, it was the Kurdistan Communist Party. However, both the KDP and PUK claim that they had been steadily returning covert groups of *peshmerga* back into Iraq in preparation to support a spontaneous uprising. See Stansfield, *Iraqi Kurdistan*, p. 180.

24. Human Rights Watch, p. 11.

25. Interview with Dr. Latif Rashid, PUK representative to London, June 14, 2002.

26. Stansfield, *Iraqi Kurdistan*, p. 181.

27. Instead of the two party leaders taking the two main government/legislative positions of Prime Minister and Parliamentary Speaker, they were instead given to subordinate party members. The Prime Minister of the First Cabinet was the PUK Political Bureau member Dr. Fu'ad Massoum, and the Speaker of the KNA was the KDP Political Bureau member Jawher Namiq Salim. Each had a deputy from the other party with equivalent power.

28. The attack was aimed at destroying the Iraqi V Corps stationed at the Iraqi–Kurdish dividing line, and then capture Mosul and Kirkuk, promoting a national uprising against Saddam.

29. See Stansfield, *Iraqi Kurdistan*, pp. 98–99.

30. See Gareth Stansfield, "The Iraqi Kurds: A New Start or Repeated History?" in *RUSI Newsbrief*, vol. 23, no. 4, April 2003, pp. 40–41. London: Royal United Services Institute for Defence Studies.

31. The KDP and PUK agreed to reassemble a joint KNA in Erbil in October 2002. The reunification of the KNA was called for by the Washington Agreement of 1998 and it is thought that the U.S. applied pressure to unite the Kurds in advance of regime change in Iraq.

32. Human Rights Watch, p. 12.

## CHAPTER 8

1. Bruce Anderson, "The Champion of Human Rights is in the White House." *The Independent*, February 17, 2003, p. 15.
2. Bruce Anderson, "The Unexpectedly Benign Consequences of Having Delayed the Conflict in Iraq." *The Independent*, March 10, 2003, p. 14.
3. www.guardian.co.uk/usa/story/0,12271,904085,00.html.
4. See Thomas Carothers, "The End of the Transition Paradigm." *Journal of Democracy*, vol. 13, no. 1, January 2002, for a critique of the "no preconditions" school of thought in the study of democratization.
5. Francis Fukuyama, "The Primacy of Culture." *Journal of Democracy*, vol. 6, no. 1, 1995, p. 7.
6. *Ibid.*, p. 8.
7. *Ibid.*, p. 9.
8. Obviously, there are troops from other countries present in Iraq (Britain and Poland, for example), but the assumption is that the U.S. will seek to dominate the process of reconstruction, and, therefore, that the success or otherwise of plans for the future of Iraq will hinge around how long the U.S. is prepared to maintain a significant troop presence.
9. International Crisis Group, *Iraqi Briefing: Voices from the Iraqi Street*, Amman /Brussels, December 4, p. 6.
10. A further significant problem is that power-sharing schemes cannot just be limited to the *political* institutions of government. The officer corps of the armed forces, long a bastion of Sunni Arabs and for long periods the ultimate arbiter in Iraqi politics; key organs of social influence, such as the Department of Education; and the state's coercive instruments (the internal security services) have played important political roles in Iraq's history and will need similar treatment.
11. "The Declaration of the Shi'a of Iraq," June 2002, (www.al-bab.com/arab/docs/ iraq/Shi'a02a).
12. For a useful summary of the requirements of sustaining federalism, see Daniel Elazar, "International and Comparative Federalism." *PS: Political Science and Politics*, vol. 26, issue 2, June 1993.
13. *Ibid.*, p. 193.
14. *Ibid.*, p. 192.
15. John W. Dower, *Embracing Defeat. Japan in the Wake of World War II*. New York: W.W. Norton & Company, 1999, p. 27.
16. *Ibid.*, p. 23.
17. Fukuyama, p. 8.
18. *Ibid.*, p. 8.
19. Robert D. Putnam, *Making Democracy Work: Civic Traditions in Modern Italy*. Princeton, New Jersey: Princeton University Press, 1993, p. 167.
20. Fukuyama, p. 8.
21. Several Arab states have experimented with democracy (Algeria and Lebanon, for example), but these experiments have tended to end in disaster and bloodshed.
22. Another important issue concerns weapons of mass destruction (WMD). The assumption is that removing Saddam's regime will eliminate the driving force behind Iraq's lengthy struggle to obtain WMD. There is some logic here in that Iraq's efforts in this direction did not take serious shape until about 1974. On

the other hand, this may mis-characterize the dynamics involved. The driving figure was Saddam Hussein, but the driving force was the desire to negate the strategic advantage enjoyed by Israel as a consequence of its nuclear deterrent. The only way to ensure that states in the region do not possess WMD is to have a heavily policed WMD-free zone in the Middle East. But this would require Israel to give up its nuclear weapons, which is inconceivable. An emerging Iraqi democracy will find itself in the midst of a region awash with WMD. Not counting Israel's nuclear weapons, Iran almost certainly has chemical and biological weapons, as do Egypt, Libya, and Syria. Iran's apparent pursuit of nuclear weapons will also change the strategic profile of the region. The assumption that a democratically elected government will be less inclined to seek WMD simply flies in the face of the reality. Of the eight countries known to possess nuclear weapons, five are fully functioning, stable democracies (Britain, the U.S., France, Israel, and India), two others (Russia, Pakistan) occupy a gray area, and only one (China) is an authoritarian regime. Changing the domestic political structure does nothing to alter the strategic environment surrounding the country. And it is the strategic environment that provides the rationale behind a state's decision to seek WMD.

23. (Almost) unbelievably, the Pentagon's Office of Reconstruction and Humanitarian Development proposed that a U.S. Administration in Iraq would run a "Ministry of Religious Affairs," with a mandate "to oversee mosques and other religious activities" (see www.cnn.com/2003/WORLD/meast/03/13/sprj.irq.sectors/index.html).

24. Both are taken from President Bush's speech to the American Enterprise Institute (of Feb 26 2003), as quoted in full on *National Review Online*, February 27, 2003 (www.nationalreview.com/document/document022703.asp).

## EPILOGUE

1. Quoted in Bill Berkowitz, "One Hundred Days of Ineptitude," *WorkingFor-Change.com*, August 18, 2003. (www.alternet.org/print.html?StoryID=16615).

2. Quoted in Gerry J. Gilmore, "'Success' Is Exit Strategy in Iraq, Rumsfeld Says," *DefenseLink*, November 10, 2003. (www.defenselink.mil/news/Nov2003/n11102003_2003111010.html).

3. See www.cpa-iraq.org/essential_services/health.html.

4. "Another vacuum opens up," *The Economist*, November 8, 2003, p. 45.

5. In the months leading up to the invasion, the State Department engaged in an extensive and systematic effort to plan for the postwar reconstruction of Iraq that might have produced better results. Ultimately, though, these efforts were ignored and control over the reconstruction process was placed in the hands of the Defense Department.

6. The representatives on the IGC are: *Religious Shi'a:* Abdul Aziz al-Hakim (SCIRI); Mohammad Bahr al-Ulloum (Najaf cleric); Essedine Salim (al-Da'wa head from Basra); Ibrahim al-Ja'afari (al-Da'wa) Abdel Karim Mahmoud Al-Mohammedawi (Iraqi Hizballah); Mouwafak Al-Rabii. *Secular Shi'a:* Ahmed Chalabi (INC); Ahmed al-Barak (lawyer from Hillah); Hamid Majid Mousa (Iraqi Communist Party); Raja Habib al-Khuzaai (woman, medical doctor); Aquila al-Hashimi (woman, assassinated September 25, 2003); Iyad Allawi (INA); Wael Abdul Latif (judge from Basra). *Sunni Arab:* Adnan Pachachi (minister in the 1960s); Naseer al-Chaderchi (National Democratic Party); Samir

Shakir Mahmoud (al-Sumaidy clan); Gazi Mashal Ajil Al-Yawer (al-Shamar tribal federation); Mohsen Abdul Hamid (Iraqi Islamic Party); Dara Noor Alzin (judge). *Kurds:* Jalal Talabani (PUK); Massoud Barzani (KDP); Mahmoud Othman (independent); Salahadin Ba'hadin (KIU). *Assyrian:* Younadem Youssif Kana (Assyrian Democratic Movement). *Turcoman:* Sondul Chapouk (woman, engineer).

7.  The one exception here was the Council's staunch refusal to accept Turkey's offer of 10,000 troops to police the Sunni areas of Iraq.

8.  The Council was originally a 25-member body, but the assassination of Aquila al-Hashimi in September 2003 reduced the number to 24. At press time, no replacement had yet been appointed.

9.  Figures such as Barzani and Talabani would understandably strongly object to being called "exiles" as they remained in Iraq throughout the 1990s. However, in effect, "exiles" is what they are as Kurdistan was, to all intents and purposes, another country.

10. Since the occupation began, Shi'a clerics have emerged as by some distance the most influential voices within the Shi'a community as a whole. In particular, Grand Ayatollah Ali Sistani appears to have a *de facto* veto over proposals for the political reconstruction of Iraq. As a "quietist," Sistani would never involve himself directly in the process of drawing up a constitution, but his seal of approval would be absolutely essential to convince much of the Shi'a community of any constitution's legitimacy.

11. L. Paul Bremer III, "Iraq's Path to Sovereignty," *The Washington Post*, September 8, 2003, p. A21.

12. All quotes from www.cpa-iraq.org/audio/20031115a_final.html.

13. Terence Hunt, "Bush Says U.S. Forces Won't Leave Iraq," Associated Press, November 10, 2003 (news.yahoo.com/news?tmpl=story2&cid=544&u=ap/20031117 . . ./us_iraq).

14. See Juan Cole, "The United States and Shi'ite Religious Factions in Post-Ba'thist Iraq," *Middle East Journal*, vol. 57, no. 4, Autumn 2003, pp. 543–566.

15. Robert Collier, "Shiite Clerics Stand in Constitution's Path, Political Goals in Iraq Hinge on 2 Theocrats," *San Francisco Chronicle*, November 17, 2003 (sfgate.com/cgibin/article.cgi?file=/c/a/2003/1 . . ./MNGB633LAH1.DTL&type).

16. Maggy Zanger, "Kurds Keep Iraq at Arm's Length," *Iraq Crisis Report*, vol. 35, November 14, 2003 (http://www.iwpr.net).

17. "Text of Bush speech to the National Endowment for Democracy," Associated Press, November 7, 2003 (http://www.pittsburghfirst.com/pg/pp/03311/237683.stm).

# INDEX

Abdullah, Hamza, 165
Aburish, Said, 37, 238*n*, 239*n*, 240*n*, 242*n*
Afghanistan, 100, 196
Aflaq, Michel, 66
Agragrian Reform Law of 1958, 45
Ahmed, Ibrahim, 164–65, 169
Al Qaeda, 3, 175
Albright, Madeline, 98, 99
Algiers Agreement, 56, 60, 169
al-Ali, Salah Umar, 71
Allawi, Iyad, 175, 252*n*
Alzin, Dara Noor, 253*n*
Amin, Nawshirwan Mustafa, 168
Ammash, Salih Mahdi, 51
Anderson, Bruce, 251*n*
Anfal campaign, 23, 72, 81, 94, 101, 169, 170,
    180, 187, 249*n*
Anglo-Iraq Treaty, 16–17
Ansar al-Islam, 175
anti-Zionism, 71, 204, 208
Arab demographics, 6
Arab nationalism, 26, 66–67
Arab-Israeli conflict of 1973, 55
Arab-Israeli War of 1967, 40
Arabism, 66, 106, 146. *See also* pan-Arabism
Arabization, 181–82
Arif, Abdel Rahman, 40, 43, 45, 46, 52, 124
Arif, Abdul Salaam, 32–34, 37, 39–40, 45, 46,
    124
Assyrian massacre, 24–25, 28, 71
Atatürk, Mustafu Kamal, 15
al-Awda, 46
Axis of Evil, 3
al-Ayubi, Salah al-Din, 245*n*
Aziz, Mulla Ali Abdul, 169
Aziz, Sheikh Othman Abdul, 169
Aziz, Tariq, 73, 85, 243*n*, 246*n*

Ba'ath Party/Regime, 6, 8, 31–32, 34, 36–40,
    42, 48, 49–50, 188, 226–27, 239*n*
    controlled by Saddam Hussein, 58–59

disintegration of, 85, 87–89, 95, 100,
    102, 106, 108, 111
and Iran, 60–62
and the Kazzar coup attempt, 55
and the Kurds, 45, 52–53, 166–69,
    181–82, 56
legacies of, 62–80, 203
and modernization, 57–58
and the military, 50–52
and oil, 54–54
organization of, 241*n*
as a secular regime, 103, 196
and Shi'a Muslims, 46, 53–54, 123,
    125–30, 132, 135
and Sunni Muslims, 46, 139, 141–42,
    145–47, 149
and tribalism, 105
and violence, 44, 45, 69–74, 109, 114
Babylon, 75, 242*n*
Baha'adin, Salahadin, 174–75, 228, 253*n*
al-Bakr, Ahmad Hassan, 38, 39, 50, 51, 55,
    58–59, 63, 125, 145, 147
Bapir, Mulla Ali, 175
al-Barak, Ahmed, 252*n*
Baram, Amatzia, 145, 148, 150, 241*n*, 242*n*,
    245*n*, 246*n*, 247*n*, 248*n*
Barzani, Idris, 168, 169
Barzani, Massoud, 162, 168, 172, 173, 253*n*
Barzani, Mulla Mustafa, 40, 44, 53, 56, 72,
    94, 96, 105, 123, 168, 169, 173, 228,
    235, 249*n*, 250*n*
Barzani, Nechervan, 177
Basra Oil Company, 54
Batatu, Hanna, 248*n*
Bednarz, Dieter, 245*n*
Bengio, Ofra, 149, 243*n*, 245*n*, 247*n*, 248*n*
Bin Laden, Osama, 2, 3, 99
Blair, Tony, 134
Bosnia, 229
Bremer, Paul, 151, 226–27, 228–30, 235,
    253*n*

British rule, 16, 24, 26, 28, 43, 143
Bush, George H. W., 86, 87, 91, 98, 99
Bush, George W., 3, 99–100, 178, 186, 211,
    225, 233, 236, 253n
    administration of, 2–5, 181, 185, 190,
    191, 206, 209, 210, 220, 225–29,
    230, 232, 234, 252n
Butler, Richard, 98
Byman, Daniel, 237n

Carothers, Thomas, 251n
Castro, Fidel, 8
al-Chaderchi, Naseer, 252n
Chalabi, Ahmed, 91–92, 95, 96, 175, 176,
    192, 193, 212, 229, 252n
Chapouk, Sondul, 253n
Chelkowski, P. J., 248n
Churchill, Winston, 23
Clinton administration, 2–3, 98–99, 244n
Coalition Provisional Authority (CPA), 152,
    226, 228, 229, 231
Cockburn, Andrew, 241n, 243n, 244n, 245n
Cockburn, Patrick, 241n, 243n, 244n, 245n
Cold War, 33, 55
Cole, Juan, 133, 247n, 253n
Collier, Robert, 235, 253n
communism, 8, 35–36, 44–47, 52, 55, 66–67
containment, policy of, 2
Coughlin, Con, 240n, 242n
coups and coup attempts, 16, 18, 19, 55–58,
    87–93, 96–97, 104, 148, 150, 200
    of 1958, 20, 27, 28, 31–43
    of 1963, 124, 166
    of 1968, 50–51

Da'ud, Ibrahim Abd al-Rahman, 50–51
Dann, Uriel, 247n, 248n
Danner, Mark, 4, 237n
al-Dawa (The Party of the Islamic Call), 46,
    53, 72–73, 123–32, 134, 187, 193, 210,
    214, 222, 228, 234
Dawood, Hosham, 245n
Dayton Peace Accords, 10
Declaration of the Shi'a of Iraq, 135, 195
democracy, 9–10, 15–16, 21, 39, 43, 52, 63,
    69, 102, 112–16, 117, 152, 158,
    190–92, 192–200, 236, 251n
Democratic Domino theory, 186
Department of General Intelligence, 9
Dodge, Toby, 244n, 245n, 248n
Dower, John W., 251n
al-Dulaymi, Mohammad Mazlum, 150
Dulles, Allen, 44
al-Duri, Sabir, 149

education, 45, 69, 77–78, 103, 111, 114, 202,
    226
Egypt, 33, 38, 40
Ekeus, Rolf, 95, 98
Elazar, Daniel, 251n
Everest, Larry, 243n

Fahd, King, 86
Faisal I, King, 14–17, 143–44, 238n
Faisal II, King, 19
Farouk, King, 33
Farouk-Sluglett, Marion, 247n
Fedayeen (Men of Sacrifice), 9, 108, 109, 113,
    149, 233
Francke, Rend Rahim, 245n, 246n
Free Officers, 32–35, 43, 144
Friedman, Menachem, 246n
Fukuyama, Francis, 190, 191, 192, 200, 203,
    204, 251n
Fuller, Graham, 245n, 246n
Fundamental Law (FL), 231, 236

Gaddis, John Lewis, 4–5, 237n
Garner, Jay, 227
Gates, Robert, 91
Ghaydan, Sa'dun, 50
Ghazi, King, 17–18
Gulf Cooperation Council (GCC), 122
Gulf War of 1991, 7, 9, 91, 101, 107, 109,
    157, 226, 243n
Gulf War, second, 89–90

al-Haeri, Ayatollah Kadhim, 235
Hajji, Aziz Al, 52
al-Hakim, Abdul Aziz, 128, 228, 252n
al-Hakim, Ayatollah Mohammad Baqir, 228
al-Hakim, Ayatollah Muhsin, 123–25, 128–30
Halabja, gassing of Kurds at, 2, 23, 72, 131,
    156–57, 170, 187, 249n
Hamid, Mohsen Abdul, 229, 253n
Hammadi, Sa'dun, 101
Hannum, Hurst, 249n
Hariri, Franso, 175
al-Hashimi, Aquila, 252n, 253n
al-Hashimi, Yasin, 18
Hashimite monarchy, 13–29, 32, 206
Hashmi, Sohail, 249n
al-Haza, Mohammad Fayzi, 149
Hiro, Dilip, 240n, 241n, 243n
Hiyawi, Hussein, 150
Hunt, Terence, 253n
Hussein, Qusay, 94, 95, 148
Hussein, Saddam:
    and Algiers Agreement, 56, 60

American support for the overthrow
of, 1
assumes leadership (1979), 31
and the Ba'ath Party, 23, 32, 37, 50,
63
"Butcher of Baghdad," 1
and coup of 1968, 50–52
demonization of, 1, 13, 23
and education, 77
fall of, 185–91
end of presidency, 114
escape from capture (1959), 36
family of, 94–95
and Iran-Iraq War, 60–62
and the Kurds, 52–53, 71–72, 156–62,
166–72, 174–82
invasion of Kuwait, 83, 85–87
legacies of, 7–10, 62–81, 100–114
and modernization of Iraq, 57–58
and nationalization of oil, 54–55
as one-man ruler, 58–59
and pan-Arabism, 74–76 156, 210
paranoia of, 65
popularity of, 242n
as "pious Muslim," 103, 106
and "oil for food" deal, 92, 97, 98,
177, 182
a "post-Saddam" Iraq, 187, 189, 191,
192–94, 204, 210
and the Republican Guard, 39
and the second Gulf War, 90–91
and the Shi'a, 53–54, 72, 117–18, 123,
124, 127–38
"stick and carrot" approach to
governance, 85, 97
and Sunni Muslims, 139–53
as a survivor, 8
titles of, 58–59, 102–103, 246n
and UNSCOM, 98–99
and tribalism, 63
as vice-president, 124
and violence, 23, 25, 38, 69–70,
73–74, 198
and women and the family, 78
See also Ba'ath Party/Regime
al-Hussein, Sharif Ali Bin, 152, 248n
Hussein, Uday, 94, 95, 108, 149

Ilah, Abdul, 19, 43
"Imam," 245n
Iran, 3, 4, 11, 110, 111, 173, 174–76, 180–81,
208, 210, 214, 217, 221, 223, 235,
240n
Islamic revolution, 73, 118, 126, 169

and the Kurds, 45–46, 55–58 167,
17
relations with Iraq, 49, 52–53, 58
and SCIRI, 88–89, 127–33, 136
and Shi'a Muslims, 118–19, 122, 124,
127, 142, 152, 196, 207
See also Iran-Iraq War
Iran-Iraq War, 2, 9, 60–62, 65, 72, 80, 83, 85,
101, 107, 118, 128–31, 181, 188, 189,
226, 244n
Iraq, as "first Arab democracy," 4
Iraq, geographical outlines of, 6
Iraq, history of as a political entity, 5–6
Iraq, modernization of, 57–58
Iraq Liberation Act, 98
Iraq Petroleum Company (IPC), 54
Iraqi Communist Party (ICP), 8, 22–23,
32–38, 41–46, 52, 55, 57, 66–70, 92,
105, 123–24, 144–46
Iraqi demographics, 6, 9–10, 117
Iraqi economy, 84–85
Iraqi Governing Council (IGC), 227–31, 235,
252n
Iraqi identity. See national identity
Iraqi Kurdistan Front (IKF), 72, 88, 90
Iraqi National Accord (INA), 92, 95–97, 101,
104, 175, 243n
Iraqi National Congress (INC), 91–92,
95–96, 128, 175–76, 195, 206, 212
Islam, 119–21. See also Shi'a Muslims; Sunni
Muslims
Islamic Movement of Kurdistan (IMK), 169,
174, 175
Israel, 33, 40, 46, 51, 53, 55, 56, 67, 71, 74,
188, 193, 202, 207
Istiqlal (Independence) Party, 22
Izady, Merhdad, 249n

al-Ja'afari, Ibrahim, 252n
al-Jabar, Faleh Abd, 245n, 246n, 247n
Jamalat al-Ulama, 46, 124
Japan, 201, 202, 205
Jerome, Carole, 243n
Jews, pogroms against, 18
July Revolution, 50, 58

Kamel, Hussein, 89, 94–95, 97, 107, 244n
Kana Younadem Youssif, 253n
Karsh, Efraim, 240n
Kazzar, Nadhim, 55
Kelidar, Abbas, 247n
Kessler, Glenn, 247n
Khadduri, Majid, 247n
al-Khafaji, Isam, 242n

al-Khalil, Samir, 238n, 239n, 241n, 242n
al-Khoei, Ayatollah Qasim, 100–101, 108,
    113, 121, 125, 129, 134
Khomeini, Ayatollah, 60–61, 73, 121, 122,
    125, 126, 245–46n
al-Khuzaai, Raja Habib, 252n
Kirkuk Massacre, 25
Kissinger, Henry, 83
al-Klibi, Chadli, 243n
Kosygin, Premier, 52, 54
Kurdish demographics, 6
Kurdish government, formation of, 172–74
Kurdish uprising, 7, 129, 170
Kurdistan, 11, 15–16, 52–53, 56, 69, 72, 76,
    80, 88, 90, 95, 101, 105, 114, 249n
    as an independent state, 217–24
Kurdistan Democratic Party (KDP), 72, 88,
    92, 95, 96, 123, 162, 164–70, 172–79,
    250n
Kurdistan Islamic Union (KIU), 174–75, 228
Kurdistan National Assembly (KNA), 172
Kurdistan Popular Democratic Party
    (KPDP), 169
Kurdistan Regional Government (KRG),
    173–74
Kurds, 15–16, 31, 34, 35, 38, 40–48, 52–53,
    122–23, 128–131, 155–59, 235–36
    as agent provocateur, 155
    gassing of at Halabja, 2, 23, 72,
        156–57, 170, 187
    social and political context, 159–61
    as victims, 155
    See also Kurdistan; Kurdistan
        Democratic Party
Kuwait, 83–88, 90, 97, 104, 110
    invasion of, 86–87, 170, 171, 177

Lake, Tony, 96
Latif, Wael Abdul, 252n
"Lawrence of Arabia," 238n
League of Nations, 15–17
Lebanon, 41
Lukitz, Liora, 245n

Mackey, Sandra, 242n
Mahmoud, Samir Shakir, 252–53n
al-Majid, Ali Hassan ("chemical" Ali), 72, 94,
    108, 113, 169, 250n
Makiya, Kanan, 246n
Mallat, Chibli, 246n
managed partition of Iraq, option of, 213–19
March Agreement, 166–67
March Manifesto, 52–53, 56, 71
Marr, Phebe, 238n, 239n, 240n, 242n, 248n

Marsh Arabs, 130–31
Mashadi, Muhie Abdal, 50
mass mobilization, 33
McDowall, David, 250n
Mesopotamia, 75, 80
military, 20, 33
Miller, Judith, 244n
Mohamedou, Mohammed-Mahmoud, 243n
al-Mohammedawi, Abdel Karim Mahmoud,
    252n
Momen, Moojan, 246n
monarchical rule, legacies of, 19–28
Mosul, 6, 15–16
Mosul Revolt of 1959, 35, 36, 44, 47
Mousa, Hamid Majid, 252n
al-Mudarissi, Ayatollah Muhammad Taqi,
    127
Mufti, Malik, 143, 247n, 248n
Muslim Brotherhood, 175, 228
Mylroie, Laurie, 244n

Nakash, Yitzhak, 238n, 246n
Namiq, Jawher, 173
Nasser, Gamal Abdul, 33, 38
National Council of the Revolutionary
    Command (NCRC), 37, 40
National Defense Council, 40
National Democratic Party (NDP), 22, 32,
    42
National Guard, 37–39
national identity, 11, 16, 19, 25–27, 46–47,
    49, 74–75, 80, 118–19, 188, 216
National Progressive Front, 55, 69
National Security Strategy (NSS), 4
national unity as a historical legacy, 25,
    45–47, 74–80, 109–114. See also
    national identity
Nayif, Abd al-Razzaq, 50–51
neo-tribalism, 204
North Korea, 3, 99

oil, 15, 54–55, 57, 85
"oil for food" deal, 92, 97, 98, 177, 182
Operation Desert Fox, 3, 98
Operation Desert Storm, 87
Operation Iraqi Freedom, 1, 175, 185
Organization of Petroleum Exporting
    Countries (OPEC), 85, 167
Othman, Mahmoud, 228, 253n
O'Toole, Pam, 249n
Ottoman Empire, 6, 14, 19–20, 186–87, 237
    n, 238n

Pachachi, Adnan, 152, 252n

pan-Arabism, 27, 33–39, 41, 44, 46, 47, 74, 76, 118, 143, 144, 193, 208, 237*n*, 238*n*
Patriotic Union of Kurdistan (PUK), 72, 88, 92, 95, 96, 164, 168–79
Peimani, Hooman, 247*n*
Pelletiere, Stephen, 249*n*
People's Court, 37, 42
Pfaff, Richard H., 241*n*
Pico, François Georges, 14
Pinault, David, 245*n*, 246*n*
political parties, 32–34, 42, 45, 48
Pollack, Ken, 248*n*
Popular Army, 62, 65, 79
Popular Resistance Force, 37, 42
Powell, Colin, 100
Pragner, R. J., 248*n*
Priest, Dana, 247*n*
Project for the New American Century (PNAC), 3
prolonged occupation, option of, 201–205
puppet regime, option of, 209–13

Qassim, Abdul Karim, 27, 31, 33–38, 41–42, 44–48, 52, 53, 70, 123–24, 144, 145, 165–66, 239*n*

al-Rabii, Mouwafak, 252*n*
al-Rahdi, Husain Ahmed, 44
Rahman, Sami Abdul, 166, 169, 250*n*
Randall, Jonathan, 248*n*
Rashid, Latif, 249*n*, 250*n*
Rasoul, Kosrat, 173, 176
Rautsi, Inari, 240*n*
regime change, American policy of, 2, 88–89, 91–92, 95, 97–98, 100
Republican Guard, 9, 39, 40, 48, 50, 63, 65, 75, 81, 87, 89, 100, 104, 108, 113, 148, 149, 171, 176, 191, 201, 243*n*
"Results in Iraq: 100 Days Toward Security and Freedom," 225
Revolutionary Command Council (RCC), 50, 51, 59, 62, 63, 68, 80
Riley, John, 1
Ritter, John, 244*n*
Roberts, Paul W., 242*n*
Royal Air Force (RAF), 26
Rumsfeld, Donald, 99, 225, 233

al-Sa'id, Nuri, 43
al-Sadi, Ali Salih, 37
al-Sadr, Ayatollah Muhammad Sadiq, 113, 132, 133, 138
al-Sadr, Muhammad Baqir, 53, 73, 124–25, 128, 132, 134, 246*n*

al-Sadr, Muqtada, 133–34, 136, 189, 234–35
Salih, Barham, 175, 177
Salim, Essedine, 252*n*
Salim, Jawher Namiq, 250*n*
al-Samarra'i, Wafiq, 87, 243*n*
sanctions, U.N., 2–3, 83, 90–93, 98–99, 101, 103, 108, 110, 111, 178–79
Saudi Arabia, 84, 86
September 11, 2001 terrorist attacks, 3, 5, 99, 178–79, 185, 190
Sha'ban, Hamid, 150
Shi'a Muslims, 6, 53–54, 117–20, 187
    and Ba'ath Regime, 46, 53–54, 123, 125–30, 132, 135
    Declaration of the Shi'a of Iraq, 135, 195
    demographics, 117
    development of Iraqi political Shi'ism, 122–31
    discrimination against, 134–35
    and the future of Iraq, 187–89, 193–196, 210–212, 216, 222–23, 234–35
    and Iran, 118–19, 122, 124, 127, 142, 152, 196, 207
    as Iraqi nationalists, 118
    key issues, 134–36
    major players, 136
    origins of Sunni/Shi'a divide, 120–22, 239*n*
    resurgence of Shi'a communal identity, 131–33
    and Saddam Hussein, 53–54, 72, 117–18, 123, 124, 127–38
    Shi'a in post-Saddam Iraq, 133–34
    unifying factors, 135–36
Shi'a rebellions, 24, 148
Shikara, Ahmed, 248*n*
Sidqi, Bakr, 18, 24–25, 27
Simmons, Geoff, 238*n*, 239*n*, 240*n*, 243*n*
Simon, Steven, 244*n*, 245*n*, 248*n*
Sistani, Ayatollah Ali, 121, 133, 134, 230, 234–35, 253*n*
Sivan, Emmanuel, 246*n*
Six Day War, 40
Slaibi, Sa'id, 39
Sluglett, Peter, 247*n*
socialism, 65–67, 69, 103, 124, 125, 135
Soeterik, Robert, 240*n*
Soviet Union, 33, 52, 55, 66, 67, 188, 207
Special Republican Guard, 9, 94, 96, 104, 148, 191, 201
Special Security Organization (SSO), 141, 148

Special Security Service, 9
Stalin, Joseph, 8
Stansfield, Gareth, 246n, 247n, 249n, 250n
Steel, Mark, 7, 237n
"stick and carrot" approach to governance,
    85, 97
Sumaida, Hussein, 243n
Sunni Muslims, 139–46
    ascension of, 143
    and Ba'ath Regime, 46, 139, 141–42,
        145–47, 149
    in Baghdad and Mosul, 6
    dominance of, 19–21, 41, 62–64,
        100–101
    insurgency, 232–34
    key issues, 152–53
    in post-Saddam Iraq, 150–52
    and Saddam's regime, 139–53
    origins of Sunni/Shi'a divide, 120–22,
        239n
    synonymous with Iraqi government,
        140
    Tikritis and associated tribes, 141,
        147–50
Sunni Triangle, 233
Supreme Council for the Islamic
        Revolution in Iraq (SCIRI), 88, 89,
        92, 100, 127–31, 134, 136, 187, 189,
        192, 197, 210, 214, 222, 223, 228,
        234, 243n
Sykes, Mark, 14
Sykes-Picot Agreement, 14
Syria, 14, 33, 36, 38, 40, 47, 56, 57, 59, 66,
        69, 71, 74, 75, 143, 145, 174, 207–9,
        214–15, 217, 227, 222

Talabani, Jalal, 162, 164–65, 167–69, 172–73,
        175–76, 228, 235, 253n
al-Tikriti, Hardan, 51
al-Tikriti, Ibrahim Hamash, 149

Transitional National Assembly (TNA), 231,
        233, 236
Treaty of Friendship and Cooperation, 54
Treaty of Sevres, 15
Tripp, Charles, 22, 238n, 239n
Turkey, 7, 11, 15
Tutwiler, Margaret, 85–86

"ulama," 246n
al-Ulloum, Mohammad Bahr, 252n
United Arab Republic (UAR), 33–36
United Nations inspections, 3, 91, 94, 98, 110
United Nations sanctions against Iraq, 132
United Nations Security Council Resolution
        678, 86
United Nations Security Council Resolution
        688, 171

Van Bruinessen, Martin, 250n
violence, 7, 13, 23–25, 43–45, 69–74, 80,
        188–89, 194, 205–9, 210, 220. See also
        Ba'ath Party/Regime: and violence;
        Hussein, Saddam: and violence

Wallace, Ray, 237n
war on terror, 2, 4
wathbah, 25, 239n
weapons inspectors, 3
weapons of mass destruction (WMD), 3, 91,
        94, 95, 97, 107, 251–52n
Wiley, Joyce, 246n
Windfuhr, Volkhard, 245n
Wolfowitz, Paul, 133
women, treatment and position of, 45, 77–78
Woodward, Bob, 244n

al-Yawer, Gazi Mashal Ajil, 253n

Zanger, Maggy, 235, 253n
Zayid, Shaikh, 152